THE FRIGHTFEST GUIDE TO EXPLOITATION MOVIES

Second pressing published by FAB Press, 2023
(First published by FAB Press, August 2016)

FAB Press Ltd.
2 Farleigh
Ramsden Road
Godalming, Surrey
GU7 1QE
England, U.K.

www.fabpress.com

Author's Dedication: For Paul, Ian and Greg.

Edited and Designed by Harvey Fenton

Film cast and crew credits, additional research and index courtesy of Francis Brewster

Front cover illustration:
Artwork from the US one-sheet movie poster for Silent Madness adapted for this cover design by Harvey Fenton.

Frontispiece illustration:
Key art for the 2008 edition of FrightFest, an original painting by Graham Humphreys.

Printed in India

A CIP catalogue record for this book is available from the British Library.

hardcover: ISBN 978 1 903254 89 9

paperback: ISBN 978 1 903254 87 5

- THE DARK HEART OF CINEMA -

FRIGHTFEST® GUIDE

EXPLOITATION MOVIES

Alan Jones

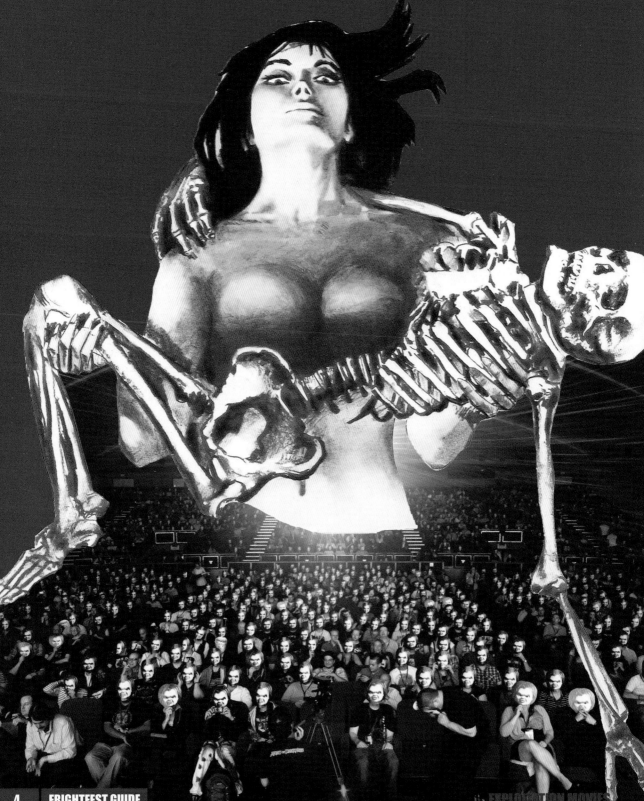

TERROR THAT RIPS THE SCREAMS RIGHT OUT OF YOUR THROAT!

EXPLOITATION MOVIES

-THE DARK HEART OF CINEMA -
FRIGHTFEST ®

FrightFest is the biggest, best and most prestigious horror fantasy event in the United Kingdom. Created by Paul McEvoy, film exhibitor Ian Rattray, film critic, international journalist, author and broadcaster Alan Jones, and veteran PR man Greg Day, the main FrightFest event takes place annually over the August Bank Holiday in London.

Beginning in 2000, and now a permanent resident at the Cineworld Empire in Leicester Square, the heart of London's glittering West End, FrightFest has organised various one-off events (including **The Descent** world premiere with Neil Marshall, 2005, the UK launch of **Drag Me to Hell** with Sam Raimi, 2009, the **Cold in July** premiere with Jim Mickle, 2014, and in conjunction with Amazon Studios, both **Master** and **Nanny** in 2022), an annual Halloween extravaganza that sometimes travelled to other key UK cities and has a tentpole weekend position every March as part of the Glasgow Film Festival. FrightFest also organised UK wide publicity tours on behalf of Universal, eOne and Vertigo for **American Mary** with the Soska sisters, **Insidious** with James Wan and Leigh Whannell, and **The Children** with Tom Shankland.

Notable attendees over the years include Christopher Nolan, George A. Romero, Dario Argento, John Landis, Guillermo del Toro, Brian Yuzna, Alan Moore, Tobe Hooper, Clive Barker, Rob Zombie, Ben Wheatley, Robert Englund, Park Chan-wook, Danny Boyle, Edgar Wright, Barbara Crampton, Buddy Giovinazzo, Paco Plaza, Frank Henenlotter, Gemma Arterton, Saoirse Ronan, Larry Fessenden, Jessica Alba, Bernard Rose, Danny Huston, Alexandre Aja, Ti West, Nacho Vigalondo, Eli Roth, Jaume Balguero, Chris Smith, Adam Wingard, Gareth Edwards, Claudia Gerini, Federico Zampaglione, Ed Speelers, Tom Six, Melissa George, Cristian Solimeno, Andy Nyman, Adam Green, Joe Lynch, Alfonso Cuaron, Maika Monroe and Caroline Munro.

'The FrightFest Guide to Exploitation Movies' is the first volume of an ongoing series including its companion 'The FrightFest Guide to Grindhouse Movies'. Other genre subjects covered in the critically acclaimed series are Vampires, Monsters, Ghosts, Werewolves and Mad Doctors, each intended to build the knowledge of the curious spectator and the cult connoisseur alike. But FrightFest is not just a film festival or the friendliest community you could ever wish to join. It's an ever-expanding brand that includes FrightFest Presents, our multi-platform/VOD entertainment label that has released such diverse and popular titles as **Some Kind of Hate** (2015), **My Father Die** (2016), **Boar** (2017), **The Siren** (2019), **Videoman** (2018), **The Wind** (2018), **12 Hour Shift** (2020), **Bitch Ass** (2022), the cultural phenomenon **The Love Witch** (2016) and the critically acclaimed **Relic** (2020), **You Are Not My Mother** (2021) and **The Harbinger** (2022).

ALAN JONES

Alan Jones is an internationally renowned reporter on the Horror Fantasy genre in all media. He travels the world to cover the making of movies in production. The first movie he covered on location was the original **Star Wars** in 1977, the latest, Federico Zampaglione's **The Well** (2023).

He was the sole London correspondent for the seminal 'CFQ' magazine from 1977 to 2002, reviewed every genre release for 'Starburst' between 1980 and 2008, was a featured film critic for 'Film Review' for two decades, contributed set-reports to 'Fangoria' for a decade and is currently a featured film critic in the 'Radio Times', the UK's biggest selling magazine. He was editor of 'Shivers', 'Film Guide' and consultant editor of 'The Horror Collection' a New Line Cinema endorsed collectable figurine part work.

Other magazines and newspapers he has written for include 'Empire', 'Total Film', 'SFX', 'Wonderland', 'Heat', 'The Guardian', 'GQ', 'Vogue', 'FHM', 'Femme Fatales', 'The Dark Side', 'The Independent' and 'Premiere'. His 'Total Film' feature titled The Splat Pack ensured that term entered film industry jargon.

He is an active member of the London Critic's Circle, whose annual film awards gain worldwide recognition and is an in-demand expert on Horror, Punk (he worked for designer Vivienne Westwood and was the Sex Pistols' DJ) and Disco. He has appeared on, researched and written numerous programmes for television including two award-winning documentaries on the Italian horror directors Mario Bava and Dario Argento. His punk showcases include the BBC series 'Punk Britannia' and the feature documentaries **Who Killed Nancy?** and **Wake Up Punk**. His reminiscences about the Disco era have graced many BBC programmes and comprise the sleeve notes of the bestselling 25-plus CD collections 'Disco: Discharge' and 'Disco: Recharge'. He also wrote the sleeve notes for 'The Vault of Horror: The Italian Connection' vinyl albums of rare soundtracks.

He has been a member of the critic's jury at the Sitges (Spain), Fantasporto (Portugal), Paris, Rome, Strasbourg, Neuchatel (Switzerland), RazorReel (Bruges), Science+Fiction (Trieste, Italy), Motel X (Lisbon, Portugal), Fantastic Fest (Austin, Texas) and Avoriaz (France) fantasy festivals and, after co-presenting the legendary *Shock Around the Clock* festival in London, and *Fantasm* at the National Film Theatre, is now co-curator of *FrightFest*. He oversees the artistic direction of the 'FrightFest Presents' multi-platform label in conjunction with the top UK independent, Signature Entertainment. In 2022 he became the Artistic Director of the *Trieste Science+Fiction Festival*, the oldest sci-fi event in the world.

His DVD commentaries continually receive high acclaim including those for Alejandro Jodorowsky's **Santa Sangre**, Nicolas Winding Refn's **Valhalla Rising**, **Bronson** and **Fear X**, Tom Shankland's **WAZ**, Andrew Birkin's **Cement Garden**, Tony Maylam's **The Burning** and Dario Argento's **The Bird with the Crystal Plumage**, **The Card Player**, **The Stendhal Syndrome**, **Tenebrae** and **Suspiria**. Other Giallo commentaries include **What Have You Done to Solange?**, **The Bloodstained Butterfly** and **The Red Queen Kills Seven Times**. His moderated commentary with Oscar-winning actress Helen Mirren for Tinto Brass's **Caligula** is considered a milestone in the art form. He has also contributed to numerous DVD extras and documentaries for **The Keep**, **Video Nasties The Definitive Guide 1** & **2**, **Heavenly Creatures**, and the **A Nightmare on Elm Street** Blu-ray collection, to name the tip of the iceberg.

He has acted in the movies **Terror**, **Talos the Mummy** and **Shaun of the Dead**, and is the well-reviewed author of *Nekrofile*, the critically acclaimed *Saturday Night Forever: The Story of Disco* (UK, US and Italian editions), the global bestseller *Tomb Raider: The Official Film Companion*, the SGM Award-winning and Rondo Award nominee *Profondo Argento*, *The Rough Guide to Horror Movies* (UK and French editions), *The Act of Seeing* (with director Nicolas Winding Refn) and *The FrightFest Fearbook*. His update of *Profondo Argento*, re-titled *Dario Argento: The Man, the Myths & the Magic*, is continually being reprinted. He also edited, annotated and illustrated *Fear*, the English edition of Dario Argento's autobiography. *Starburst: The Complete Alan Jones Film Reviews, 1977-2008* and his autobiography *Discomania!* will be published by FAB Press in 2023 and 2024 respectively.

INTRODUCTION BY BUDDY GIOVINAZZO

Shit, about a year or so ago my friend Alan Jones told me about this book he was putting together. A book about Times Square and 42nd Street during the grindhouse days when if you said you were going to the strip, it was akin to announcing you were going to visit Caligula at a Roman bathhouse. Well, I spent a good many years of my youth going to Times Square back in the day, from when I was 10 years old with my father taking me and my three brothers, one middle-aged man with his four sons, all holding hands, to Times Square. My father might as well have taken us to Mars. My first impression of Times Square was to be hit by the blinking lights and the colors, the flashing marquees for films I'd never seen advertised on TV, the advertisements for things I was too young to understand.

I didn't know yet what peep shows or private booths were. I thought it odd that many storefronts were covered over with newspaper on the windows, even though they were open for business. I was amazed at the women on the street all dressed so colorfully and standing around in bent-over poses reminding me of characters out of Dr. Seuss. My father took us along and led us into a large shop in the middle of the street; it might have been 42nd Street but I think it was one of the side streets around it. This shop was a juvenile delinquent's wet dream. It had everything in it I was not allowed to play with. Every kind of joke and prank you could pull on someone. The wind-up hand buzzer, the fly in the ice cube, the rubber puke and mound of shit, the Groucho Marx nose and mustache, every kind of rubber snake and insect you could imagine; the possibilities were endless. And my favorite, the one I'd been seeing in the back of comic books for years: the X-Ray Glasses, where you could see through people's clothes.

I remember asking the store clerk, a stubby old guy with a soggy cigar – yes, the cliché was real! – if the glasses really worked and he rasped at me, "Kid, I just sell 'em." Well, of course I bought them and like everything that's ever been sold or would be sold on the strip, they were a rip-off. I couldn't see anyone naked with those glasses. Debbie Shiro, my first love in fifth grade, was reduced to a bunch of squiggly lines that made it seem like I was watching her skeleton. Naturally, after three days the glasses broke.

Cut to three years later. I went with my brother and some friends on our first excursion into NYC, having taken a bus to the Staten Island Ferry and from there hopping on the Number 1 IRT subway to 42nd Street. But now I knew what the boarded-up shops were selling, and now the prostitutes didn't look like candy anymore, but like old damaged women who'd been left and abandoned after the circus had left town. We started at the top of the strip, 7th Avenue and 42nd, and worked our way west. It was like a jungle to us, a jungle where we were relatively safe because we were too young for the drug dealers and the hookers; at least nobody harassed us or tried any shit. We walked past grimy fast food stands with pizza that smelled like dirty socks, there was a bin of cassette music tapes out front of one shop. My friend Vinnie Petrizzo bought two Ultimate Spinach tapes, without any idea who they were or what kind of music they played; a mistake that he probably still regrets today. The book shops had their doors open as it was very hot out, and as we passed we caught glimpses inside these shops. Businessmen in rumpled suits browsing through racks filled with every kind of sex magazine published at the time. Instead of the novelty shops, this time we discovered the Army/Navy stores. Attracted by the army helmets and mock pistols and weaponry in the window, I saw my first switchblade knife in that window. The switchblade knife was famous in our neighborhood. It was like the Holy Grail to my friends and me. Highly illegal, here it was on display in the window on 42nd Street at fifteen dollars a shot! Fifteen bucks was a fortune to us back then, but we pooled together our money and bought one. Then took turns clicking the blade open and having street fights with imaginary enemies. I bought a real hand grenade there too, but not on this trip. The hand grenade had been disarmed and was welded shut, but it was a real military weapon and one of my most prized possessions at the time. I would carry it with me for weeks before the sheer heavy weight of it became too burdensome to carry in my pocket.

After the success of our first exploratory trip to the strip, we went more frequently, at least once every two weeks. It was then that I discovered the movie theaters that lined the street on both sides. The Lyric, the Liberty, the Selwyn, several others whose names escape me. The movies on 42nd Street were fucking cheap. It was amazing! For between 75 cents and $1.50, we could sit through a double or triple bill watching really bad movies, then afterward step out into a world that was nearly as depraved as the films we'd just watched. The triple bill that still stands out in my mind as being the most wild was a showing of **The Corpse Grinders**, **The Undertaker and His Pals**, and **The Embalmer**.

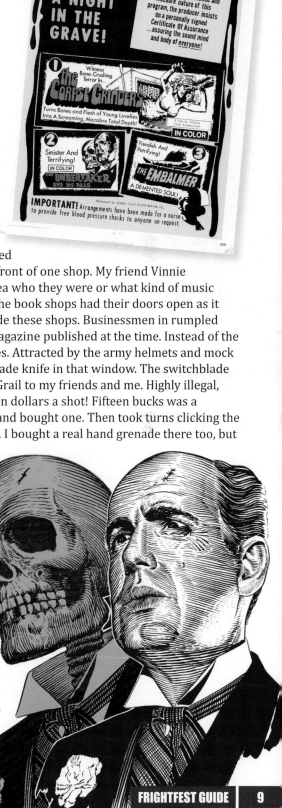

2000 A.D. PRODUCTIONS
PRESENTS

AMERICAN NIGHTMARES

A Film By Buddy G.

90 mins/color

NOW PLAYING

COMBAT SHOCKER!

The theater was grimy, rundown and smelled of disinfectant; the same disinfectant I would smell in the peep shows and bookstores and of course, in Show World a few years later. The floors were wet with small puddles all throughout the room; you could see the water reflected from the projection off the screen. During the pause for the second film I saw why. The workers there would never clean the floors; they would dump pails of water down the aisles hoping the soapy water would wash away the filth and take the stench of sweat, alcohol and piss with it. There must have been a revolving circuit of exploitation films at those theaters, because for nearly two years, **The Embalmer** was the film at the end of every bill. I sat through that cheap Italian mess at least six times without ever understanding what it was about. I remember a monk in black robes slinking through the canals of some dark Italian city, and that's pretty much all that I remember of it.

Films like **Two Thousand Maniacs!** and **Horrors of Spider Island** were a staple of the theaters there. For a number of the 42nd Street denizens, these cheap theaters were substitute living rooms, as I often saw the same faces, or figures (because a lot of the clientele was hunched over, sleeping or passed out in the seats) at different films, and they certainly weren't there for the screenings. The theaters were never emptied out at the end of the show. For your admission fee you could sit there all day and all night (some theaters were open 24 hours), show after show, and sleep, shoot up, jerk off, or have sex. The management never showed its face in the theater; so as long as no one was screaming for the police, everything was fine inside. There were a few times where I could see someone shooting up a few rows in front of me. I could see the flame cook the drug, then it would go out and the room was dark again. I heard a soft groan, then the occupant would slowly slump down in his seat and stay there without moving. For hours. For a junkie, 42nd Street was the cheapest shooting gallery in town, and relatively safe; although I can imagine many a junkie got rolled in a drug stupor sleeping there as **The Embalmer** trudged through a projector.

At the bottom of 42nd Street and the corner of 8th Avenue sat 3 floors of pornography, depravity and sleaze. Show World was there as long as I could remember, until it succumbed to the New York City cleanup under Mayor Guiliani, which is more disgusting than anything that ever took place at Show World. In the late '70s Show World was a sex superstore where you could buy sex toys, see peep shows, watch live sex and have lap dances (though at the time they weren't called lap dances). On the bottom floor was the carousel, a circle jerk where for the price of a 25 cent token,

you could watch two completely naked women dance on a stage. Every cubicle had a coin slot and an opaque screen. You put in your token and the screen rose up, revealing the girls dancing on a platform behind Plexiglas. The cubicles formed a circle and you could see the other guys across from you watching the girls. The girls would come up to your window and shake their asses in your face, and after a minute or so, the curtain would fall, prompting you to throw another token into the slot. It was sort of bizarre really. The girls were completely untouchable, but there was a tiny speaker like a transistor radio, so you could hear them talking to you. What was truly fascinating was watching guys across the way. As the curtain lowered they would crouch down peeking under the edge, trying to get every last second of naked chick for the price of their token. Outside the carousel was a corridor of rooms where girls would ask you inside for a private date. That was the catchphrase on the strip back then. "Wanna date?"

In October, 1986 my first feature film **Combat Shock** played at two theaters in Manhattan. One was a first-run twin theater on Broadway and 49th Street, a relatively normal theater that was also showing a Klaus Kinski movie, **Crawlspace**. But now in hindsight, the more important screening – though at the time I had higher hopes for my film – was at the Liberty Theater in the middle of 42nd Street on a triple bill with **Missing In Action** and **P.O.W. The Escape**.

In front of the theater they had a small stand with a TV monitor showing clips from the film; you can see it in the photo on this page, just to the left of the marquee. I stood there that day watching people watch clips of the mutated baby and the wife getting shot. The reactions were priceless: Shock, disgust, followed by a "get the fuck outta here" hilarity, especially every time the baby appeared. I stood there for a few hours just soaking in the depravity, happy in the thought that for a few seconds out of the day I could warm the souls of the downtrodden, the luckless people who fall through the cracks; the denizens of the strip. My people, if not in physical circumstances, at least in emotional harmony. I don't know why I find these characters so compelling and so sympathetic. I don't know what draws me to them; perhaps it's better not to know. Some things are better kept in the heart, unexplained; it's what makes the mystery of life so fascinating.

When I go to 42nd Street now all I feel is alienated, and anxious, displaced by all the high-end restaurants and the ridiculous sterile multiplexes. I don't feel at home there anymore, I feel pushed out by the tourists and their children strolling along in wide-eyed wonder at the bright and shiny neon lights, lights that no longer announce "Girls! Girls! Girls!", but instead promise some Disney-fied illusion of happiness and "Life is fair"-ness and I want to scream at them that it's all a lie and a trick and it's numbing their brains and soon there won't be anything left to explode out of their skulls when they do finally pull the trigger. But I don't. Because after all, who am I to crush anyone's fantasies. I'm certainly

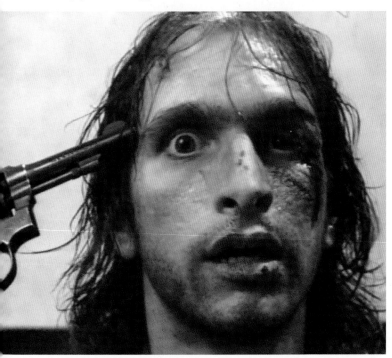

no model of joy and contentment. Instead I scream through my films. I feel honored to have had my first feature film, **Combat Shock**, premiere on 42nd Street. And although they may have chased Frankie Dunlan and his ilk off the strip, taken away their refuge and replaced it with a paradise for the rich and the rich only, Frankie Dunlan is a state of mind, a state that lives in every city in America. Just read the papers any day of the week, there are hundreds of Frankie Dunlans still out there, ticking time bombs, roaming around, struggling to survive, just trying to find some moment of peace and a place to call home. 42nd Street in the grindhouse days was for me just such a place. I fucking miss it.

— Buddy G.

A TO Z

OF
EXPLOITATION

From the first moment movies began the exploitation film existed. Instantly, fearless grifters, ex-carneys and dodgy businessmen filled gaps in the new entertainment market by selling what the big studios wouldn't dare: sex and violence, sin and sensation, 'Uncensored', 'Unashamed' and 'For Adults Only'. The first exploitation titles were built around simple concepts; **Chinese Opium Den** (1894), **The Kiss** (1896) and **Fatima's Belly Dance** (1897) showed exactly what they described in the title to appalled Victorians convinced the early kinetoscopes and 'flickers' were the devil's instruments anyway.

From that moment on titillation under the guise of moral instruction percolated throughout the early part of the 20th century with the likes of **Traffic in Souls** (1913), **Human Wreckage** (1923), **Bootleg Babies** (1940) and **Skid Row** (1943). But the skindependent sleaze industry exploded during the 1950s when shifts in censorship and the changing liberal attitudes of the times meant every whispered taboo became an easy target for prurient abuse. Untold amounts of money started being made by an intrepid bunch of gutsy showmen known by more reputable motion-picture distributors, continually outraged ratings boards and law enforcement officials as 'The Forty Thieves'. These carpetbaggers of cinema salaciousness promoted their dubious wares with extravagant claims ('Like nothing – but nothing you've seen before – EVER!' – **The Orgy at Lil's Place**, 1963), over-blown advertising copy ('Scarlet girls chained to the vultures of vice – It blasts the truth before your eyes!' – **Gambling with Souls/ The Vice Racket**, 1936) and lurid poster designs,

usually featuring semi-clad damsels in distress, promising far more than their Poverty Row budgets could ever deliver. And they raked it in for a good thirty years as such cheap thrill operations reached their zenith in the Swinging

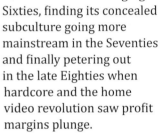

Sixties, finding its concealed subculture going more mainstream in the Seventies and finally petering out in the late Eighties when hardcore and the home video revolution saw profit margins plunge.

For every town had a drive-in cinema on its outskirts or a seedy fleapit in their red light district, the main places such backstreet B fodder made their fortunes. None more so than in New York City and that infamous intersection at Broadway and Times Square known as 42nd Street. Once the go-to place for peep shows, striptease, burlesque and 'bump 'n' grind' dancing (from where the alternative exploitation term grindhouse originates), such live attraction venues soon saw the projector light and switched to erotic screen spice instead. It enshrined the area's unsavoury reputation as one populated only by hookers, pimps, hobos, homos, barkers and hapless punters sucked in by the promises of celluloid shock, wanton lust, the sordid and the prohibited. As an oft-quoted joke during this shameless

golden era reported, "They call it 42nd Street because you're not safe if you spend more than forty seconds on it."

Notorious cinemas such as The Deuce, Selwyn, Anco, Lyric, Apollo, Liberty, Avon, Forum, Rialto, Embassy and The Doll were the places you went to sate whatever appetite you had. From the horror enthusiast seeking triple bills filled with extreme bloody violence and the Harlem hipster craving Blaxploitation to the action crowd demanding dazzling martial arts displays and lonely males just wanting to view sex in any form – the proverbial 'dirty raincoat brigade' – these fading picture palaces showed it all from dawn to late-night and often 24 hours non-stop.

Sometimes you had to be quick to see any explicit or hyped headliner. While they were usually billed 'For One Week Only', if they didn't draw the box-office footfall, they were off after a single day. You had to keep alert though as the same film would sometimes return under a different even more sensational title, occasionally three, to wring yet more cash out of the average patron's fears and desires.

Often the movie just contained a fleeting glimpse of pubic hair or a flash of the unspeakable you had to sit through 70 minutes of absolute boredom to catch. And often the movie playing was immaterial anyway. Bums would be sleeping in the auditorium having nowhere else to go and keep warm, you'd have to fight off groping hands in dark stairwells on the way to the balcony, hookers would be plying their trade in the filthy bathrooms and drug dealers would be slouched down operating in the front row.

But for those die-hard fans who frequented these run-down neon Nickelodeons such threatening and sexually charged atmospheres only added to the excitement and their metropolitan mystique. For many, just getting through the broken swing doors was a thrill in itself even before the tantalizingly controversial images unfolded on the dirty stained screen.

So welcome to 'The Greatest Productions in the History of Motion Pictures', to films that 'Exceed the imagination!', to 'Savagely realistic' spectaculars where 'Nothing so appalling in the annals of horror!' takes place. For 'This is the Real Thing!' and 'Your Head Will Spin', therefore 'We Dare You to See...'

ANGELS HARD AS THEY COME (1971), an apt description of that perennial wild one Jack Nicholson who starred pre **Easy Rider** (1969) in **Hells Angels on Wheels** (1967). Nothing like a big chopper between your legs and a motorcycle mama getting hot under the chrome and leather – especially if it's Nancy Sinatra in **The Wild Angels** (1966). Those biker boots were made for kicking! Abrupt senseless violence between rival gangs was the only plot ever needed to get the Harley motor running, heading for the highway in the genre that exploitation guru Roger Corman invented when his Edgar Allan Poe based horrors lost their lustre.

Naked Angels

BLAXPLOITATION. Who's the black private dick that's a sex machine to all the chicks? **Shaft** (1971) of course. And in his wake came **Super Fly** (1972), **Slaughter** (1972) and such Double D-cup dusky divas as **Coffy** (1973), **Foxy Brown** (1974) and **Sheba, Baby** (1975) invariably starring the genre's Queen, Pam Grier, who hacked off honky nuts to the delight of inner-city theatres and redneck-run drive-ins alike. Plus a host of hokey horrors that blackened famous monster names from **Blacula** (1972) to **Blackenstein** (1973). Even **The Exorcist** (1973) turned black in **Abby** (1974). Can you dig it?

Shaft in Africa

CANNIBALISM, the last great exploitation innovation invented in Italy. **Deep River Savages** (1972) was the first to mix real animal butchery and trashy gore into racist 'Jungle Jim' adventure. But it was the unforgettable mutilation extravaganza **Cannibal Holocaust** (1980), the first found-footage shocker wrongly accused of being a 'snuff movie' in Roman courts that became the defining standard.

Cannibal Holocaust

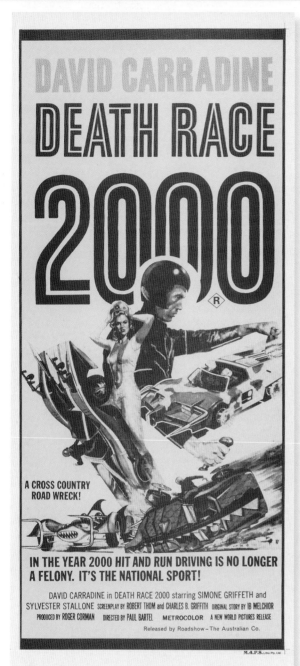

DAVID CARRADINE
DEATH RACE 2000

A CROSS COUNTRY ROAD WRECK!

IN THE YEAR 2000 HIT AND RUN DRIVING IS NO LONGER
A FELONY. IT'S THE NATIONAL SPORT!

DAVID CARRADINE in DEATH RACE 2000 starring SIMONE GRIFFETH and
SYLVESTER STALLONE SCREENPLAY BY ROBERT THOM and CHARLES B. GRIFFITH ORIGINAL STORY BY IB MELCHIOR
PRODUCED BY ROGER CORMAN DIRECTED BY PAUL BARTEL METROCOLOR A NEW WORLD PICTURES RELEASE
Released by Roadshow – The Australian Co.

M.A.P.S. Litho Pty. Ltd.

Cult of the Cobra

CULTS. **The Seventh Victim** (1943) had Greenwich Village devil worshippers eliminating former members, **Cult of the Cobra** (1955) highlighted High Priestess Faith Domergue transforming into a snake, while Scream Queen Barbara Steele oversaw **The Crimson Cult/Curse of the Crimson Altar** (1968), innkeeper Patricia Jessel ran the Satanic coven in **Horror Hotel/The City of the Dead** (1960) and Joan Fontaine fell foul of **The Witches/The Devil's Own** (1966). For a while in Exploitation Land cults were mainly about Black Magic, the supernatural, voodoo, Santeria, and were depicted in everything from **Night of the Eagle/Burn, Witch Burn!** (1962) and **Rosemary's Baby** (1968) to **The Devil Rides Out** (1968) and **The Wicker Man** (1973). But then psycho hippie Charles Manson orchestrated the 1969 Tate-LaBianca murders and before you could say 'Helter Skelter' cults became synonymous with crazed fanatical followers carrying out lunatic orders. See **Cult of the Damned/Angel, Angel, Down We Go** (1969), **Manson** (1973) and the ultimate Made in Mexico laugh-riot **Guyana, Cult of the Damned/Guyana, Crime of the Century** (1979) where Stuart Whitman as Reverend Jim Johnson (names changed to protect the innocent!) issues the "Drink the Kool-Aid" order.

CARS. Cars being instruments of death are one thing and practically every exploitation movie features an explosive crash. But when Steven Spielberg's **Duel** (1971) made a vehicle more important than the actors, the writing was on the wall. Out went the pile-ups of **The Cars That Ate Paris** (1974) and **Death Race 2000** (1975) and in came an assembly line of possessed motors including **Crash!** (1976), **The Car** (1977), **The Hearse** (1980), **Christine** (1983) and **Maximum Overdrive** (1986).

Curse of the Crimson Altar

What Ever Happened to Baby Jane?

DE SADE (1969). A major financial flop for American International Pictures was this tame biopic of the notorious Marquis who gave his name to the technique of deriving sexual arousal from inflicting pain and humiliation. Kier Dullea followed his iconic **2001: A Space Odyssey** (1968) with this moronic clunker where the height of depravity had him smearing jam on a girl's nipples while a bevy of Euro-starlets ran topless through his bedroom. All the sexual corruption, decadence and immorality director Cy Endfield couldn't whip up was instead found in such art-house shockers as Liliana Cavani's **Il portiere di notte/The Night Porter** (1974) and Pier Paolo Pasolini's **Salò o le 120 giornate di Sodoma/Salò, or the 120 Days of Sodom** (1975) while further down the exploitation chain Jesús Franco offered such studies in perversion as **Rote Lippen, Sadisterotica/Sadist Erotica** (1969), **Eugénie de Sade** (1973), **Die Marquise von Sade/Doriana Grey** (1976), **El sádico de Notre-Dame/The Sadist of Notre-Dame** (1979) and **Eugenie (Historia de una perversión)/Wicked Memories of Eugenie** (1980). Don't forget the debauched flipside either, Masochism, as named after Leopold von Sacher-Masoch, whose 1870 novel 'Venus in Furs' provided Joseph Marzano, Franco and Massimo Dallamano with fetish source material for **Venus in Furs** (1967), **Paroxismus** (1969) and **Le malizie di Venere/Devil in the Flesh** (1969) respectively.

De Sade

DIVA DRAMA. After bitch queens Bette Davis and Joan Crawford feuded through **What Ever Happened to Baby Jane?** (1962) and their Grand Guignol grotesquerie proved a massive hit, every Old Hollywood studio system vamp dusted off their CVs to turn Sixties shocker camp with varying degrees of success. Davis returned with Olivia de Havilland for **Hush, Hush, Sweet Charlotte** (1964), while the latter gouged out James Caan's eyes with her corset bones in **Lady in a Cage** (1964). De Havilland's sister Joan Fontaine graced **The Witches/The Devil's Own** (1966) as Tallulah Bankhead sashayed through **Fanatic/Die! Die! My Darling** (1965) and Geraldine Page and Agnes Moorehead asked **Whatever Happened to Aunt Alice?** (1969), Debbie Reynolds **What's the Matter with Helen?** (1971) and Shelley Winters **Whoever Slew Auntie Roo?** (1972). Other fading femme fatales went even further in the 'trash yourself terror' department – Virginia Mayo in **Castle of Evil** (1966), Veronica Lake in **Flesh Feast** (1970), Gloria Grahame in **Blood and Lace** (1971), Ruth Roman in **The Baby** (1973) and Lauren Bacall in **The Fan** (1981). Golden Era Exploitation was never ageist even if mainstream Hollywood was!

Persons under 16 not admitted. Ⓧ

TORYTOEDREAM ALOVESTORYTOEDREAM ALOVESTORYTOEDREAM ALOVESTORYTOEDREAM

DRUGS. Vintage archetypes **Reefer Madness** (1936) and **Cocaine Fiends** (1935) professed to teach the dangers of their 'torn from today's headlines' scandals while depicting worst-case scenarios in the most lurid way imaginable. They played side-splittingly fast and loose with the facts for heightened shock value, e.g. the case history of the lad high on weed axing his entire family. Seventies stoners didn't have such freak-out murder on their minds. All they wanted was to tune in turn on and drop by psychedelic hued love-ins as depicted in **The Trip** (1967) and **Hallucination Generation** (1966). "Don't go straight to these movies" was good advice given by one of the more groovy critics of the day.

EMMANUELLE as played by innocent nymphet Sylvia Kristel might have been the glossy erotic soft-core sensation of 1974. But it was **Black Emanuelle** (1975) – with one M to avoid any lawsuits – that brought the sexy brand name down to shoddy rock bottom. Gorgeous Java-born Laura Gemser floated butt-naked throughout crass vulgarity, gross violence against women, sadistic perversions and even cannibalism with hilarious hauteur – all to a glorious easy listening lounge soundtrack. The E industry was at least about equal opportunities though – **Yellow Emanuelle** arrived in 1977.

The Trip

Emanuelle and the Last Cannibals

ENTER THE DRAGON (1973). That popular chop-socky saga might have been martial artist grand master Bruce Lee's last complete feature, but its huge commercial success meant many more Asian dragons – Bruce Li, Dragon Lee, Jackie Chan, Angela Mao, Tommy Lee, Bruce Le, Sonny Chiba, David Chiang – entered the fray in a wild variety of Kung-fu, Samurai, Karate and Ninja action exploitation. From the dazzling **Jing wu men/ Fist of Fury/The Chinese Connection** (1972) to the stunning **Du bi quan wang da po xue di zi/ Master of the Flying Guillotine** (1976), nothing escaped the stars beloved by millions throughout the Far East who suddenly found a fan base in the flea-pit West too. Japanese sword slashers, Ninja dirty tricks, nunchaku blood feuds, Shaolin temple battles and Yakuza cool fuelled everything from the sublime **Shi ba ban wu yi/Legendary Weapons of China** (1982) and **Yakuza no hakaba: Kuchinashi no hana/Yakuza Graveyard** (1976) to the ridiculous **Wu long tian shi zhao ji gui/Kung Fu Zombie** (1981). Even The Hammer House of Horror got in on the act with **The Legend of the 7 Golden Vampires** and **Shatter** (both 1974).

THE STORY OF THE LOVE LIFE OF THE SIDESHOW

DWAIN ESPER PRESENTS

CAN A FULL GROWN WOMAN TRULY LOVE A MIDGET?

DO SIAMESE TWINS MAKE LOVE?

WHAT SEX IS THE HALF MAN HALF WOMAN?

FREAKS

LOUELLA PARSONS SAYS—

FOR PURE SENSATIONALISM 'FREAKS' TOPS ANY PICTURE YET PRODUCED. IT'S MORE FANTASTIC AND GROTESQUE THAN ANY SHOCKER EVER WRITTEN

EXCELSIOR PICT. CORP. NEW YORK 19, U.S.A.

FREAKS. 28 years after starring in **Freaks** (director Tod Browning's 1932 horror classic that became a grindhouse staple under the alternative title **Forbidden Love** thanks to schlock pioneer Dwain Esper), real-life Siamese twins Daisy and Violet Hilton got a second stab at sideshow fame. They danced cheek-to-cheek-to-cheek-to-cheek through the tacky murder mystery **Chained for Life** (1951). Other physically challenged vaudeville and circus acts appeared in the enforced sterilization saga **Tomorrow's Children** (1934) and the all-midget western **The Terror of Tiny Town** (1938).

Legendary Weapons of China

Enter the Dragon

GIALLO, or jet-set Euro-trash thriller. Maestro Dario Argento's stylish output – **The Bird with the Crystal Plumage** (1970), **Four Flies on Grey Velvet** (1971), **Deep Red** (1975) etc. – are the retina-dazzling benchmark. But any barmy erotica motivated plot, jazzy discotheque scene with unusual suspects – preferably Italian sex kittens Edwige Fenech and Barbara Bouchet – frugging in funky wigs to a sublime Ennio Morricone score and plentiful chic gore will do. Usually sporting the longest titles ever – **Why are those Strange Drops of Blood on the Body of Jennifer?** (1972), **Your Vice Is a Locked Room and Only I Have the Key** (1972) being just two examples – the sleazy **Strip Nude for Your Killer** (1975) is a classic.

Deep Red

Strip Nude For Your Killer

GIMMICKS. Master showman William Castle was the undisputed king of Gimmick cinema. To tempt people away from their TV sets in the 1950s he issued insurance polices covering death by fright in **Macabre** (1958), his **Homicidal** (1961) had a 'Fright Break' so scaredy-cats could leave before the shocking revelation, and **Mr. Sardonicus** (1961) allowed audiences to choose the fate of its villain with 'thumbs up/thumbs down' cards. But Castle's pioneering triumphs were 'Emergo' for **House on Haunted Hill** (1958), in which a plastic skeleton was cranked across the cinema ceiling during a key Vincent Price scene, and 'Percepto' for **The Tingler** (1959) where buzzers under seats administered mild shocks when the monster was loose. Other

notable gimmicks; 'The Fear Flasher and Horror Horn' whenever a gory scene was about to happen in **Chamber of Horrors** (1966) to warn sensitive viewers, 'The D-Test' questionnaire before sitting through

Dementia 13 (1963), 'The Final Warning Station' before entering the cinema to see **Twitch of the Death Nerve** (1971) and the subliminal messages telegraphed by 'Psychorama' in **My World Dies Screaming** (1958). Not to mention a whole host of giveaways at the auditorium doors including packets of **Torture Garden** (1967) seeds, matchboxes of **The Legend of the 7 Golden Vampires** (1974) vampire dust, masks to avoid **The Gorgon** (1964), **Mark of the Devil** (1970) sick bags, **Brides of Blood** (1968) engagement rings, **Rasputin, the Mad Monk** (1966) beards and a **Golden Needles** (1974) acupuncture kit.

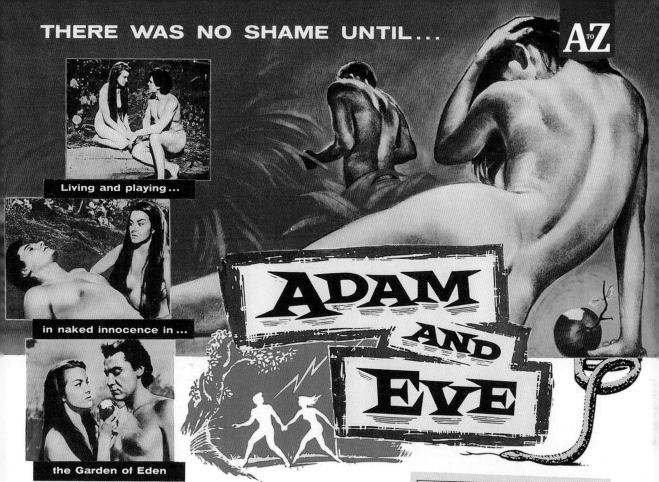

THERE WAS NO SHAME UNTIL...

Living and playing...

in naked innocence in...

the Garden of Eden

ADAM AND EVE

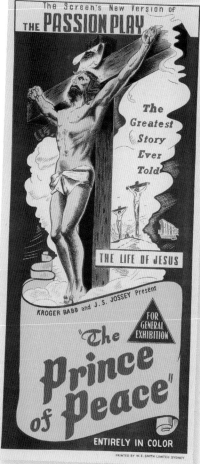

The Screen's New Version of
THE PASSION PLAY

The Greatest Story Ever Told

THE LIFE OF JESUS

KROGER BABB and J.S. JOSSEY Present

FOR GENERAL EXHIBITION

"The Prince of Peace"

ENTIRELY IN COLOR

PRINTED BY W.E.SMITH LIMITED SYDNEY

GOD TOLD ME TO (1976). That Larry Cohen masterpiece about an alien messiah introduces Godsploitation to the grindhouse grift. While most exploitation was about sex and violence, some of the Forty Thieves recognized there was a religious demographic out in the sticks not having their devout beliefs catered to. So why not peddle heavenly awe and God-fearing virtues, and if they could sell some miniature bibles in the foyer afterwards marketed by Divinity Experts (i.e. out-of-work actors in dog collars) even better. This remunerative genre was the brainchild of supreme showman Kroger Babb, who got wind of an annual passion play performed in the Wichita Mountains by the citizens of Lawton, Oklahoma. He bog-standard filmed it, including all the putting-on-a-show backstage excitement, and released it as **The Lawton Story/ The Prince of Peace** (1949). And it played the drive-in circuit for years. Most of it was God-awful, but **God Is My Partner** (1957), **I'll Give My Life** and **The Cross and the Switchblade** (1970) have their disciples. Of course it was soon noted that the Bible also had its fair share of nudity and salaciousness and **Adam and Eve** (1956), **Sodom and Gomorrah** (1962) and **The Joys of Jezebel** (1970) quickly became firm favourites with pious and penitent do-gooders. Amen to that.

EXPLOITATION MOVIES

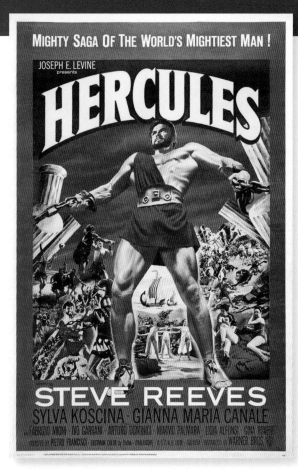

MIGHTY SAGA OF THE WORLD'S MIGHTIEST MAN!

JOSEPH E. LEVINE
presents

HERCULES

STEVE REEVES

SYLVA KOSCINA · GIANNA MARIA CANALE

Hundreds more shoddier spectaculars then swamped the grindhouse circuit for years. Other actors donning the pepla with flair include body-builders Dan Vadis/Constantine Daniel Vafiadis, Reg Park, Kirk Morris/Adriano Bellini, Alan Steel/Sergio Ciani, Gordon Mitchell and Gordon Scott/Gordon Weschkul. Best titles? Try Mario Bava's **Ercole al centro della Terra/Hercules in the Haunted World** (1961), Sergio Leone's **Il colosso di Rodi/The Colossus of Rhodes** (1961) and Giacomo Gentilomo and Sergio Corbucci's **Maciste contro il vampiro/Goliath and the Vampires** (1961). High points were always when the action ground to a halt for the ubiquitous Vestal Virgin/Slave Girl dance routines.

HERSCHELL GORDON LEWIS accidentally became the godfather of gore looking for the Next Big Thing after his violent sexed-up nudie-cuties, like **Scum of the Earth** (1963), started losing box-office appeal. So he drenched half-naked girls in gallons of stage blood and hacked up shop window mannequins in close-up on screen for **Blood Feast** (1963), a 'ghastly beyond belief' slaughterhouse of a movie. And the 'splatter' film, a term coined by George A. Romero when directing **Dawn of the Dead** (1978), was born to flow and flower through the 1970s with **Twitch of the Death Nerve/Blood Bath** (1971), **The Last House on the Left** (1972), the epochal **Friday the 13th** (1980) franchise, and onwards to the pinnacle of the genre, **Braindead/Dead Alive** (1992).

HERCULES (1958). Rippling muscles, skimpy loincloths (pepla, hence the Peplum label), fragile beauties in flimsy costumes, pointy-bearded villains, cheap monsters and evil queens in heavy eyeliner and beehive hairdos. Welcome to the sword and sandal mini-epics made at Cinecittà during the height of **La Dolce Vita** (1960). From the late 1950s for more than a decade the Italian Film Industry, mostly, churned out a vast number of budget gladiator movies in which interchangeable beefy heroes Hercules, Maciste, Samson, Goliath, Ursus and Atlas took on numerous labours and tyrants, slaying panto enemies and destroying cardboard palaces in the muscle-bound process. Producer/director Pietro Francisci chose Steve Reeves as the star of **Le fatiche di Ercole** ('The Labours of Hercules', 1958) after seeing him in the MGM musical **Athena** (1954). Following moderate success in Europe, producer Joseph E. Levine bought the US rights, marketed it simply as **Hercules**, launched an unprecedented publicity campaign, including unheard of TV spots, and thanks to his saturation booking policy, meaning no escape from a cinema showing it, turned his paltry investment of $120,000 into a massive money-maker.

Blood Feast

Two Thousand Maniacs!

HIXPLOITATION.
Poor white trash needed movies too, ones reflecting their own inbred, hillbilly lifestyles where rural morality was in a different time zone and **Deliverance** (1972) the warning to everyone not to mess with **Scum of the Earth** (1974) down **Tobacco Roody** (1970) or "Duelling Banjos" would be playing in your ears before you could scream **Mudhoney** (1965). **Child Bride** (1938), **Shotgun Wedding** (1963), **Common Law Wife** (1963), **Shanty Tramp** (1967), **Country Cuzzins** (1972), **The Pig Keeper's Daughter** (1972), **Hot Summer in Barefoot County** (1974), **'Gator Bait** (1973) and **Moonshine County Express** (1977) weren't movie titles so much as normal backwoods conversation! Sex and violence were the Hixploitation mainstays, the rougher the better, but **Two Thousand Maniacs!** (1964), **Hillbillys in a Haunted House** (1967), **The Texas Chain Saw Massacre** (1974), **The Hills Have Eyes** (1977), **Death Trap/ Eaten Alive** (1977), **Motel Hell** (1980) and **Just Before Dawn** (1981) ensured rednecks and red necks, from all the throat-slashing, populated hix-based horror hits.

I AM CURIOUS (YELLOW) (1967).
What's a story concerning a non-violent radical 20-year-old girl protesting about U.S. involvement in Vietnam and the Swedish class structure in order to forge her own identity amidst all the political and social turmoil of the late '60s doing here? Well, it contained a lengthy scene of totally naked stars Lena Nyman and Borje Ahlstedt indulging in sexual intercourse, fellatio and cunnilingus with uninhibited abandon in front of the Stockholm royal palace. While this explicit section was a legitimate part of the strident message in director Vilgot Sjoman's 'Make Love, Not War' blend of documentary and fictional footage, its frankness caused a permissive furore that eventually broke down American censorship rulings because of its serious context. While banning and controversy issues kept this taboo-breaker off art-house screens worldwide for two years, the title became instantly synonymous for everything forbidden and full frontal. The sexploitation industry cottoned on fast to this outrage-by-association and within months rip-offs like **The Curious Female** (1969) and **I Am Curious Tahiti** (1970) and started appearing with myriad come-on strap lines such as "If you are curious see..." being slapped on posters. The sequel **I Am Curious (Blue)** followed in 1968 (yellow and blue the colours of the Swedish flag) in the wake of its forerunner becoming one of the most infamous 'For Adults Only' titles ever made alongside **The Immoral Mr. Teas** (1959) and **Deep Throat** (1972).

I Spit on Your Grave

I SPIT ON YOUR GRAVE (1978). One of the most infamous titles of all time was purloined from the English translation of the 1959 French film **J'irai cracher sur vos tombes**, based on Boris Vian's novel by producer/director Meir Zarchi as an alternative to his original **Day of the Woman** moniker. It introduces the Rape Revenge genre, that ever-popular mix of carnality and carnage, which has become a staple of exploitation because it allows for wallowing in sexual violence while knowing there will be a satisfying payback. Arguably rooted by Ingmar Bergman's **Jungfrukällan/The Virgin Spring** (1960) art-house shocker, notable variations on the formula are **The Last House on the Left** (1972), **Thriller – en grym film/Thriller: A Cruel Picture** (1973), **Act of Vengeance/The Rape Squad** (1974), **L'ultimo treno della notte/ Night Train Murders** (1975), **Jackson County Jail** (1976), **Death Weekend/The House by the Lake** (1976), **La casa sperduta nel**

The Last House on the Left

parco/House on the Edge of the Park** (1980), **Ms.45/Angel of Vengeance** (1981) and **Savage Streets** (1984).

JUVENILE DELINQUENTS. Cool and crazy rebels without a cause and hot rod girls wanted to live fast and die young in the Fifties. It was the untamed youth era revolving around switchblade fights and motorway chicken runs that put the dreaded word teenager in every headline and every drive-in title. There were teenage Dolls, Monsters, Cavemen, Crime Waves, Mothers, Werewolves, Jailbait, Menaces, Zombies, Stranglers, Gang Debs, Bad Girls and even **Teenagers from Outer Space** (1959). Platinum blonde powerhouse Mamie Van Doren jived up a storm uncovering 'the stark brutal truth about today's lost generation' in such be-bop till you drop movies as **Running Wild** (1955) and the classic **High School Confidential!** (1958). And when 1955 saw the birth of Rock 'n' Roll on film in **Blackboard Jungle**, featuring Bill Haley and the Comets' 'Rock Around the Clock' blaring out on the soundtrack, the 'negro' music became shorthand for delinquency, violence, blatant sexuality and cool.

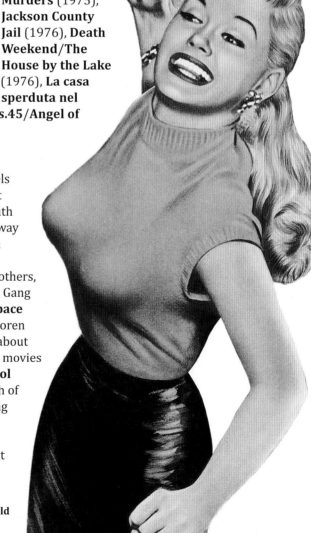

Running Wild

Killer Nun

KILLER NUN (1978).
Atypical for the genre because it's set in the modern day, **Suor omicidi/The Killer Nun** nevertheless introduces Nunsploitation to the lexicon of lurid celluloid libidinousness. The rather genteel **La monaca di Monza/The Nun of Monza** (1969) innocently set the template of a cloistered all-female convent population indulging in bad habits. The elements of physical anguish/torture, nudity and forbidden love were embroidered upon in Luchino's nephew Eriprando Visconti's 1969 same-titled version. Then when Ken Russell's **The Devils** (1971) became one of the most controversial conversation pieces of the decade, it was only a matter of time before producers jumped on the all-stops-out sacrilegious bandwagon. Pretty soon lesbianism, perversion, flagellation, sadistic Mother Superiors, demonic possession, lecherous priests and violent rituals were added to the sin and blasphemy Sister Acts all lip-smackingly on show in such postulant delights as **Le monache di Sant'Arcangelo/The Nun and the Devil** (1973), **Le scomunicate di San Valentino/The Sinful Nuns of Saint Valentine** (1974), **Flavia, la monaca musulmana/Flavia, the Heretic** (1974), **Suor Emanuelle/Sister Emanuelle** (1977), **Shûdôjo Runa no kokuhaku/Cloistered Nun: Runa's Confession** (1976) and **L'altro inferno/The Other Hell** (1981).

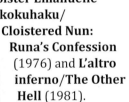

KILLER SHREWS (1959), **Killer Bees** (1974), **Killer Fish** (1979), in fact any unlikely species could cause tawdry monster mayhem. Especially animals cheaply dressed as others (dogs with fake fangs and carpets strapped on their backs for giant shrews) or plentifully supplied by Mother Nature at no extra cost. Crappy trick photography and grainy superimposition lent a hand – "Attention! Attention! Ladies and gentlemen, attention! There is a herd of killer rabbits headed this way and we desperately need your help!" Nothing comes close to **Night of the Lepus** (1972) though for the delirious depths of anti-vivisection protest and gore guffaws to match.

The Devils

KRIMI. The name given to a series of West German crime thrillers – Kriminalfilm – based on the works of British mystery novelist Edgar Wallace (1875–1932). When Wallace's work became popular post World War II in Germany (and later his son Bryan's too), Rialto Film bought all the rights to his novels based on the huge success of their first outing, **Der Frosch mit der Maske/The Fellowship of the Frog** (1959). With their shared stock themes of masked evil geniuses, Scotland Yard detectives, foggy London town, spooky castles/mansions, demure heroines in need of protection and gruesome sequences tipping into horror, contemporary critics loathed them while global audiences lapped them up. That international appetite meant 32 films were produced, making it the longest running series in German cinema history and a direct influence on the Italian Giallo. Joachim Fuchsberger, Heinz Drache and Siegfried Lowitz are most associated with the policemen roles, Karin Dor, Karin Baal, Uschi Glass and Margaret Lee their glamorous assistants/love interest, Eddi Arent and Siegfried Schürenberg the bumbling sidekick comic relief, Fritz Rasp, Gert Fröbe, Pinkas Braun and Dieter Borsche the best baddies, while the most

famous Krimi actor is force-of-nature icon Klaus Kinski. **Die Toten Augen von London/Dead Eyes of London** (1961), **Das Ratsel der roten Orchidee/The Secret of the Red Orchid** (1962), **Der Zinker/The Squeaker** (1963) and **Der Bucklige von Soho/The Hunchback of Soho** (1966) are a few of the more well-known titles.

LET ME DIE A WOMAN (1977), the quim-tessential 'whinge for a minge' sex change movie, from notorious director Doris Wishman, one of the few women to produce exploitation fare – the pinnacle of which was **Deadly Weapons** starring Chesty Morgan as the spy with a 73" bust. This leader of the snatch batch comes complete with a 'doctor' pointing at genitals stating the anatomical

obvious, tacky drag queen interviews, capped by amateur medical footage of silicone breast implants, penis removal and the testicle sac flattened into labia lining. Pass the angora sweater along with the sick bag! For another graphic beaver fever op see **Shocking Asia** (1976).

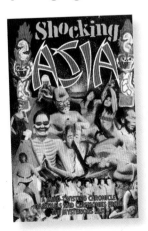

MAD DOCTORS. "It's alive!" What would exploitation be without those deranged physicians and megalomaniac scientists convinced they are creating physical abominations in the name of progress? Frankenstein may be the go-to doctor for easy horror but *en route* to the lab are Doctors Jekyll, Fu Manchu, Blood, Butcher, Death, Cyclops, Goldfoot, Orloff, Mabuse, X, Phibes, Terror, Renault and thousands more. And what was this dose of Doctors up to? One popular pastime remains raising the dead (**The Brain That Wouldn't Die**, 1960), another is eternal youth (**The Sorcerers**, 1967) and experimental plastic surgery (**Circus of Horrors**, 1960), then there's the creation of robots, giant apes (**Konga**, 1961), manimals (**The Island of Dr. Moreau**, 1977) or new sub-species (**Scream and Scream Again**, 1970) altogether. But the most outré of Doctor characters come from the fertile imagination of genius David Cronenberg and his crazed collection of brain surgeons, dermatologists, venereal disease researchers, mental disorder psychiatrists and telekinesis specialists populating **Crimes of the Future** (1970), **Shivers** (1975), **Rabid** (1976), **The Brood** (1979), **Scanners** (1980), **Videodrome** (1982) and **Dead Ringers** (1988).

MONDO CANE (1962). Stomach churning blueprint for the 'shockumentary', catalogues of war atrocities, animal killing and cruelty and weird tribal rites packaged as serious reportage. Much was faked in later 'brutal slices of primitive life' like the 'hidden camera' investigation **Mondo Bizarro** (1966) and the notorious 'banned in 43 countries' **Faces of Death** (1979). Shock, horror, it's the only 'documentawdry' category to be nominated for an Oscar – the Easy Listening Evergreen 'More', theme tune from **Mondo Cane**, written by Riz Ortolani and Nino Oliviero, recorded by Johnny Mathis.

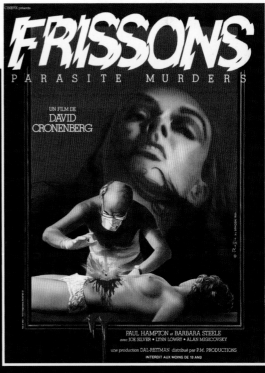

Shivers

NATURISM. Men travelled miles to see a glimpse of nipple in subtitled foreign films before the 'nudies', crude documentaries promoting 'Health and Efficiency' lifestyles. After a lengthy 1957 court case involving **Garden of Eden** (1954), it was decided that nudity on its own had no erotic content and was therefore not obscene. The censors outwitted, the floodgates opened. The formula was a rigid one – a buxom townie taught the joys of sunbathing in the raw by a nudist camp devotee. There was no sexual contact at all, the 'actors' always looked self-conscious and volleyball featured heavily because the breasts and buttocks jiggled more! And they were often endorsed by such authentic sounding, but usually bogus, organisations as 'The American Sunbathing Association'.

Naked As Nature Intended (1961), starring under-the-counter Brit pin-up Pamela Green from **Peeping Tom** (1960), and **Nudes of the World** (1961) have entered the smut-peddling Hall of Fame, but Doris Wishman's **Nude on the Moon** (1961) is perhaps the funniest of all – the lunar surface is discovered by eminent scientists to resemble the Sunny Palms nudist lodge in Florida.

Garden of Eden

NIGHT OF FEAR (1972). Australia's first excursion into the horror genre proper was that Terry Bourke directed, dialogue-free, barely an hour-long "slow descent into madness". But it was released just as Australia ended decades of draconian censorship by introducing the R certificate to cater for the flood of provocative overseas productions. And a counter-strike boom in bonzer Ozploitation began. From sex comedies **Alvin Purple** (1973) and **The True Story of Eskimo Nell** (1974) to the erotic fantasy anthology **Fantasm** (1976), the shockumentaries **The Love Epidemic** (1975) and **Australia After Dark** (1975), the crazed action adventures **The Man from Hong Kong** (1975) and **Mad Max** (1979) through the horrors of **Patrick** (1978), **Long Weekend** (1978), **Thirst** (1979), **Road Games** (1981) and **Turkey Shoot** (1982), it was fair dinkum days for budget Aussie film production launched by **Wake in Fright** (1971). Ozploitation was more explicit, violent, brasher and energetic, the broad location canvas eye-catching, the offbeat take on conventions and the outback atmosphere completely different to anything offered by any other culture. Ripper!

Blind Beast

OPERATION KID BROTHER (1967).

"The name's Connery, Neil Connery", Sean's look-alike sibling embarrassed himself in one of the many kitsch secret agent spoofs cashing in on the James Bond phenomenon. While Connery's acting ability registered minus 007, this Eurospy classic featured **Thunderball** villain Adolfo Celli, **From Russia with Love** Bond Girl Daniela Bianchi and franchise regulars Bernard Lee and Lois Maxwell. Other cheaply made but popular Euro-spy sagas include the Kommissar X, OSS 117, Jerry Cotton and Agent 077 series that made continental stars of Tony Kendall, George Nader and Frederick Stafford.

PINKU EIGA.

The Japanese Pink film, which can be Nikkatsu Roman Porno, Toei Pinky Violence or Tokyo erotica, is a style of softcore porno where many big international names first got their start. Dominating the domestic market for two decades from the mid-1960s, Pinks were mainly the product of small independents until the big studios saw the money they were raking in and got in on the act too. Dealing with overtly sexual themes like lesbianism, prostitution, adultery, masochism and sadism in a high-class way, the genre used superb artistry and lush aesthetics to tell their usually sordid stories that became critical and popular successes in their own territory, but also eminently profitable on the lowbrow exploitation market elsewhere. Best examples? Koji Wakamatsu's masterpiece entirely set on an apartment rooftop, **Yuke yuke nidome no shojo/Go, Go Second Time Virgin** (1969), Yasuzô Masumura's **Môjû/ Blind Beast** (1969), about a sightless sculptor kidnapping women, Noboru Tanaka's **Jitsuroku Abe Sada/A Woman Called Sada Abe** (1975), the first Sada Abe film beating Nagisa Oshima's more famous **Ai no corrida/ In the Realm of the Senses** (1976), and Masaru Konuma's ritual torture classic **Ikenie fujin/Wife to Be Sacrificed** (1974).

POLIZIOTTESCHI. **Rome Armed to the Teeth** (1976), **Calibre 9** (1972), **Shoot First, Die Later** (1974), **Almost Human/The Death Dealer** (1974) and **How to Kill a Judge** (1975) are just five of the hundreds of *poliziotteschi* movies the Italian film industry churned out during the turbulent 1970s once the Spaghetti Western and Giallo trends subsided. Begun by director Steno's **Execution Squad** (1972), first they aped the American crime hits of the day like **Dirty Harry** (1971), but soon they morphed into addressing typically Italian issues like the Mafia, Camorra and the Red Brigade. Rushed production methods meant local stars (Maurizio Merli and Tomas Milian the most prominent) and borrowed American names (Henry Silva, Richard Conte, Charles Bronson) performing their own stunts, regular directors like Fernando Di Leo and Umberto Lenzi stealing shots in urban places, no live sound recording and a rapid bleed-over between real crime taken from newspaper headlines and violent movie action. The exciting mayhem depicted ruled the 1970s box-office in Italy and ensured the films found their way to 42nd Street as Eurocrime gold.

QUEER STUFF. Forget anything homoerotic; queers on film were strictly swishy, the worst flaming stereotypes this side of Fairyland in such limp-wristed camp fare as **The Gay Deceivers** (1969) and **The Pink Angels** (1971). No, hot-blooded AC/DC sexploitation was all about steamy girl-on-girl action. Predominantly male audiences never had a problem with women lusting after each other and lipstick lesbians became an adult movie staple in the Swinging Sixties – see **Sin in the Suburbs** (1964) and the

ultimate pudenda pairing **Fanny Hill Meets Lady Chatterly** (1967). Real dykes preferred angst in their pants rather than bi-girl erotica aimed at straight men – **The Fourth Sex** (1962) for example, although **The Girl with the Hungry Eyes** (1967) was more typical because it killed off its lesbian lead as a lesson to those with a craving for 'unnatural desires'. Anything truly gay – **Pink Narcissus** (1971) with bulging posing pouches, tight toreador trousers and window dresser scenarios – was classed as Underground and on a completely different art-house circuit.

Pink Narcissus

RACISM. The frighteningly honest, tense social drama **The Intruder** (1962), starring extremist William Shatner decrying desegregation, was director Roger Corman's only commercial failure. No wonder then that the exploitation film mainly reinforced racist stereotypes rather than seriously explore relevant issues. And there were many Afro-American topics begging to be displayed in all their lurid glory when it came to miscegenation, passing for white, the Ku Klux Klan, white oppression, slavery, honky hatred and bigotry. **Is the Father Black Enough?** (1972) had a white girl pregnant by her black lover whose racist brother insists she has an abortion. **Addio zio Tom/Farewell Uncle Tom** (1971) was an astonishing exploration of race relations in America as it time-travelled between slave trade atrocities and Black Power radicalisation. **Black Love** (1971) was a hardcore mockumentary detailing of exactly that. **High Yellow** (1965) finds a light-skinned black girl pretending to be Caucasian. **Brotherhood of Death** (1976) has a group of black Vietnam vets taking on the KKK. **Mandingo** (1975) puts slave Ken Norton in demand in white bedrooms and bare-knuckle fighting rings. As for **Nigger Lover** (1973), enough said!

un trio de SUPERWOMEN avec bottes, boucles et ceinturons

RUSS MEYER. Creator of the nudie-cutie – **The Immoral Mr. Teas** (1959), master of the roughie – **Faster, Pussycat! Kill! Kill!** (1965), and the cause of millions of hard-ons in everything from **Wild Gals of the Naked West** (1962) and **Vixen!** (1968) to **Cherry, Harry & Raquel!** (1969) and **Beneath the Valley of the Ultra-Vixens** (1979). Give it up for King Leer, the cult sexploiter of all time who put big tits and big hair into cartoon plots so ludicrous all you could do was laugh along with his raunchy trips down mammary lane. His bona-fide cult masterpiece was, of course, **Beyond the Valley of the Dolls** (1970).

SPAGHETTI WESTERNS. Hollywood's cowboy contingent were in a perilous state until 'Rawhide' TV star Clint Eastwood went to Italy to headline as The Man With No Name in a low-budget horse opera for one-time peplum director Sergio Leone. And thanks to the radical interpretation of the genre in **A Fistful of Dollars** (1964) – where gun-fighting, blood-spilling and a haunting Ennio Morricone soundtrack combined for an aria of savage violence – the Spaghetti Western rode the international success range through the next decade. In the wake of Leone's mythic massaging, soon the likes of Ringo (**A Pistol for Ringo**, 1965), **Django** (1966), **Sabata** (1969) and Trinity (**They Call Me Trinity**, 1970) appeared in stetsons making stars of Giuliano Gemma, Lee Van Cleef, Franco Nero, Terence Hill and Bud Spencer as titles got ever more convoluted – **Ed ora... raccomanda l'anima a Dio!/And Now... Make Your Peace with God** (1968), **Se incontri Sartana prega per la tua morte/If You Meet Sartana Pray for Your Death** (1968) and **Crisantemi per un branco di carogne/Chrysanthemums for a Bunch of Swine** (1968). The last shoot-'em-up gasp? The 3-D spectacular **Comin' At Ya!** (1981).

Death Rides a Horse

SS. Imagine all the perverted corrupt evil of the Third Reich crammed into one movie and that's Don Edmonds's **Ilsa, She Wolf of the SS** (1975), a classic of the roughie, kinky and ghoulie genre. Awash in tasteless Gestapo gore, Nazi nastiness and concentrated camp because it was 'Based on documented fact', it made a star out of jackbooted dominatrix Dyanne Thorne and spawned two equally revolting sequels, **Ilsa, Harem Keeper of the Oil Sheiks** (1975) and **Ilsa the Tigress of Siberia** (1977). Other key Nazisploitation: **Love Camp 7** (1969) from the depraved dynamic duo Lee Frost and Bob Cresse, **The Beast in Heat** (1977), **SS Experiment Camp** (1976) and **Red Nights of the Gestapo** (1977). It's this genre that contains one of the ultimate **S**hock **S**equences of all time. In **Deported Women of the SS Special Section** (1976), a prisoner shoves a cork studded with razorblades up her vagina so the next German officer who rapes her gets his penis slashed to ribbons!

STALK AND SLASH. Conceived by Alfred Hitchcock (**Psycho**, 1960), cultivated by Tobe Hooper (**The Texas Chain Saw Massacre**, 1974) and set-in-stone by John Carpenter (**Halloween**, 1978), the stalk and slash horror exploded after Paramount Pictures took the unprecedented step of releasing **Friday the 13th** (1980), the first time a legit studio decided to get down-and-dirty with the indie shocker brigade, and made an absolute mint. From **He Knows You're Alone** (1980) and **Happy Birthday to Me** (1981) to **My Bloody Valentine** (1981) and **Terror Train** (1980), the near-supernatural maniac menaces every promiscuous teenager in sight until the Final Girl makes a stand. Still an industry staple with sequels, reboots, remakes and self-referentials ticking all the boxes.

THE TOUCH OF HER FLESH (1967). Which alongside its two equally infamous sequels **The Curse of Her Flesh** (1968) and **The Kiss of Her Flesh** (1968) introduces two of the most notorious filmmakers in the annals of exploitation, the husband-and-wife team of Michael and Roberta Findlay. Together they unleashed some of most violently perverted antics seen in all the roughie, kinky and ghoulie genres. Roberta, under the name Anna Riva,

often starred in their early movies like **Satan's Bed** (1965), with the then unknown Yoko Ono, and **Take Me Naked** (1966), before moving behind the camera and taking up residence as director of photography. Michael directed under the pseudonym Julian Marsh and starred as Robert West in their **Flesh** trilogy, legendary for concocting inventive ways of murdering nude women. The threesome chronicles the exploits of psycho misogynist Richard Jennings (Michael under his West nom-de-plume) who kills assorted mistresses, prostitutes and strippers with poisoned roses, toxic cat's claws, razor-studded dildos and electrically charged earrings. Bizarre deaths became a Findlay trademark – see **A Thousand Pleasures** (1968), **Invasion of the Blood Farmers** (1972) and **Shriek of the Mutilated** (1974) – while their crowning achievement was the ultimate exploitation movie con trick, **Snuff** (1976).

UNDER AGE (1964), a classic 'White Coater', so called because once the film ended, a lecture started conducted by a "community expert on family affairs". Afterwards appropriate literature was peddled so more money could be extracted from a gullible public who actually thought the hot topic story of a mother on trial for 'raping' her 14-year-old daughter had socially redeeming features. 'Raping' in this Texas Law instance meant enforced sex with her boyfriend so they would be married "in the eyes of God". The most famous 'White Coater' is genius exploiter Kroger Babb's **Mom and Dad** (1945), a sex education quickie culminating in birth-of-a-baby footage. Shown to segregated male and female audiences for over thirty years, at each performance Dr. Elliott Forbes was on hand to give hygiene lectures and answer embarrassing questions. There were up to twenty Elliot Forbes' altogether, each a stand-up comedian making extra bucks flogging the rhythm method ovulation chart pamphlets. Or 'Vatican Roulette' as the scam became known.

ONCE..IN A LIFETIME.. Comes A Presentation That TRULY PULLS NO PUNCHES!

Now YOU Can SEE The Motion Picture That DARES DISCUSS and EXPLAIN SEX As NEVER BEFORE SEEN and HEARD!

THE ONE, THE ONLY, THE ORIGINAL...

MOM and DAD

Truly The World's Most Amazing Attraction!

Extra - IN PERSON ELLIOT FORBES "THE SECRETS OF SENSIBLE SEX"

NO ONE UNDER HIGH SCHOOL AGE Admitted Unless Accompanied By Parents!!

EVERYTHING SHOWN! EVERYTHING EXPLAINED!

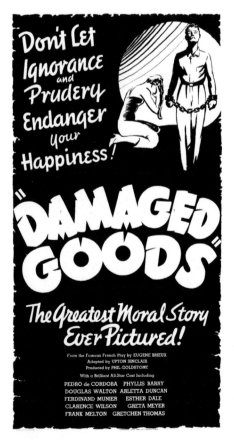

VD. "Tonight – Romance! Tomorrow – Remorse! Forever – Regrets!" screams the trailer for **Damaged Goods** (1961), or as its original title put it more bluntly **V.D.** Produced by the King of the Classroom Scare flick, Sid Davis, who had already warned the new teenage demographic about hoodlums, **Gang Boy** (1954), child abuse, **Age 13** (1955), and predatory homosexuals, **Boys Beware** (1961) came the cautionary tale of the consequences of sleeping around with the wrong partner. It's hard to believe that gonorrhoea discharges, syphilis symptoms and venereal sores were once exhibited as forms of erotic entertainment. But 'Clap Operas' were often the only way Joe Public could view genitalia in the old days. While infection exploitation dated back to the silent days in the likes of **The Spreading Evil** (1918) and **The Scarlet Trail** (1918), where armed forces returning from decadent Europe after World War I were urged to get tested if they had partaken of prostitution, they weren't that graphic. Until the original **Damaged Goods** (1937) – "One Moment of Ecstasy – A Lifetime of Sorrow!" – dared show syphilis bacteria at the end of a microscope lens and John Ford's **Sex Hygiene** (1942) – yes that John Ford! – the preventive measures needed if you caught said lurgy. It halted all thought of back row heavy petting that's for sure, and who knew what you might catch off the seats in the foyer toilets! Incredible, but true, many of the films mentioned here were still being shown to American GIs in 1970 as a tour of duty precaution at the height of the Vietnam War.

WOMEN IN PRISON. Reform school dykes, bitch wardens and glamorous cell inmates kitted out in kinky Frederick's of Hollywood outfits. Plus rape, riot and revenge... **Caged** (1950) began the WIP genre, informed by lurid correctional facility melodrama splashed about in pulp novels of the post World War II era. As censorship relaxed, more extreme jailhouse shocks were depicted until Jesús Franco's **99 Women** (1969) set the seal on the whole female captive kit and caboodle. From **Women's Prison** (1955) and **The Big Bird Cage** (1972) to **Ebony Ivory & Jade** (1976) and **Black Mama White Mama** (1973), the cookie cutter plots devolved into having an innocent girl sent to a penitentiary run by a sadistic male or lesbian warden, both usually running an inmate prostitution ring. Group strip searches, scantily-clad hard labour, group showers, down-and-dirty cat-fights, group fire-hosing, Sapphic orgies, brutal punishments, Nazis/Japanese commandants/Filipino jungle gangs – delete where applicable – also had to feature somewhere. Throw in Agnes Moorehead, Linda Blair, Edy Williams, Brigitte Nielsen or Lina Romay. Result **Chained Heat** (1983), **Hellhole** (1985) and **Barbed Wire Dolls** (1975) where "white-hot desires melt cold prison steel..."

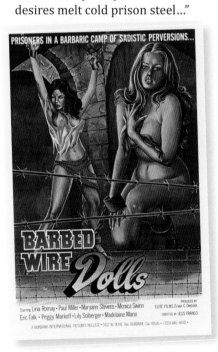

X RATING.

In the United States the X originally referred to a non-trademarked rating that indicated a film contained content unsuitable for children, such as extreme sex and violence. From 1968 when it was first introduced it could be self-applied to any film by a distributor certain their film contained material minors (those under 18 years old) shouldn't see. Prior to this legislation an Adults Only warning sufficed. While mainstream movies like **Midnight Cowboy** (1969) and **A Clockwork Orange** (1971) adopted the X rating for the appropriate reasons, the exploitation gang leapt on it solely to hype the adult nature of their bargain basement merchandise. This reached ludicrous proportions when pornography began to become chic as Triple X ratings started being used to give the impression hardcore entertainment was more graphic than your average X. In Great Britain where the X certificate had existed since 1951, distributors used the forbidding sounding letter as a promotional tool to pull in the punters, like the Hammer House of Horror who incorporated a bright red X as part of the campaign for their sci-fi shocker **The Quatermass Xperiment** (1955). Their American counterparts never used this marketing tool; the hardcore industry staked sole claim to the X as they used the R rating, meaning children could be accompanied by adults for extra revenue.

YOG: MONSTER FROM SPACE (1970) – "Spewed from intergalactic space to clutch the Earth in its tentacles" – and all the other Z-movie Martians, mutants, mind-melding extraterrestrials and alien nightmares from across the cardboard diorama sci-fi galaxy. Ed Wood's infamous **Plan 9 from Outer Space** (1959), the one with the Bela Lugosi stand-in once the horror great died, is considered the worst ever. But don't forget **Robot Monster** (1953), with its titular threat a man in a gorilla suit wearing a deep-sea diving helmet, **Fire Maidens from Outer Space** (1956) where British astronauts visit an all-female community on a Jupiter moon, complete with cars driving by in the background, or the obvious shag-pile carpet creature in **The Creeping Terror** (1964). Those who couldn't even compete with those bottom-of-the-barrel plastic fantastic special effects just waved a lobster in front of a torch and used the wriggling shadows for giant 'Gargon' creatures in **Teenagers from Outer Space** (1959). Or draped tripe over a clotheshorse for **Caltiki, the Immortal Monster** (1959)!

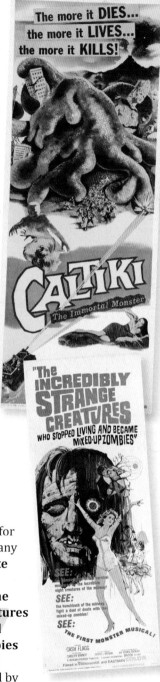

Yog: Monster from Space

ZOMBIES, that horror perennial invented solely for the film medium without any genesis in literature. **White Zombie** (1932) was the first, the most peculiar **The Incredibly Strange Creatures Who Stopped Living and Became Mixed-Up Zombies** (1964). Yes, it's 'The First Monster Musical' directed by hackmeister Ray Dennis Steckler presented in 'Hallucinogenic Hypnovision'. What was this fabulous gimmick (or gaff in exploitation-speak) competing with the 'Hypnovista' of **Horrors of the Black Museum** (1959) and fragrant Aromarama of **Behind the Great Wall** (1958)? All available usherettes wearing phosphorescent masks of star Cash Flagg (Steckler again) running through the auditorium happy slapping startled patrons. 'Not 3-D. Don't Miss It'. Altogether now, 'Let's do 'The Mixed-Up Zombie Stomp' again'…

Right, you've read the rough guide overview of the entire exploitation movie industry with all its many monumental permutations – accent on the mental and mutations!

Now, are you ready for more...
"Blasts of bold truth before your traumatized eyes"?

For a further...
"New height in daring adult delight"?

For extra...
"Shattering studies of the shameless sick set"?

For additional...
"Throbbing dramas of shackled youth"?

For supplementary...
"Electrifying horror torn from today's headlines"?

Dare you face...
"Spine-tingling shock after shock after shock"?

If so, join FrightFest on a fast and furious road to sensation in our following in-depth look at 200 of the most infamous, the most obscure and the most unusual exploitation movies ever made.

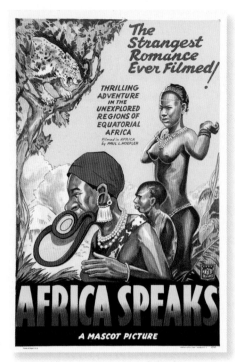

AFRICA SPEAKS

USA, 1930
Director: Walter Fuller. Producer: Paul L. Hoefler, Walter Fuller.
Screenplay: Walter Fuller. Cinematography: Paul L. Hoefler.
Cast: Paul L. Hoefler, Harald Austin, Lowell Thomas (narrator).

Jungle exploiters, or 'goona-goonas' in early grindhouse jargon (taken from Andre Roosevelt's 1932 movie of the same name) before the term shockumentary took over, were repeatedly played by unscrupulous carnies for decades. No matter how silent, dated or black-and-white they were, documentaries featuring exotic locations, wild animals, native nudity and fleeting moments of shock barbarity and atrocity footage could be repackaged, re-grifted and still coin it in. Many were culled from assorted early 20th century travelogues, shot in the era when intrepid cameramen combed the globe to capture never-before-seen vistas. **Lady Mackenzie's Big Game Pictures** (1915), **Headhunters of the South Seas** (1922), **Chang** (1928), **Ingagi** (1930), **Rama/Cain** (1930), **Congorilla** (1932), **Baboona** (1935), **Forbidden Adventure** (1937), **Karamoja** (1954) and **Mau Mau** (1954) were just a few titles Forty Thief supremos like Dwain Esper and Kroger Babb mercilessly pillaged to line their pockets. **Africa Speaks** was Colorado-based explorer Paul L. Hoefler's record of his 1928 African Expedition and featured jumping impalas, a swarm of locusts devouring everything in its path, tsetse fly dangers, salt-eating pygmies of the Ituri forest, and the duck-billed women of the Ubangi, disfigured by discs placed in their lips so they are useless as slaves to hostile Dark Continent tribes.

THE WAGES OF SIN

USA, 1938
Director: Herman E. Webber. Producer: Willis Kent. Cinematography: Harvey Gould.
Cast: Constance Worth, Willy Costello, Blanche Mehaffey, Clara Kimball Young, Carleton Young, Paula Bromleigh.

Ace Forty Thief Willis Kent was a prolific producer of Adults Only fare throughout the Depression Era, where one person's abject degradation made hard-pressed audiences feel

better in comparison. Kent chose stories about abortion rackets and black market adoptions solely for their exploitation value and came up with an absolute stormer with this Louis Sonney (**Maniac**, 1934) co-production. The story was the roadshow 'Awful Warning' model one about menial laundry worker Marjorie Benton (B movie starlet Constance Worth) trying to make ends meet for her lazy family. Out on the town one night at the Hideaway club, vice boss Tony Kilonis (Willy Castello) sees her potential, gets her fired from her job, and sweet talks her into working for him as a prostitute at Fat Pearl's brothel. Eventually dumped, she escapes the bordello, tracks her pimp down and shoots him dead in front of his latest conquest. A cliffhanger ending finds Marjorie on trial awaiting the verdict of an all-male jury. Kent's gimmick was inviting audiences to send in essays stating their opinion for or against with the lure of $1000 for the best one. No one is sure if anyone actually did win, but knowing Kent, it's doubtful.

BREAKING ALL RECORDS — FROM — COAST TO COAST!☆

Is **SEX** a **SIN**?

The WORLD'S MOST AMAZING ATTRACTION!

MOTHERS Bring Your Daughters' FATHERS Bring Your Sons' IT ANSWERS THEIR EVERY QUESTION

Bold! Fearless!
Shocking beyond Description!
EXCLUSIVE SHOWING!
The Most Revealing Picture Ever Filmed!!

"THE **Wages** OF **SIN**"

TECHNICOLOR SCOPE [R]
EXCLUSIVE ROADSHOW ENGAGEMENT

You may faint but you will learn about the . . . "FACTS of LIFE"

I Urge and Urge You Implicitely To See It ! !

● MANY WILL FAINT! DON'T COME ALONE!
● BREAKING RECORDS FROM COAST TO COAST!
● SEE IT FIRST . . .
  THEN TELL OTHERS WHAT WE CAN'T!!

2nd Shocker!

A DRAMATIC THUNDERBOLT!

Bold! UNCUT! UNCENSORED!

THE MOST BREATHTAKING BIRTH SCENES EVER SHOWN TO THE PUBLIC.
the Secret 'COLOR'
MIRACLE OF BIRTH'

STRANGE LOVE...

SETS THE PACE FOR THIS MOST UNUSUAL SUSPENSE MYSTERY

"INSIDE A GIRLS' DORMITORY"

INSIDE A GIRLS' DORMITORY

France, 1953
Director: Henri Decoin. Producer: Raymond Eger. Screenplay: Henri Decoin, François Chalais.
Music: Georges Van Parys. Cinematography: Robert Lefebvre.
Cast: Jean Marais, Françoise Arnoul, Denise Grey, Jeanne Moreau, Noël Roquevert, Dany Carrel.

Before he stunned the world with the suspense masterpiece **Diabolique** (1955), French director Henri-Georges Clouzot had adapted two books by Flemish author Stanislas-André Steeman into the highly successful thrillers **The Murderer Lives at Number 21** (1942) and **Quai des Orfèvres** (1947) based on his novel 'Légitime Défense'. Taking over from Clouzot in the Steeman business came director Henri Decoin, who adapted his novel '18 Fantômes' into the screenplay for this highly regarded mystery filmed under the title **Dortoir des grandes**. French superstar and frequent Jean Cocteau collaborator Jean Marais headlined as Detective Désiré Marco, sent to investigate the strangulation of a popular pupil at an exclusive boarding school for girls. The headmistress is convinced it was an outside intruder but Marco isn't so sure and soon uncovers a variety of motives and suspects as it is revealed some sadistic bondage games were played in the dormitory the night of the murder. One of the main suspects is a female mathematics teacher with an 'unnatural' affection for her wards (including Jeanne Moreau and Dany Carrel) and it was this story thread that ensured Decoin's blackly comic film noir ended up on 42nd Street as the more luridly titled **Inside a Girl's Dormitory**.

SATELLITE IN THE SKY

UK, 1956
Director: Paul Dickson. Producer: Edward J. Danziger, Harry Lee Danziger.
Screenplay: John Mather, J.T. McIntosh, Edith Dell. Music: Albert Elms.
Cinematography: Georges Périnal, James Wilson.
Cast: Kieron Moore, Lois Maxwell, Donald Wolfit, Bryan Forbes, Jimmy Hanley,
Thea Gregory.

1956 was the year **Forbidden Planet** was hailed a science-fiction landmark, **X the Unknown** consolidated The Hammer House of Horror's reputation, Roger Corman's **It Conquered the World** established the cult director as a major genre player. Clinkers included Cy Roth's **Fire Maidens from Outer Space** and this fellow British import that went straight down the 42nd Street toilets, remarkable only for showcasing the effective special visual effects work of Wally Veevers, who would go on to **2001: A Space Odyssey** (1968) glory. A predictable blending of British stiff-upper-lip heroics and outer space melodrama, six astronauts (future director Bryan Forbes among them) man a rocketship to explode an

experimental Tritonium bomb above the stratosphere. Unfortunately the bomb becomes attached to the vessel and the crew try desperately to dislodge it until its inventor (noted Shakespearean actor Sir Donald Wolfit slicing the ham thickly) does the decent thing, climbs outside, and pushes the nuclear weapon into the galaxy, sacrificing himself in the hackneyed process. Failing to rise above its moribund earthbound script and trite dialogue, 'Picturegoer' magazine reviewed it thus: "As a comedy this is a four-star riot. But horror of horrors, I don't think it was meant to be".

TEENAGE BEAUTY ON THE RUN
AND LOST IN THE WILDERNESS
—MEETS A NATURE LOVER

TWO
IN A
SLEEPING
BAG

IN
BLUSHING
TECHNICOLOR

A Holt International Release

TWO IN A SLEEPING BAG

West Germany, 1956
Director: Rainer Geis. Screenplay: Joachim
Wedekind. Music: Franz Grothe. Cinematography:
Klaus von Rautenfeld.
Cast: Claus Biederstaedt, Susanne Cramer,
Eva Kerbler, Hans Nielsen, Dietmar Schönherr,
Heinrich Gretler.

Two years after directing
the adult farce **School for
Connubial Bliss** (1954),
Rainer Geis was after the
newly emerging German
teenage demographic with
this youth comedy, **Kleines
Zelt und große Liebe** or to give its literal
translation, **Small Tent, Big Love**. Anything
remotely taboo became manna from heaven
to the 1950s grindhouse so this lederhosen
lark found itself launched onto 42nd Street
under yet another
suggestive title hinting
at forbidden relations
under the stars.

Karin Faber (Susanne
Cramer) is a spoiled
student who runs away
from boarding school to
be with her fiancé Ferry (Dietmar Schönherr).
But to get to The Inn camping ground where
he is, she has to hitch a canoe ride
with Peter Camper (Claus
Biederstaedt). The nature-
loving Camper and his
rich-bitch passenger make
an unlikely couple but soon
the ice melts between them,
especially when they are
forced to sleep together in

the Fifties sharing sense. Upon arrival at The
Inn, Karin's father takes to Peter, she forgets all
about Ferry and the
camping continues.
Ill-fated Teutonic
starlet Susanne
Cramer had the
most tumultuous
private life – three
bad marriages, two
suicide attempts, one discovery of a possible
murder victim and an early death in 1969.

GOLIATH AND THE BARBARIANS

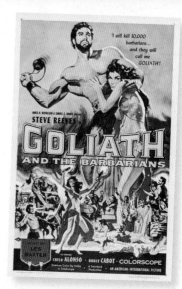

Italy/USA, 1959
Director: Carlo Campogalliani. Producer: Emimmo Salvi. Screenplay: Carlo Campogalliani, Gino Mangini, Nino Stresa, Giuseppe Taffarel. Music: Carlo Innocenzi, Les Baxter (US version). Cinematography: Bitto Albertini.
Cast: Steve Reeves, Chelo Alonso, Bruce Cabot, Giulia Rubini, Luciano Marin, Livio Lorenzon.

Bronzed body builder Steve Reeves followed up his massive worldwide hits **Le fatiche di Ercole/Hercules** (1958) and **Ercole e la regina di Lidia/Hercules Unchained** (1959) with this rousing tale directed by Carlo Campogalliani as **Il terrore dei barbari**. Campogalliani was a perfect choice because he directed two silent Maciste movies, **Maciste I** (1919) and **Maciste contro la morte** (1920), starring Bartolomeo Pagano in his spin-off strongman character from **Cabiria** (1914).
After this one he would stay in peplum, with **Maciste nella valle dei Re/Son of Samson** (1960), **Ursus** (1961) and **Rosmunda e Alboino/Sword of the Conqueror** (1961) until his 1964 career end. Reeves plays Emiliano (Goliath for export), a 587 AD lumberjack in a small Italian village who takes on the evil Barbarian army pillaging, raping and plundering all who stand in the way of their invasion. Of course, in one of peplum's clichés, he falls for Landa (Chelo Alonso, **Sign of the Gladiator**, 1959), daughter of head Barbarian Alboino (Hollywood import Bruce Cabot). And in another he's strapped to two horses pulling in opposite directions, designed to split him apart. AIP bolstered the budget in return for the US distribution rights and it made them a fortune.

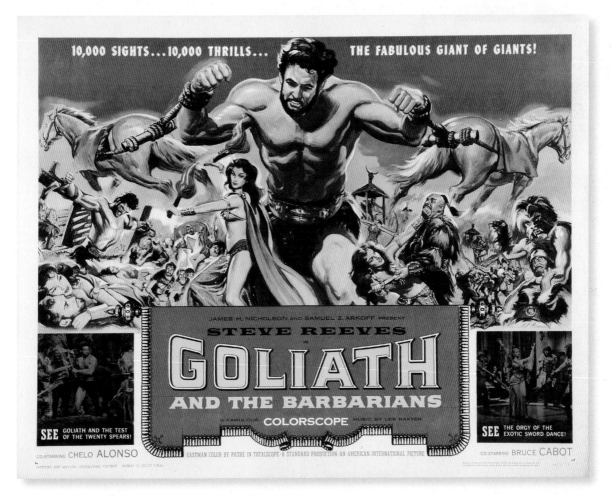

I SPIT ON YOUR GRAVE

France, 1959
Director: Michel Gast.
Producer: Janny
Gérard [uncredited].
Screenplay: Boris Vian,
Jacques Dopagne.
Music: Alain Goraguer.
Cinematography:
Marc Fossard.
Cast: Christian
Marquand,
Antonella Lualdi,
Paul Guers,
Renate Ewert,
Jean Sorel,
Fernand Ledoux.

Before this title became synonymous in 1978 with one of the most notorious exploitation shockers ever, it was sported by director Michel Gast's French adaptation of Boris Vian's 1947 literary hoax. In the novel's preface Vian pretended he was merely the translator of the thriller supposedly written by black American author Vernon Sullivan. Once the scam was made public the hard-boiled noir became a bestseller. Future **Candy** (1968) star/director Christian Marquand played Joe Grant, the light-skinned black African investigating his brother's lynching in the Deep South. When he sets sights on the beautiful daughters of a local plantation owner, a plan for terrible revenge against the society that murdered his kin is put into action. He sleeps with both sisters, turning them against each other and humiliating them, before a climactic orgy of violence. Vian hated the movie and had already disowned it when he attended the first preview screening in Paris. In an ironic twist of fate, ten minutes into the movie, Vian allegedly sneered, "These guys are supposed to be American? My ass!" before collapsing back into his seat and suffering a fatal heart attack. Little did he know how infamous his title would actually become!

THE DEAD ONE

USA, 1960
Director: Barry Mahon. Producer: Barry
Mahon. Screenplay: Barry Mahon.
Cinematography: Mark Dennis.
Cast: John McKay, Linda Ormond, Monica
Davis, Clyde Kelley, Darlene Myrick, Lacey Kelly.

Prolific Adults Only creator Barry Mahon
strikes again with this horrendously
acted, scripted and directed excuse for a
zombie movie. After an elongated tour of
New Orleans strip joints and jazz palaces
undertaken by John Carlton (Mahon's
pal John McKay from **Cuban Rebel Girls**,
1959) and his new bride Linda (Linda
Ormond, who like McKay, was obviously
too thick to respond to any other name
than his/her own), the paper-thin story
begins… Furious that the marriage means
she loses the family plantation she's run
single-handedly for many years, cousin
Monica (Monica Davis, ditto) uses voodoo
rituals to resurrect her dead brother Jonas
(Clyde Kelley), ordering him to kill Linda.
But during their tourist cruise of Bourbon
Street, the newlyweds picked up exotic
dancer Bella Bella (the appallingly bad
Darlene Myrick) and it's her Jonas kills
by mistake. Investigating the death, John
crashes his cousin's voodoo ceremony,
halts the incessant drum beat by throwing
the instrument out of the window, and the
'exciting climax' continues with the dapper
Jonas in suit and bowtie disintegrating in
the sun while police shoot high priestess
Monica. Priceless dialogue: John finding
Bella's corpse saying, "She's dead", Linda
responding, "But can't we help her?"

LA C.C.B. présente

CC

DE BLANKE NEGERIN

"I PASSED FOR WHITE"

SONYA WILDE

JAMES FRANCISCUS

FRED M. WILCOX

PRODUCTION , RÉALISATION ET SCENARIO

LA NÉGRESSE BLANCHE

EDICOLOR ... Bruxelles ... Tél . : 54.78.71

I PASSED FOR WHITE

USA, 1960
Director: Fred M. Wilcox. Producer: Fred M. Wilcox. Screenplay: Fred M. Wilcox.
Music: John Williams, Jerry Irvin [uncredited]. Cinematography: George J. Folsey.
Cast: Sonya Wilde, James Franciscus, Patricia Michon, Elizabeth Council, Griffin
Crafts, Isabel Cooley.

Alfred Hitchcok's **Murder!** (1930), both versions of **Imitation of Life**
(1934/59) and **Show Boat** (1936/51), and the Oscar-winning **Pinky**
(1949) all dealt with the subject of persons of mixed-race heritage trying
to be accepted as white for socially advantageous reasons. None of those
'Dark Secret' classics entered the grindhouse circuit though. This was
the first that did, based on Mary Hastings Bradley's factional biography
about an African-American woman, given the alias Reba Lee in the
book, Bernice Lee in the film, who lived a white life until her pregnancy
with her rich white, and very racist, Chicago husband threatens to expose her lie if the baby is born
black. The last movie directed by Fred McLeod Wilcox of **Forbidden Planet** (1956) stature, it caused
much controversy because the star was white Sonya Wilde, who played High Yellow, another popular
phrase at the time for such racial blurring. James Franciscus plays Rick Leyton, her oblivious other
half, who never gets suspicious about Bernice's family continually being on holiday in South America.
The handsome matinee idol would later appear in such exploitation winners as **The Valley of Gwangi**
(1969), **Beneath the Planet of the Apes** (1970) and **The Cat O'Nine Tails** (1971).

ANATOMY OF A PSYCHO

USA, 1961
Director: Brooke L. Peters [Boris Petroff]. Producer: Brooke L. Peters [Boris Petroff].
Screenplay: Jane Mann, Don Devlin. Music: Manuel Francisco [Michael Terr].
Cinematography: Joel Colman.
Cast: Darrell Howe, Ronnie Burns, Pamela Lincoln, Judy Howard, Russ Bender,
Pat McMahon.

Post 1960, every wannabe horror movie trying to penetrate the commercial
conscious and make money felt it had to allude to Alfred Hitchcock's shock-
buster **Psycho** somehow. And so it was with this routine juvenile delinquency
crime melodrama, outlining vocalist Darrell Howe (star of the 1958 'Teenage Idol'
sitcom) in the role of Chet, compiling a list of people who helped send his brother
to the state gas chamber. With assistance from sadistic sexpot Judy (**Ghost of
Dragstrip Hollow**, 1959) Howard, he plans to take nasty revenge on those who
convicted his sibling. Surprise, surprise, his brother was guilty of murder as
charged, but that fact doesn't stop
the unhinged Chet chasing after
his girlfriend's sweetheart's father

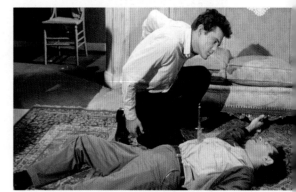

who gave the crucial witness testimony. George Burns and
Gracie Allen's adopted son Ronnie Burns plays Mickey, the
victim of the final ludicrous frame-up. From the director
of the mad doctor mutant farrago **The Unearthly** (1957)
Brooke L. Peters (in reality Russian émigré Boris Petroff),
this 'terrifying state of a twisted mind with a frenzied
desire for revenge' piles on the agony by including
snatches of music over key moments from the Ed Wood Jr.
fiasco **Plan 9 from Outer Space** (1959).

HALF-MAN...HALF-WOLF...

He fought the hideous curse of his evil birth, but his ravished victims were proof that the cravings of his beast-blood demanded he kill...*Kill*...<u>*KILL*</u>!

The CURSE OF THE WEREWOLF

in Eastman **COLOR**

Even the innocent girl who loved him was not safe ...once the full moon rose!

Starring **CLIFFORD EVANS · OLIVER REED · YVONNE ROMAIN · CATHERINE FELLER**

Screenplay by JOHN ELDER · Directed by TERENCE FISHER · Produced by ANTHONY HINDS · Executive Producer MICHAEL CARRERAS

FILM PRODUCTION · A UNIVERSAL·INTERNATIONAL RELEASE

THE CURSE OF THE WEREWOLF

UK, 1961
Director: Terence Fisher. Producer: Anthony Hinds.
Screenplay: John Elder [Anthony Hinds]. Music: Benjamin Frankel. Cinematography: Arthur Grant.
Cast: Oliver Reed, Yvonne Romain, Catherine Feller, Clifford Evans, Anthony Dawson, Josephine Llewellyn.

The Hammer House of Horror virtually had the late 1950s/60s pretty much sewn up with their conveyor belt of crisply produced, classy costume horror beginning with the epochal **The Curse of Frankenstein** (1957) that married gore, colour and terror together for the very first time. Guy Endore's 1933 lycanthropic ground zero novel 'The Werewolf of Paris' was transported to 1730s Spain (mainly because Hammer had already built sets for a stalled shocker about the Inquisition) in director Terence Fisher's ravishing looking and superior version starring an excellent Oliver Reed who turns into a tormented monster when sexually frustrated. His birth, the result of a mute servant girl being raped by a raddled creature in a prison cell, put Hammer and the British Board of Film Censors at each other's throat for their most serious skirmish regarding graphic visuals and context. In Britain it would remain extensively cut until the mid 1980s and was reviewed very badly, the 'Monthly Film Bulletin' calling it, "A singularly repellent job of slaughterhouse horror." In America only four scenes were slightly trimmed, making it 3 minutes longer, and the trade bible 'Variety' called it "Exceptional... a triumph". So, clear absolute proof that censorship is bad!

YOU'LL SEE WHAT GOES ON... AND COMES OFF...INSIDE THE PAGES OF ONE OF "THOSE" MAGAZINES !

Miss PAGAN

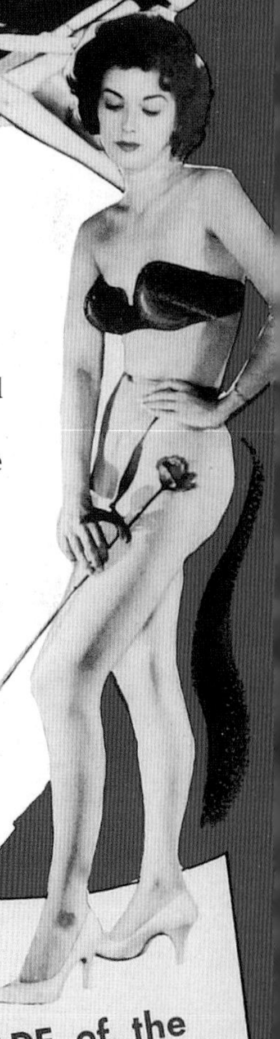

LIVING VENUS

USA, © 1960, first public screening 1961
Director: Herschell Gordon Lewis.
Producer: Herschell Gordon Lewis,
David F. Friedman [uncredited].
Screenplay: James McGinn,
Herschell Gordon Lewis, Seymour Zolotareff.
Music: Martin Rubinstein.
Cinematography: Arthur Haug.
Cast: William Kerwin, Danica D'Hondt,
Harvey Korman, Jeanette Leahy,
Lawrence J. Aberwood, Robert Bell.

Although the future Wizard of Gore's debut feature **The Prime Time** (1960) entered the grindhouse market at pretty much the same time, this nudie-cutie was the first to sport the credit 'Produced and Directed by Herschell Gordon Lewis'. This exercise in sporadic titillation – some partially nude scenes were shot but they only wound up in the pressbook – starred Lewis perennial William Kerwin as Jack Norwall, a character based loosely on 'Playboy' magazine publishing magnate Hugh Hefner. Fired from his job on 'Newlywed' magazine, Norwall starts his own For Men Only monthly 'Pagan'. The skin rag's logo is the Venus de Milo statue and when he meets model Peggy Branson (Danica D'Hondt, a busty Canadian TV game show hostess) he realises she is the living Venus equivalent and persuades her to become the 'Pagan' mascot. Many romantic complications later as the magazine's success goes to Norwall's head, he dumps his fiancée, steals Peggy's heart from his favourite photographer and marries her while still playing away. In time-honoured **Sunset Boulevard** (1950) tradition, the mortified Peggy ends up face down in a swimming pool having committed suicide. The moral? Being a sex addict will cost you your friends, your loves and your business empire.

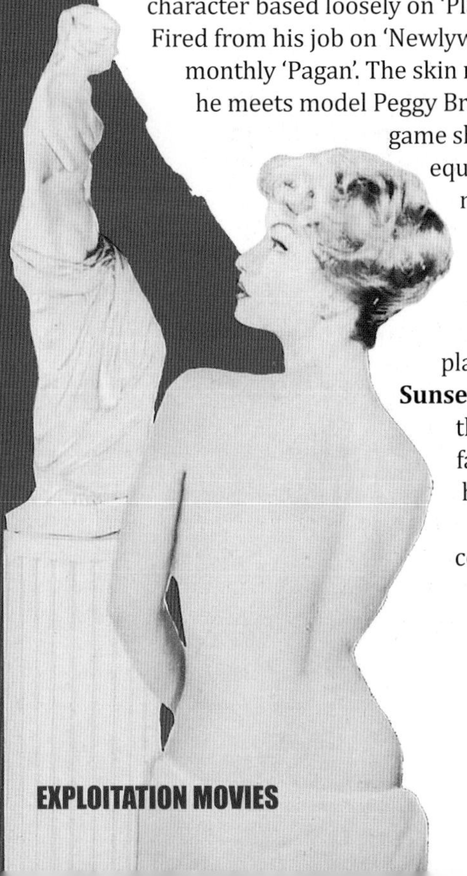

LIVING Venus

plus

A PARADE of the PULCHRITUDINOUS PETS WHO PEER PASSIONATELY FROM THE COVERS and CENTER-FOLDS of the SLICK, RED-HOT MAGAZINES!

The Show That Separates the Men from the Boys

The Howlarious Story of 2 Guys who Make a NUDIE MOVIE

THE PICTURE THAT TAKES OFF WHERE ALL THE OTHERS LEFT UP!

BOIN-N-G!

USA, 1963

Director: Lewis H. Gordon [Herschell Gordon Lewis]. Producer: Davis Freeman [David F. Friedman], Stanford S. Kohlberg. Screenplay: Davis Freeman [David F. Friedman], Lewis H. Gordon [Herschell Gordon Lewis]. Music: Herschell Gordon Lewis. Cinematography: Marvin Lester [Herschell Gordon Lewis]. Cast: Thomas Sweetwood [William Kerwin], William R. Johnson, Vickie Miles [Allison Louise Downe], Christina Castel, Robbie Bee, Lawrence Wood.

Director Herschell Gordon Lewis's personal favourite movie from his early nudie period was this amusingly self-aware affair that satirised the entire sexploitation industry of the times. William Kerwin (who married **Blood Feast**, 1963, star Connie Mason) and William R. Johnson (who would appear in **Goldilocks and the Three Bares** the same year) play two aspiring filmmakers convinced they can make it in the nudie-cutie world. After watching a grindhouse double-bill of Lewis's own **The Adventures of Lucky Pierre** (1961) and **Daughter of the Sun** (1962), the bumbling duo figure they can direct something similar as long as their poster is a truth-stretching doozy. So they audition some voluptuous girls, get them to strip off, film them by a lake, pile on the T&A and broad comedy and package their product for would-be distributors to view. It ends with a sequence in which the amateur nudie film within the bawdy lampoon is screened to potential exhibitors. As their truly awful attempt finishes unspooling through the projector, a distributor comments, "That's the worst picture I ever saw. I'll buy it!" And so ended producer David F. Friedman and Lewis's wry observation on the business they were both so heavily invested in.

FREE, WHITE AND 21

USA, © 1962, first public screening 1963
Director: Larry Buchanan. Producer: Larry Buchanan. Screenplay: Cliff Pope, Harold Dwain, Larry Buchanan. Music: Joe Johnson & His Orchestra.
Cinematography: Ralph K. Johnson.
Cast: Frederick O'Neal, Annalena Lund, George Edgley, George R. Russell, Johnny Hicks, Hugh Crenshaw.

Director Larry Buchanan started out as assistant director for George Cukor – **The Marrying Kind** (1952) – and blanket applied his notorious guerrilla-style of filmmaking to sci-fi junk for AIP TV and more hard-hitting subjects. Like his **High Yellow** (1965), this courtroom melodrama dealt with the sensitive issues of race relations. Black motel owner Ernie Jones (Frederick O'Neal, a 'Car 54, Where Are You?' sit-com regular) is accused of raping Swedish Greta Mae Hansen (Annalena Lund from **Mr. Sardonicus**, 1961) in Texas to join the civil rights movement as a Freedom Rider. Just like what happened in the William Castle horror **Mr. Sardonicus**, Buchanan stops the movie during the climax to poll the jury/audience for its verdict. Theatre staff dressed as policemen handed out ballots with tear-off 'Innocent' and 'Guilty' stubs, which then were collected and supposedly counted in the lobby, however the only verdict filmed went in the defendant's favour. For taking the trouble to cast your vote you were given a three-inch long wood-coloured plastic mini-gavel (cost, only $32 per 1000!) And the main advertising gimmick suggested? Papering local downtown areas with realistic printed subpoenas summoning the interested to sit in judgement on 'The State vs. Ernie Jones' case.

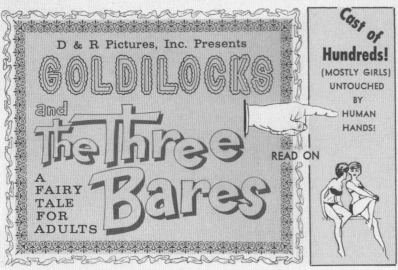

GOLDILOCKS AND THE THREE BARES

USA, 1963
Director: Lewis H. Gordon [Herschell Gordon Lewis].
Producer: Thomas J. Dowd, Davis Freeman [David F. Friedman].
Screenplay: William R. Johnson. Music: Lathrop Wells.
Cinematography: Marvin Lester [Herschell Gordon Lewis].
Cast: Vickie Miles [Allison Louise Downe], Rex Marlow,
Thomas Sweetwood [William Kerwin], Joey Maxim,
Netta Mallina, Craig Maudslay Jr.

Great title, same old conversion to naturism story, and
nothing remotely to do with the fairy tale. Director
Herschell Gordon Lewis and
producer David F. Friedman ground
out nudist movies like conveyor
belt sausages in the early Sixties.
This one was made to order for
Chicago exhibitor Tom Dowd, who
wanted to get a premiere edge in
his area's grindhouse circuit. On
Dowd's insistence the star of the
show had to be his protégé, nine-
fingered crooner Rex Marlow,
in the hope it would provide a
vehicle to springboard the lounge
singer into the big-time. It speaks
volumes about this would-be nudie
musical that Marlow's only other
screen appearance came in the
Arch Hall Jr. western vanity project
Deadwood '76 (1965). Ironically,

in that film Marlow does no singing at all. Weirdly set in the 1920s, Marlow plays Miami nightclub
singer Eddie Livingstone who finds out via comedian pal Tommy that his press agent girlfriend is a
secret nudist. Eddie is horrified, naturally, but Tommy has his interest piqued by the information and
throws himself wholeheartedly into the healthy lifestyle. Soon he's convinced Eddie to give it a go in his
role as Cupid to get the distant lovers back together.

A Ride with Her was A 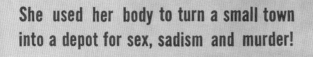 Ride to Hell!

She used her body to turn a small town into a depot for sex, sadism and murder!

HIGHWAY PICK-UP

France/Italy, 1963
Director: Julien Duvivier.
Producer: Robert Hakim,
Raymond Hakim.
Screenplay: René Barjavel, Julien
Duvivier. Music: Georges Delerue.
Cinematography: Léonce-Henri Burel.
Cast: Robert Hossein, Jean Sorel,
Catherine Rouvel, Georges Wilson,
Lucien Raimbourg, Sophie Grimaldi.

Director Julien Duvivier was one of the greatest figures in the history of French cinema, responsible for such world famous classics as **Pépé le Moko** (1937) and **Tales of Manhattan** (1942). His penultimate movie before being killed in a car crash was this fine example of *film noir* based on the novel 'Come Easy, Go Easy' by the master of his hard-boiled art, James Hadley Chase. Two safe crackers get caught by a security guard on a job: one kills the guard and flees, leaving his partner Daniel (Robert Hossein) behind to take the heat. The abandoned accomplice is convicted but eventually escapes prison and sets out to get revenge on his partner Paul (Jean Sorel). Finding refuge in a remote garage in the Alps, he's hired as a mechanic by the owner Thomas (Georges Wilson). But when his gold-digging wife Maria (Catherine Rouvel) discovers his true identity, she blackmails him into breaking open her husband's vault so she can steal his cash. In the ensuing discovery scuffle, Thomas is killed, but Maria still has an ace up her sleeve. Although reminiscent of the Chase masterpiece 'The Postman Always Rings Twice', it's edgy pulp fiction of the grittiest order.

THE MAD EXECUTIONERS

West Germany, 1963
Director: Edwin Zbonek. Producer:
Artur Brauner. Screenplay: Robert A.
Stemmle. Music: Raimund Rosenberger.
Cinematography: Richard Angst.
Cast: Hansjörg Felmy, Maria Perschy,
Dieter Borsche, Rudolf Forster,
Harry Riebauer, Chris Howland.

Austrian director Edwin Zbonek's **Der Henker von London** is a suitably eerie, atmospheric example of the Krimi but a tale of two distinctly separate halves. One part of this thriller, the fourth of ten in the German CCC Film series based on Bryan Edgar Wallace's novels – here the source material was 'George and Jojo/The White Carpet' – concerned a secret society passing judgment on criminals seemingly beyond the reach of the law. Hanged by a noose stolen from Scotland Yard's infamous Black Museum, the victims are dumped in the foggy Thames after summary sentencing. Is a member of the police force one of the hooded court meting out illegal justice? The second, more fantastic, string to this black-and-white Ultrascope production concerned a serial killing mad scientist decapitating young women and attaching their heads to a robot's body back in his lab. As with all the Krimi, the combination of thriller, horror and fantasy makes for a heady Hitch-cocktail, the creepy mock trials and explanation regarding how the rope is appropriated from a locked safe adding extra delicious frissons. Headliner Maria Perschy endured all grindhouse genres from Nazisploitation – **Ordered to Love** (1961) – to Eurospy – **Kiss Kiss, Kill Kill** (1966).

THE SADIST

USA, 1963
Director: James Landis. Producer: L. Steven Snyder.
Screenplay: James Landis. Music: Paul Sawtell, Bert Shefter.
Cinematography: Vilmos Zsigmond.
Cast: Arch Hall Jr., Richard Alden, Marilyn Manning, Don Russell,
Helen Hovey, Joan Howard.

BANNED IN THE U.K FOR 22 YEARS

Arch Hall Jr. owed his film career solely to efforts by his scam
artist father Hall Sr. (alias William Watters) – said to be the
inspiration for the comic novel and movie **The Last Time I Saw
Archie** (1961) – who founded Fairway International Pictures
in 1960 to make exploitation fodder star vehicles for his pug-
nosed son. The result was usually lame trash: the delinquent
drama **The Choppers** (1961), the prehistoric caveman
Eegah (1962), the rock'n'roll fable **Wild Guitar** (1962), the
spy comedy **The Nasty Rabbit** (1964), the cowboy clinker
Deadwood '76 (1965). But one in the Fairway run actually
worked and showcased Hall Jr.'s limited talents well – **The Sadist** (also known as **Sweet Baby
Charlie**). Directed by James Landis, who also helmed the minor gem **Rat Fink** (1965), Hall Jr. plays
thrill-killing maniac Charlie Tibbs, loosely based on real-life mass murderer Charles Starkweather, also
the inspiration for Terrence Malik's masterpiece **Badlands** (1973). Charlie and his dim-witted girlfriend
terrorize a trio of lost schoolteachers at a desert scrapyard on their way to an LA Dodgers game. Packing
a punch due to its suspense mechanics playing out in 'real' time, Hall Jr. overdoes the crazed leering as
the trigger-happy psycho, but even that can't derail a bona fide drive-in classic.

Hey, Sweet Baby
What makes you so sweet...
The blood on your hands...
or the snake at your feet?

JERRY GROSS
Presents

SWEET
BABY
CHARLIE

Sweet Baby's toy was a rattler...

Starring ARCH HALL Jr. with HELEN HOVEY, RICHARD ALDEN
a JERRY GROSS presentation · Written and Directed by JAMES LANDIS
Distributed by CINEMATION INDUSTRIES

THE THRILL SEEKERS

UK, 1963
Director: Robert Hartford-Davis. Producer: Robert Hartford-Davis. Screenplay: Donald Ford, Derek Ford. Music: Malcolm Mitchell. Cinematography: Peter Newbrook.
Cast: Jacqueline Ellis, Annette Whiteley, Iain Gregory, Douglas Sheldon, Georgina Patterson, Raymond Huntley.

The first British independent sexploitation movie was **The Yellow Teddybears**. It was directed by Robert Hartford-Davis, whose career making cheap exploitation films in every genre hit as many high notes – **The Black Torment** (1964), **Corruption** (1968), **The Fiend** (1972) – as low ones – **Gonks Go Beat** (1965), **The Smashing Bird I Used to Know** (1969). Sleaze-merchant and future Tigon producer Tony Tenser could always sniff out a commercial proposition and in 1963 he read a newspaper report about a group of schoolgirls who had taken to advertising their loss of virginity by wearing the golliwog brooches given away as a sale promotion by the Robertson jam company. Given to Derek and Donald Ford to flesh out into a script, the end result was not quite what Tenser had in mind as they had written a social drama questioning the sex education methods in schools. But this edifying treatment of a scandalous subject impressed the British censors and attracted not only sensation seekers but also teachers who took their students to see it as a warning. The movie did big business in Britain and was sold all around the world, released in America under this title and later **Gutter Girls**.

What does The TEDDY BEAR mean?

Fast **Funny** **Wacky** * WITH PLENTY of **BOOM BOOM** and **GO GO** *

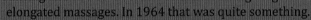

ARTIST'S STUDIO SECRETS

USA, 1964
Director: J.M. Kimbrough. Producer: Lou Campa.
Cinematography: George Cirello.
Cast: J.M. Kimbrough, Madeleine, Lou Campa,
Judy Jennsen, Debra Darcy, Gigi Darlene.

When he wasn't directing tacky T&A like **Mini-Skirt Love** (1967), **Sock It to Me Baby** (1968) and **C'mon Baby, Light My Fire** (1969), Lou Campa made the odd cameo appearance in his own productions under the alias Louis Champion. Here he is in one for his pal J(ack) M. Kimbrough (who doubles up himself playing Percy Green) in an adult tale of bohemian life in New York's Greenwich Village. It wasn't all beatniks, Bob Dylan and folk singing venues according to this time capsule historical document. No, this silent black-and-white nudie-cutie posits one of sexploitation's all-time burning questions; are women more sexy wearing just their underwear or stark naked? The usual mind-numbing narration argues both sides of the case as Gigi Darlene and Debra Darcy strut their stuff in bra and panties while ensuring they don't reveal too much skin while posing nude. A tacked-on sub-plot of sorts has the perplexed artist's zany wife keeping a close watch on both her husband and younger brother who gets too close to the comely models for comfort. 'Highlights' include Darlene's erotic go-go dancing and two of the featured female cast giving each other elongated massages. In 1964 that was quite something.

BOLD NEW NUDIE EXPOSÉ! OF WILD STUDIO PARTIES

LORNA

USA, 1964
Director: Russ Meyer. Producer: Russ Meyer. Screenplay: James Griffith.
Music: James Griffith [uncredited]. Cinematography: Russ Meyer.
Cast: Lorna Maitland, Mark Bradley, James Rucker, Hal Hopper,
Doc Scortt, James Griffith.

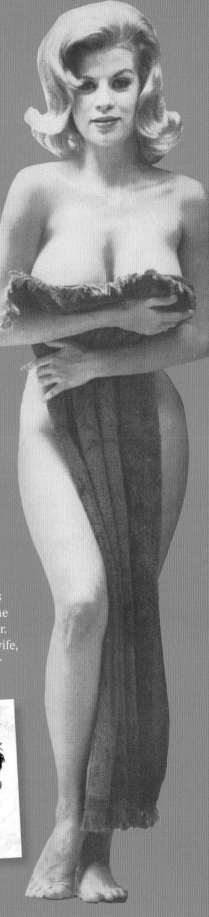

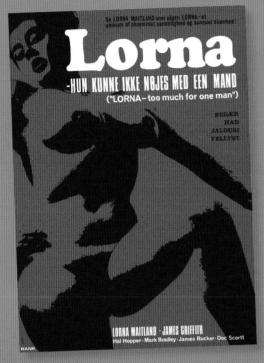

Marking the end of Russ Meyer's nudie period complete with buffoonish macho humour, this rural sex fantasy was the self-appointed King Leer's first foray into serious filmmaking. And despite the tragic death struggle ending, it's the Prince of Pulchritude's most romantic film. Barbara Popejoy was a Las Vegas showgirl when she answered an advert in 'Daily Variety' about playing the lead in an upcoming erotic drama. She was one of 132 actresses who applied but her audition photos were initially overlooked until Meyer's original choice was fired on the first day of shooting for looking too flat chested in camera. At that time, Barbara was three months pregnant, which augmented her already very large breasts, so she got the job by default. As the movie was always titled **Lorna**, that's what Meyer chose to rename his latest discovery, the Maitland surname selected to add a touch of class to the backwoods roots of the character. Set in Tobacco Road USA, it told the brutal tale of a lonely, frustrated wife, the handsome but dumb husband who doesn't appreciate her need for constant sexual attention, and the convict who rapes her in the woods causing her best climax ever.

MOONSHINE MOUNTAIN

USA, 1964
Director: Herschell Gordon Lewis. Producer: Herschell Gordon Lewis. Screenplay: Charles Glore. Music: Chuck Scott [Charles Glore], Herschell Gordon Lewis [uncredited]. Cinematography: Herschell Gordon Lewis.
Cast: Chuck Scott [Charles Glore], Adam Sorg [Gordon Oas-Heim], Jeffrey Allen, Bonnie Hinson, Carmen Sotir, Ben Moore.

With the nudie-cuties far behind him, and his landmark gore movie **Blood Feast** (1963) creating heated controversy and censorship problems, hackmeister Herschell Gordon Lewis needed to earn money so decided to create another genre. His brainchild was the 'good ole boy' hillbilly family picture packed with cornball action and hoedown excitement. Pandering to his core audiences, Lewis set the movie in the American South, added country and western music and, because he knew they would expect it, a smattering of dialled-down sex and violence. Scriptwriter Charles Glore played country star Doug Martin, back in hicksville for some down home musical inspiration. There he hooks up with the Basham and Carpenter families whom, with Sheriff Potter, own the biggest illegal moonshine still in the area. Falling in love with Carpenter daughter Laura, Doug finds that he has to deal with his fiancée Delia when she turns up for a visit. Laying her dismay on the line, Delia makes an attempt to leave town but is killed by Potter after she rejects his sexual advances. Dumping her body in the still – like he has with so many other snooping federal agents – it seems it's this special added ingredient that gives their White Lightning its magic potency.

WHITE LIGHTNIN' FLOWS JES' LIKE WATER ON...
Moonshine Mountain
A HERSCHELL GORDON LEWIS production
COLOR
Thar's sing'n, danc'n, shoot'n 'n fight'n too! It gets real excit'n when th' world's biggest still is busted!
Starring CHUCK SCOTT ADAM SORG JEFFERY ALLEN
and introducing
BONNIE HINSON CARMEN SOTIR
FILMED IN THE BEAUTIFUL CAROLINAS

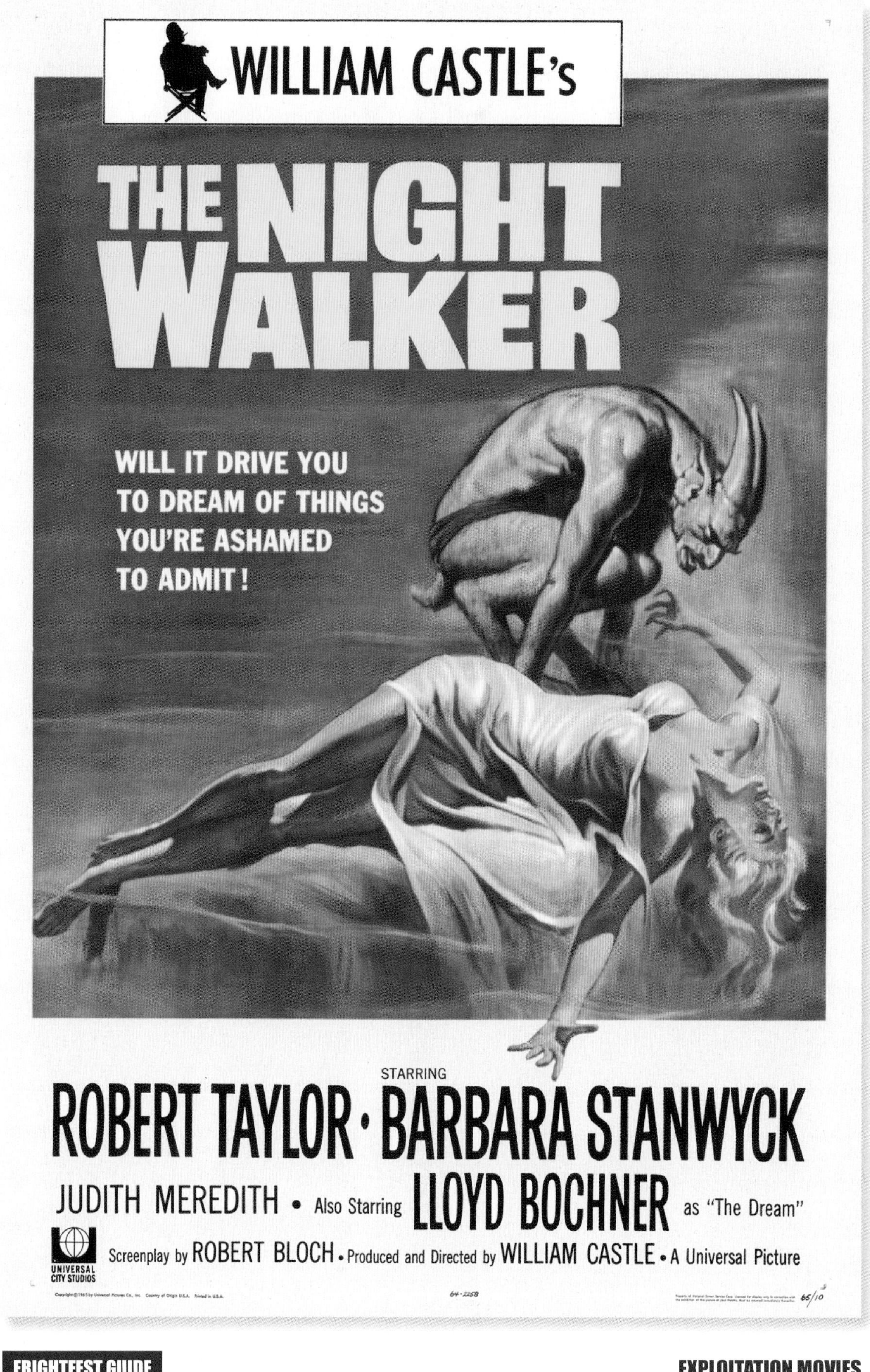

WILLIAM CASTLE's
THE NIGHT WALKER
WILL IT DRIVE YOU TO DREAM OF THINGS YOU'RE ASHAMED TO ADMIT!
STARRING
ROBERT TAYLOR · BARBARA STANWYCK
JUDITH MEREDITH • Also Starring LLOYD BOCHNER as "The Dream"
UNIVERSAL CITY STUDIOS
Screenplay by ROBERT BLOCH • Produced and Directed by WILLIAM CASTLE • A Universal Picture
Copyright © 1965 by Universal Pictures Co., Inc. Country of Origin U.S.A. Printed in U.S.A.
64-2258
65/10

THE NIGHT WALKER

USA, 1964
Director: William Castle. Producer: William Castle. Screenplay: Robert Bloch. Music: Vic Mizzy. Cinematography: Harold E. Stine. Cast: Robert Taylor, Barbara Stanwyck, Judi Meredith, Hayden Rorke, Rochelle Hudson, Marjorie Bennett.

After exhausting ever more arcane gimmicks for **13 Ghosts** (1960) – the 3-D variant 'Illusion-O', **Zotz!** (1962) – plastic coins to flip, and **I Saw What You Did** (1965) – seatbelts to strap audiences down to withstand the shock, master showman producer/director William Castle turned to **Psycho** (1960) imitations just like Hammer did with their **Maniac** (1963), **Paranoiac** (1963), **Nightmare** (1964) and **Hysteria** (1965) roster. This contrived shocker (scripted by **Psycho**'s Robert Bloch) starred Hollywood diva Barbara Stanwyck (in her last movie role) as a woman accused by her blind husband of being unfaithful with her solicitor (played by real-life ex-husband Robert Taylor). When he dies in an explosion, his disfigured face haunts her guilty nightmares, until it's all revealed to be an elaborate inheritance scam. Prefaced by a ludicrous lecture on the real meaning of dreams and the nature of the subconscious, this was shoddy stuff enlivened only by Stanwyck's earnest performance. The poster art is a complete rip-off of the famous 1782 painting 'The Nightmare' by Gothic romantic artist Fuseli, depicting an incubus sitting on top of a reclining woman. Ken Russell's **Gothic** (1986) also used the same pose. Not that any regular 42nd Street habitué would know that...

UNDER AGE

USA, 1964
Director: Larry Buchanan. Producer: Harold Hoffman. Screenplay: Larry Buchanan, Harold Hoffman. Cinematography: Henry A. Kokojan. Cast: Anne McAdams [Annabelle Weenick], Judy Adler, Roland Royter, George R. Russell, John Hicks, George Edgley.

Larry Buchanan strikes again. The **Mars Needs Women** (1967) hackmeister put a divorced Texas mother on trial for encouraging her 14-year-old daughter to have sex with her sweet sixteen Mexican beau in this 'sizzling courtroom drama'. Just like his **Free, White and 21** (1963), Buchanan made the audience the jury by using what was promoted as a 'novel photographic trick', i.e. the actors pleading their testimonies directly towards the camera lens. All this and the ditties 'Boil Them Cabbage Down' by The Alpine Trio, 'Turtledove Song' by The Lost River Trio and the title theme co-written by Buchanan. Suggested gimmicks other than the post credits lecture conducted by a 'community expert on family affairs' included hiring a local store window, blacking it out from the inside apart from peepholes, over which was emblazoned 'Do You Know What Your Daughter Is Doing Right Now?' The curious who looked in would see a stills and poster display. More startling was having a local radio disc jockey run a contest in which a listener sending in the longest list of terms synonymous with the words **Under Age** won tickets. San Quentin Quail – meaning jailbait – was one given as an acceptable example!

AGENT 3S3: PASSPORT TO HELL

Italy/France/Spain, 1965
Director: Simon Sterling [Sergio Sollima]. Screenplay: Simon Sterling [Sergio Sollima].
Music: Piero Umiliani. Cinematography: Carlo Carlini.
Cast: George Ardisson, Barbara Simons, Georges Rivière, Seyna Seyn, Franco Andrei, Dakar.

After directing an episode in the erotic comedy anthology **L'amore difficile/Sex Can Be Difficult** (1962), Sergio Sollima made his feature debut proper with **Agente 3S3: Passaporto per l'inferno**, an average Eurospy effort under the alias Simon Sterling. Giorgio/George Ardisson (the 1961 Mario Bava duo **Ercole al centro della Terra/Hercules in the Haunted World** and **Gli invasori/Erik the Conqueror**) is debonair Walter Ross Agent 3S3 (meaning secret agent 3 of the 3rd Special Division), assigned to cosy up to Jasmine von Witheim (Barbara Simons) to find out the whereabouts of her Most Wanted spy ring mastermind father, codenamed Mr. A. Turns out he was killed a year earlier by Professor Steve Dickson (Georges Rivière, **La vergine di Norimberga/Horror Castle**, 1963) and his lover Jackie Vein (Seyna Seyn, **Se tutte le donne del mondo/Kiss the Girls and Make Them Die**, 1966) and they have been perpetuating his existence ever since to camouflage their hostile takeover. Shot in Vienna and Lebanon, outlandish gadgets include a pendant transmitter, the receiver in a pair of spectacles, a needle-shooting compact case and special litmus paper to detect poisonous cocktails. Sollima and Ardisson returned for **Agente 3S3: massacro al sole/Agent 3S3: Massacre in the Sun** (1966).

ALL MEN ARE APES!

USA, 1965
Director: Joseph P. Mawra. Producer: Barnard L. Sackett.
Screenplay: Charles E. Mazin, Barnard L. Sackett.
Cinematography: Richard E. Brooks.
Cast: Stephanie De Passe, Mark Ryan, Grace Lynn, Steve Woods, Lawrence Adams [Steve Vincent], Tom O'Horgan.

From **Olga** series mastermind Joseph Mawra comes this campy caper devoid of nudity but emphasizing the director's proclivity for arbitrary violence. The filmstrip image poster was a modish one during the mid-Sixties – movies with New Wave pretensions used it to position their entertainment as something fresh and cineaste. This bog-standard wayward stripper chronicle was neither, as star Steffie De Passe is behind bars reminiscing about the time her two-bit agent pressurized her into becoming a 'Beauty and the Beast' burlesque novelty act with Harry the Ape. Insanely trying to evoke fond memories of **King Kong** (1933) and **Blonde Venus** (1932), this teasing trifle featured a highly unusual male strip, ho-hum back-story concerning De Passe's slut-on-wheels mother and a daft ending with a twist in the tale. A third generation of the do-wop group The Ink Spots

(their hits 'If I Didn't Care' and 'Whispering Grass') get shoehorned into the risible antics taking place at many famous Greenwich Village watering holes of the era including The Bitter End. Playing wild beatnik Marcel Fires is Tom O'Horgan who, three years after appearing in this pot-boiler, would change the face of Broadway history by directing the landmark American Tribal Love-Rock Musical 'Hair'.

THE FARMER'S OTHER DAUGHTER

USA, 1965
Director: John Hayes. Producer: Paul Leder, William W. Norton. Screenplay: William W. Norton. Music: Victor Pierce. Cinematography: Paul Hipp.
Cast: Judy Pennebaker, William Michael, William Guhl, Harry Lovejoy, Jean Bennett, Ernest Ashworth.

Cult director John (Patrick) Hayes moved from psychological melodrama (**Shell Shock**, 1964) to explicit erotic drama (**Help Wanted Female**, 1968) before arriving at the **Grave of the Vampire**(1972)/**Garden of the Dead** (1972) offbeat horror strand he's most remembered and celebrated for. Between the first two titles came this transitional Hixploitation effort that echoed the traits of the many raunchy White Trash comedies of the day. Poor Farmer Brown (Harry Lovejoy) plans to sell his beautiful daughter June ('Star of Tomorrow' Judy Pennebaker) to rich travelling salesman Jim Huckleberry (William Michael), organiser of a July 4th bathing beauty contest. But when the flimsy swimsuits disintegrate in the rain, Jim just about avoids being lynched to help stop Farmer Brown having his small holding seized by the greedy town sheriff. He does this by applying for Farm Aid from the government, but due to bureaucratic mistakes gets given Foreign Aid instead. Ho, ho, ho. A queasy mix of cornpone humour, stabs at political satire, child bride concerns, slapstick comedy and sedate erotica, the country and western music from the Kentucky Colonels, with Ernest Ashworth, of the long-running 'Grand Ol' Opry' radio show, only helps run its rural stereotypes further into the ground.

HIGH YELLOW

USA, 1965
Director: Larry Buchanan. Producer: Clyde Knudsen. Screenplay: Larry Buchanan.
Cast: Cynthia Hull, Warren Hammack, Kay Taylor, Bill McGhee, Anne MacAdams [Annabelle Weenick], Bob Brown.

Shlockmeister Larry Buchanan was a mainstay of trailer-led trash in the early 1960s addressing topically taboo issues such as teenage sex and racial relations. This unyielding potboiler fell into the latter category, inspired by studio hits **Pinky** (1949) and **Imitation of Life** (1959). Future TV staple Cynthia Hull ('The Mod Squad', 'The Flying Nun') is the light-skinned negro maid intent on passing for white after working for the wealthy Langley family. Unfortunately the household head is a sexually frustrated tyrant, his son has suffered military expulsion on homosexual charges, his teenage daughter is a nymphomaniac, their handyman is a sadist and the black chauffeur is trying to escape his past too. Can Cindy escape this cruel madhouse as 'The Explosive Story of the Year' culminates in 'Tender moments of modern racial decision'? Not with Buchanan at the helm she can't! Best remembered for a spate of poverty-stricken TV remakes of AIP science-fiction fillers, including **Zontar: The Thing from Venus** (1966) and **Mars Needs Women** (1967), Buchanan was obsessed by conspiracy theories and made a couple of paranoia movies purporting to tell the 'truth' about subjects the government and Hollywood hushed up, **The Trial of Lee Harvey Oswald** (1964) and **Goodbye, Norma Jean** (1976).

A female half breed who is too white to be black... too black to be white!

She didn't cross the color line she walked right down the middle!

HIGH YELLOW

Rx: A prescription for something you'll never believe!

WOMEN THEIR DESIRE, GOLD THEIR OBJECTIVE AND A WAR-TORN COUNTRY THEIR BATTLEGROUND!

THE RAVAGERS

USA/Philippines, 1965
Director: Eddie Romero. Producer: Eddie Romero.
Screenplay: Cesar Amigo, Eddie Romero. Music: Tito Arevalo.
Cinematography: Nonong Rasca.
Cast: John Saxon, Fernando Poe Jr., Bronwyn Fitzsimmons,
Michael Parsons, Kristina Scott, Robert Arevalo.

Director Eddie Romero's international reputation rests
chiefly on the low budget horror, Blaxploitation and
action movies he made during the 1960s and '70s
like the 'Blood Island' trilogy, **Beast of the Yellow Night**
(1971), **The Twilight People** (1972), **Beyond Atlantis** (1973),
Black Mama White Mama (1973), **Savage Sisters** (1974) and
Sudden Death (1977). Exploitation movies aside, Romero also
tackled Filipino issues in war dramas such as **Lost Battalion**
(1962), **Intramuros** (1964) and **Manila, Open City** (1968).
Named a National Artist of the Philippines in 2003, Romero
was born 1924 in Dumaguete City and began his film career
with **Ang kamay ng Diyos** (1947) just as The Philippines were
recovering from the devastation of World War II. That movie
starred Gerardo de Leon who turned director and with Romero
later made Filipino fantasy a viable global brand. His most
prestigious film is the musical drama **Ganito kami noon…
Paano kayo ngayon?** (1976), winner of the Filipino Academy
of Movie Arts and Sciences' Best Director Award, and Metro
Manila Film Festival Awards for Best Director and
Screenplay. **The Ravagers** was a Pacific War drama
in the brutal style of **The Camp on Blood
Island** (1958) starring one-time juvenile
delinquent movie mainstay John Saxon.

THE STORY OF
BLACKS & WHITES in COLOR!

A TIMELY PICTURE ON A TOUCHY SUBJECT!
★★★★★★★★★★★★★★★★★★★★★★★★★★★★★★★★★★★★★★

UNCLE TOM'S CABIN

West Germany/Italy, 1965
Director: Géza von Radványi. Producer: Aldo von Pinelli. Screenplay: Fred Denger, Géza von Radványi. Music: Peter Thomas. Cinematography: Heinz Hölscher.
Cast: John Kitzmiller, O.W. Fischer, Herbert Lom, Eleonora Rossi-Drago, Juliette Gréco, Mylène Demongeot.

In the 1930s the infamous travelling exploitation roadshow partnership of Howard Russell Cox and Howard Underwood ('Child Bride'/'Dust to Dust', 1938, was their pinnacle grift, centered around the 1935 film **High School Girl**) discovered a copy of a silent version of the Harriet Beecher Stowe classic in an unclaimed railway freight auction. Eliminating the inter-titles, they added a soundtrack with a Lincoln-esque voice relating the plot, plus old recordings of Stephen Foster songs, and it cleaned up in the Deep South for three years. Finally copyright owners Universal tumbled to the piracy but it was too late as the Forty Thief duo had milked it dry. One of their employees, a certain Kroger Babb, followed their template in 1970 when a Euro pudding version of the 1852 anti-slavery saga had been languishing on sales agents' shelves. With a cast of thousands, including Herbert Lom and Juliette Gréco, great visuals and stirring symphonic score it was superbly appointed but the dubbing was hilarious. Babb redubbed it with proper southern accents and pitched it as the first civil rights crusading story. In the aftermath of Martin Luther King Jr.'s assassination, it hit the mood of the times, made a fortune and was the **Mom and Dad** (1945) legend's last hurrah.

WIFE SWAPPERS

USA, 1965
Director: Richard W. Bomont. Screenplay: Terrance Michaels.
Cinematography: Karl Prince.
Cast: Judette Banket, Robert Chambers, Margaret MacPherson,
Ken McDonald, Rudy Gome, Rosalie Saunders.

For just over twenty years from 1955 the independent West
Coast based company Emerson Film Enterprises peddled
their dubious wares on the grindhouse circuits of America.
Some of the movies they distributed were interesting – Anthony
Asquith's British crime thriller **Two Living, One Dead** (1961)
and the eccentric cult sci-fi **The Creation of the Humanoids**
(1962) – but most of their repertoire was of the low-grade
The Doctor and the Playgirl (1965), **Manos: The Hands
of Fate** (1966) variety and the infamous **Psyched by the
4D Witch (A Tale of Demonology)** (1973). Like this
completely generic item with a psycho twist from San
Francisco-based director Richard W. Bomont revealing in
laborious detail what goes on at a wife swapping party.
Nothing much it turns out above the normal ponderous
boozing, dancing and off to the bedrooms for some chaste
simulated sex action, while the narrator attempts to add
characterisation to the no-account actors. It was such dud
movies that forced manager Joe Emerson to broaden his
company's catalogue and handle the release of 'difficult'
international product as the Charles Bronson Euro-hit
Cold Sweat (1970), Sam Fuller's **Dead Pigeon on
Beethoven Street** (1972) and the British sex comedy
Spanish Fly (1976).

SPICY! BAWDY! WILD!

Life can be dull unless you find new excitement!

The wife wh
bed-bounced
herself
between the
two men!

Nothing is too good or too sacred
for a man who is your best friend!

Released by William Mishkin

"WILD, WILD PLANET"

It begins with the incredible... and that's just the beginning!

THE WILD, WILD PLANET

Italy, 1965

Director: Anthony Dawson [Antonio Margheriti]. Producer: Joseph Fryd, Antonio Margheriti. Screenplay: Ivan Reiner, Renato Moretti. Music: Angelo Francesco Lavagnino. Cinematography: Riccardo Pallottini. Cast: Tony Russell, Lisa Gastoni, Massimo Serato, Franco Nero, Carlo Giustini, Enzo Fiermonte.

The way out Swinging Sixties meets the far-out 21st Century in director Antonio Margheriti's psychedelic blast of pop art sci-fi fantasy. Shot back-to-back with its prequel **War of the Planets** (1965), this It-alien adventure is full of marvellous ideas, cheap but cheerful sets, **Flash Gordon** rockets-on-strings, surprisingly good make-up effects and hilariously wooden acting from transplanted American Tony Russell, peplum heroine Lisa Gastoni and future **Django** (1966) Franco Nero. In 2015 AD, Earth is ruled by rival factions: The Corporations super-power and the United Democracies. The former send out robot minions to capture the latter's citizens, shrink them down to suitcase size and transport them to the Gamma 1 space station for hideous human experiments. An entertainingly schlocky B movie sporting mini-skirted, beehive haired women with super-human strength, bald four-armed heavies in black leather raincoats and dark sunglasses and a gorgeously slimy performance from Massimo Serato as the evil miniaturizing crazed scientist Mr. Nurmi. The fantastic poster suggests more of a **Barbarella** (1968) go-go atmosphere – that Jane Fonda space opera was still a few years away from release. But the campaign is a characteristic-of-the-day 'See, See, See' kind where all possible selling points were listed to promote attendance.

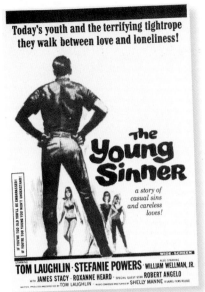

THE YOUNG SINNER

USA, 1965
Director: Tom Laughlin. Producer: Tom Laughlin. Screenplay: Tom Laughlin. Music: Shelly Manne. Cinematography: Ed Martin, Sven Walnum. Cast: Tom Laughlin, Stefanie Powers, William Wellman Jr., Robert Angelo [Robert Fuca], Linda March, James Stacy.

Shot in Milwaukee in 1960 and screened for exhibitors as **Like Father, Like Son**, this story of "Today's youth and the terrifying tightrope they walk between love and loneliness", didn't find a wide release until the title change in 1965. By then filmmaker Tom Laughlin (Seventies indie **Billy Jack** sensation) had made more of a name for himself in TV series like 'Wagon Train', and co-stars Stephanie Powers (Hammer's **Fanatic**, 1965), William Wellman Jr. ('Rawhide') and James Stacy (the beach party **A Swingin' Summer**, 1965) were much better known to the teenage set. This was the first and only chapter in an aborted Godsploitation trilogy made under the umbrella title **We Are All Christ**, the gimmick being the parables were all told via confession booth flashbacks. Laughlin plays small-town football star Christopher Wotan, who gets expelled from school after being found in a compromising position with a 14-year-old choir sexpot and in bed with a poor little rich girl. His sporting life over, and further complications due to his drunken father consistently being thrown into jail, he wrecks the church altar and smashes up a religious statue until a priest comes to his aid showing him the path to redemption.

SHOWMAN'S SUGGESTIONS
LITTLE EFFORT — BIG PAYOFF!

POSTER CONTEST
Get city school system, public library system, newspaper, Girl and Boy Scout organizations or large department store to sponsor a poster contest based on "The Young Sinner" theme. Entrants limited to students. Winning poster would receive cash award. Display poster in theatre lobby, use in newspaper ads.

SCHOOL PAPER REVIEWS
Invite schools to set up contest for high school and college newspaper editors and reporters. Invite them to special screening of picture. Have them write for their paper a review of "The Young Sinner." Give prize for winning review (judged by exhibitor or motion picture editors of local newspapers). Prize could be a year's free pass to theatre.

FREE RADIO PROMOTION
Have local radio stations play Shelly Manne albums and singles—and announce that his music is background for "The Young Sinner" at your theatre.

CROWD BUILDER
Build crowds by inviting local teen-age combos to play in front of theatre or in foyer an hour before show time. The combos will draw crowds. The teen combos won't charge. They like audiences, too.

"IDEAL FAMILY" CONTEST
Tie in with your local newspaper on "The Ideal Family" contest. Newspaper readers write letters recommending a family they think deserves the honor. Cooperate with newspaper in setting up panel of town's leading citizens to select winning family. Award engraved plaque to "Ideal Family." Get mayor or newspaper publisher to make presentation of plaque on theatre stage final night of run. Present family with gift book of free admissions to your theatre . . . promote restaurant for once-a-month dinner for year. Check other merchants for prizes for "The Ideal Family."

FATHER AND SON NIGHT
Son admitted to theatre free when accompanied by his father.

TEEN-AGE TV PANEL SHOW
Get local television station to put on teen-age panel discussion show. Panel could discuss such topics as . . . "Who's Really To Blame For Juvenile Delinquency?" . . . "Are Today's Parents Square?" . . . "Are Teen-age Morals Different Today From 20 Years Ago?" . . . "Will Marriage Soon Be Outdated?" For another approach, pit teenagers against adults in discussing the same topics.

GIRL ON A CHAIN GANG

USA, 1966
Director: Jerry Gross. Producer: Jerry Gross. Screenplay: Jerry Gross. Music: Steve Karmen. Cinematography: George Zimmermann.
Cast: William Watson, Julie Ange, Ron Charles, Arlene Farber, Ron Segal, Peter Nevard.

Entering the sexploitation industry as the producer of **Vice Girls, Ltd.** (1964) Jerry Gross's first attempt at directing was this dire melodrama about three young people framed, arrested and imprisoned by corrupt Southern police. It had absolutely nothing going for it except two great gimmicks, and boy did it need them! On entering the theatre each patron was given two items. One was a pink envelope you unfolded to read a handwritten plea by the raped Jean Rollins (Julie Ange) character begging her boyfriend to come see her on the Chain Gang where she was the only white girl. This evidence then had to be destroyed according to the instructions. The other was a 'Certificate of Jury Service' which had to have the patron's name printed on it so they could never reveal the shocking contents of the motion picture they were about to see under oath. Purportedly shot under extremely adverse conditions in the Deep South, the movie was actually made in New Jersey. Gross next helmed **Teenage Mother** (1967) but after **Female Animal** (1970) abandoned directing altogether in favour of producing and distributing such curios as **I Drink Your Blood** (1970), **Zombie** (1979) and **The Boogeyman** (1980).

A SHOCKER!...

THE FILM THAT UNCOVERS THE LID OF SMALL TOWN HATE...!

"When you come back from the fields to-night, I'm going to give you the beating of your life!"

"They said I could go off with her to Perkin's Motel and she'd be real co-operative!"

"Nellie the town's plaything, she passed for white and they loved it!"

STARRING
WILLIAM WATSON | **JULIE ANGE** | **R. K. CHARLES** | Original Story by **DON OLSEN** | Associate Producer **NICHOLAS DEMETROULES**

Produced, Written & Directed by **JERRY GROSS**   **A JERRY GROSS PRESENTATION**

UNBELIEVABLE! The girls with MINI-SKIRTS and MINI-MORALS who follow THE BIG BLAST of the HARD ROCK MUSIC GROUPS!

BLAST-OFF GIRLS

USA, 1967
Director: Herschell Gordon Lewis. Producer: Herschell Gordon Lewis. Screenplay: Herschell Gordon Lewis.
Music: Larry Wellington. Cinematography: Roy Collodi.
Cast: Dan Conway, Ray Sager, Tom Tyrell, Ron Liace, Dennis Hickey, Harland Sanders.

Herschell Gordon Lewis's **A Hard Day's Night** (1964)? Not quite. More like a wrong-headed **Gonks Go Beat** (1965). Fluffy cotton candy movies featuring pop idols of the day were big business in the mid Sixties. Billy Fury starred in **I've Gotta Horse** (1965), The Dave Clark Five in **Catch Us If You Can** (1965), Freddie and the Dreamers in **Every Day's a Holiday** (1964), Joe Brown in **Three Hats for Lisa** (1965) and The Monkees in **Head** (1968). But Lewis didn't have any such luminous chart-toppers to headline his music biz saga. Instead he made do with The Faded Blue, rechristened them The Big Blast, and threw them headlong into a stupid plot about their manipulative manager Boojie Baker (Dan Conway) doing everything he can to make them stars and make himself rich. Those plans include the band's titular groupies rushing the stage and ripping their clothes off, providing the right record industry people with sexual favours, and one-off gigs for Mr. Kentucky Fried Chicken himself, Colonel Harland Sanders. Boojie's idiot assistant Gordie is played by Ray Sager, future Montag the Magnificent in **The Wizard of Gore** (1970). As for The Faded Blue, well, they just simply faded…

A COLT IS MY PASSPORT

Japan, 1967
Director: Takashi Nomura. Screenplay: Hideichi Nagahara, Nobuo Yamada.
Music: Harumi Ibe. Cinematography: Shigeyoshi Mine.
Cast: Jô Shishido, Jerry Fujio, Chitose Kobayashi, Toyoko Takechi, Asao Uchida,
Takamaru Sasaki.

Part Nikkatsu Studio gangster noir and part Sergio Leone-style
spaghetti western, Takashi Nomura's **Koruto wa ore no pasupooto**
was yet another spin on the tried-and-tested Yakuza formula where
a gang member is betrayed and fights back. Here, it's lonely hitman
Kamimura (Jô Shishido, who in 1956 underwent plastic surgery to give
him his distinct and always employable apple-cheeked look) hired by the Tsugawa gang to assassinate
the Shimazu family crime boss. But after he methodically targets his prey, the rivals form a truce and
as part of the deal the Tsugawas give up Kamimura to the other side, forcing him to go on the run with
his guitar-strumming sidekick Shun (Jerry Fujio). The memorably thrilling finale has our hero fighting

off a fistful of riflemen on a beach with cars, explosives and
carefully laid traps detonating. An archetypal example of the
mukokuseki akushon, the 'borderless action' genre deliberately
fusing Eastern and Western styles together to appeal to the
Japanese baby boomer audience fed up with ancient history
lessons, **A Colt Is My Passport** is a fun, zippy crowd-pleaser
that looked forward to the ubiquitous output of director Takashi
Miike, marrying generics with artifice, style, invention and
consummate creativity.

THE GLORY STOMPERS

USA, 1967
Director: Anthony M. Lanza. Producer: John Lawrence. Screenplay:
James Gordon White, John Lawrence. Music: Davie Allan, Mike Curb.
Cinematography: Mario Tosi.
Cast: Dennis Hopper, Jody McCrea, Chris Noel, Jock Mahoney, Casey
Kasem, Jim Reader.

From 1966 to 1972 American International Pictures were the main
makers of motorcycle melodramas thanks to the massive success of
The Wild Angels (1966). As writers searched for new activities to
involve rebel bikers, the stories became more like westerns with a
Harley haze. Scripter James Gordon White borrowed the plot from
James Stewart's **Winchester '73** (1950) for his **Hell's Belles** (1969)
mainly because he had already successfully mined the formula for
this Anthony M. Lanza B picture where horses were simply traded
for choppers. While Jock Mahoney, TV's 'The Range Rider' and star of numerous 1950s westerns like
The Kid from Broken Gun (1952), took to the standard revenge framework easily, it was Dennis
Hopper, in his first biker flick, who had the most to learn about all things Angel in his pre-**Easy Rider**
(1969) days. Hopper plays Chino, leader of the Black Souls, who capture rival Stompers' head Darryl
(**Beach Party** regular Jody McCrea) and his girlfriend Chris (Chris Noel). With Darryl beaten up and left
for dead, Chino drags Chris off to be sold on the Mexican white slavery market. But Smiley (Mahoney)
discovers Darryl on the roadside and joins his former buddy on the revenge manhunt.

HILLBILLYS IN A HAUNTED HOUSE

USA, 1967
Director: Jean Yarbrough. Producer: Bernard Woolner. Screenplay: Duke
Yelton. Music: Hal Borne. Cinematography: Vaughn Wilkins.
Cast: Ferlin Husky, Joi Lansing, Don Bowman, John Carradine, Lon Chaney
Jr., Basil Rathbone.

The sequel nobody wanted to **The Las Vegas Hillbillys** (1966) was
this redneck musical comedy that wasted the talents of once-popular
horror stars Lon Chaney Jr., Basil Rathbone and John Carradine. It was a poor but fitting last film for
Jean Yarbrough, who started out in the film industry as producer Hal Roach's chauffeur, progressed
to Abbott and Costello comedies and tumbled to Poverty Row quickies like **The Devil Bat** (1940) and
King of the Zombies (1941). Here, three country and western music stars, Ferlin Husky (famous for his

1950 smash hit 'Wings of a Dove'), Don Bowman (the original host of
radio's top-rated 'American Country Countdown') and Joi Lansing (a
regular on 'The Beverly Hillbillies' sit-com) break down on the way to
Nashville and stay the night in a haunted mansion. If that wasn't bad
enough the place is the HQ for an international spy ring searching
for a secret rocket fuel formula. There's the prerequisite Mad
Doctor, Yellow Peril in the shape of Madame Wong, leading 'gorilla
performer' George Barrows in an ill-fitting hairy suit who rules the
basement and 14 mediocre songs, although a couple of them are sung
by outlaw C&W legend Merle Haggard.

THE TORRID STORY OF THREE GALS OF THE TRADE

HOW THEY MAKE MEN PAY ...AND PAY!

ADULTS ONLY

TEASING, TAUNTING, POWER-PACKED!

THE HOOKERS

USA, 1967
Director: Jalo Miklos Horthy. Producer: Jalo Miklos Horthy. Screenplay: William Rose.
Cinematography: Sean O'Reilly.
Cast: Fleurette Carter, Monica Lee [Monica Davis], Shan Benedict [Sharon Kent], Jay Martin [Joel Holt],
Lucky Kargo, Linda Lavell.

What would movies be without The World's Oldest Profession? No matter the completely misleading title – it's not about hardened prostitutes at all, just the stories of three compromised women in dire straits – this is a well done and well acted street-walk on the wild side, and a perfect example of mid Sixties sexploitation craft. First up is young black secretary Callie Sue (Fleurette Carter from **Aroused**, 1966) who arrives in the big city from the Deep South after unwanted attention from a much older white co-worker has caused her to recall the redneck rape that cost her virginity. Next is wannabe actress Julie (nudie cutie staple Sharon Kent as Shan Benedict, whose prior 1967 film was **Julie Is No Angel**) who finds the casting couch beckoning if she is serious about her ambitions. Last is housewife Barbara (Monica/Pat Davis from Joe Sarno's **The Swap and How They Make It**, 1966) whose gambling debts mean she owes a fortune to a sleazy loan shark (Lucky Kargo, star of many Barry Mahon quickies) happy to take sexual advantage of her addiction. Joel Holt narrates the sexcapades, also appears as Barbara's husband, and was the most famous trailer voiceover talent of the era.

THE LOVE-INS

USA, 1967
Director: Arthur Dreifuss. Producer:
Sam Katzman. Screenplay: Hal Collins,
Arthur Dreifuss. Music: Fred Karger.
Cinematography: John F. Warren.
Cast: Richard Todd, James MacArthur, Susan
Oliver, Mark Goddard, Carol Booth, Marc Cavell.

Despite containing ample drug use, Arthur
Dreifuss's Hollywood plastic look at Haight
(H)Ashbury hippies didn't
come under fire because it
purportedly showed the
seamy side of psych-out
lifestyles. German-born
choreographer Dreifuss
migrated to America
in 1928, became a
Broadway theatrical
producer, but soon
headed for Tinsel
Town, first as a
dance director, then
from 1939 as director
of a steady stream of
B-movies. He retired in
1968, significantly a year
after this feebly scripted
and cast LSD cautionary
tale. Astonishingly **The
Dam Busters** (1955) star
Richard Todd plays a Timothy
Leary-type who advocates
acid for religious meditation
on a local TV show and
becomes a hero in San
Francisco. But after forcing
his student girlfriend
Susan Oliver to have an
abortion and charging
$5 for admissions to his
Happenings, his public
image tarnishes.

THE TRIP-OUT!

THE SLEEP-IN!

THE FREAK-OUT!

Until James MacArthur, on the eve of 'Hawaii Five-0' TV stardom, kills him for stealing Oliver away, and
Todd quickly becomes a martyr for the hippie cause. It falls into that familiar category of dope opera
made extra dopey for being made by people completely at the other end of the generation gap it's
supposedly truthfully
portraying, but the
hallucinogen-induced
ballet of 'Alice in
Wonderland' is an
absolute laugh-riot.

THE LOVE-iNS

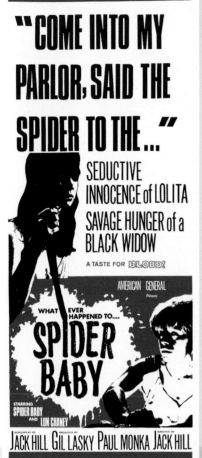

SPIDER BABY, OR THE MADDEST STORY EVER TOLD

USA, 1967
Director: Jack Hill. Producer: Paul Monka, Gil Lasky. Screenplay: Jack Hill.
Music: Ronald Stein. Cinematography: Alfred Taylor.
Cast: Lon Chaney Jr., Carol Ohmart, Quinn Redeker, Beverly Washburn,
Jill Banner, Sid Haig.

Any film that has B-movie horror icon Lon Chaney Jr. singing the title song has to be special. And this minuscule-budgeted excursion into depravity and dementia doesn't disappoint, mainly because the stark black-and-white photography, twisted performances and self-aware humour all converge into a warped vision of insanity. Director Jack Hill kept drive-ins and grindhouses in business with such classic exploitation fare as **The Big Doll House** (1971) and **Foxy Brown** (1974) and an early example of his craft was this mental horror comedy ironically named after the Biblical epic **The Greatest Story Ever Told** (1965). At the age of ten each member of the Merrye family is afflicted with a rare mysterious syndrome that causes their brains to rot and turn them cannibal (**The Liver Eaters** was an alternate title at one point). So when a pair of gold-digging distant relatives turn up to Merrye House to lay claim to the mansion, they have no idea they will be subjected to a range of horrific torture. Though graphic violence is kept to an off-screen minimum, the constant creepiness of the Merrye Family, clearly modelled on the more demure Addams one, and the game of Spider is alternately scary and funny.

THE FILM THAT DARES TO EXPLAIN WHAT MOST PARENTS CAN'T...

SEE Life Begin!...SEE The Actual Birth Of A Baby! IN COLOR!

TeenAge Mother
—MEANS 9 MONTHS OF TROUBLE!

She did her homework in parked cars!

TEENAGE MOTHER

USA, © 1966,
first public screening
1967
Director: Jerry Gross.
Producer: Jerry Gross.
Screenplay: Jerry Gross. Music:
Steve Karmen. Cinematography:
George Zimmerman, Richard E. Brooks.
Cast: Arlene Sue Farber [Arlene Farber],
Frederick Riccio, Julie Ange, George
Peters, Howard Le May, Matt Reynolds.

One of three movies Jerry Gross directed before finding his forte in outrageously promoting seminal exploitation fare like **I Drink Your Blood** (1970), **I Eat Your Skin** (1964) and **I Spit on Your Grave** (1978). Essentially an update of the classic white-coater **Mom and Dad** (1945) complete with post screening lecture and actual baby birth footage, only this time in colour. Arlene Farber stars as the oldest-looking 15-year-old ever in this rancid hilarious story of 'a girl who wasn't careful'. Her supposed pregnancy is actually blamed on the new Swedish Sex Health teacher, Erika Petersen (Julie Ange) who comes to Claremont High to teach anatomy and hygiene. However the school's principal, faculty and PTA have problems with her forward attitudes, so when Arlene is rumoured to be in the family way it becomes her fault due to her progressive methods. None of this matters a jot to Arlene who is basically playing her school sweetheart Tony (Howard Le May) off against greaser bad boy Duke (Frederick Riccio) and faking her condition. It all ends with Arlene and Tony watching Miss Petersen's classroom presentation of crude live birth footage safe in the knowledge it won't happen to them. Yet!

THE VIOLENT ONES

USA, 1967
Director: Fernando Lamas. Producer: Robert Stabler. Screenplay: Doug Wilson, Charles Davis. Music: Marlin Skiles. Cinematography: Fleet Southcott. Cast: Fernando Lamas, Aldo Ray, Tommy Sands, David Carradine, Lisa Gaye, Melinda Marx.

For his second film as a director (the first **Magic Fountain**, 1963, with wife Esther Williams), Argentine matinee idol Fernando Lamas chose this over-baked rape melodrama. In the small Mexican town of Santa Rita, an 18-year-old girl is raped and brutally beaten – her last words before slipping into a coma and dying explain to her distraught father that her attacker was a "gringo". So Deputy Sheriff Manuel Vega (Lamas) rounds up the only white folk in the entire area: Polish troublemaker Joe Vorzyck (horror sleaze staple Aldo Ray), wise-ass drifter Lucas Barnes (pre 'Kung Fu' TV David Carradine) and dishonourably discharged soldier Mike Marain (teen idol Tommy Sands, just divorced from Nancy Sinatra). As a lynch mob forms and Vega worries about the safety of his prisoners, it soon becomes vital to get the chained trio of suspects to Silver City where they will stand a fair trial. But when their transport is cut off by the mob, the four men are left on foot in the arid desert. Will Vega get the guilty man to confess in the heat of the night? Melinda Marx, daughter of famed comedian Groucho, made her film debut as Juanita in this bland Tex Mex mix.

BRAND OF SHAME

USA, 1968
Director: B. Ron Elliott [Byron Mabe]. Producer: B. Ron Elliott [Byron Mabe], David F. Friedman [uncredited]. Screenplay: Gene Radford, David F. Friedman. Music: Billy Allen [William Allen Castleman]. Cinematography: I.C. Freely. Cast: Donna Duzzit [Samantha Scott], Steve Stunning [Steve Vincent], Bart Black [Steve Allen], Vanessa Van Dyke [Marsha Jordan], Paula Pleasure [Cara Peters], Ora Fiss [Lynn Hall].

In 1968 rival producers Bob Cresse and David F. Friedman locked horns over play dates at Vince Miranda's highly profitable Pussycat Theatre chain. Miranda had two slots open, July and August, and both exploitation behemoths were vying for the more lucrative earlier opening. Cresse won the argument and sunk more money than usual into producing and promoting R. Lee Frost's **Hot Spur**, convinced it would inaugurate the 'roughie' Western genre. Super showman Friedman took note, rushed a similar Western into production, and cut an absolutely fabulous trailer making sure it was played before every screening of **Hot Spur**. Within a month of non-stop ballyhoo anticipation **Brand of Shame** ended up out-performing **Hot Spur** because Friedman cannily coasted off Cresse's sexy confection without spending a cent. Despite a terrific poster, the fact **Brand of Shame** was a pretty poor Peckinpah show was neither here nor there, unfolding the saga of schoolteacher Samantha Scott (future **Beyond the Valley of the Dolls**, 1970, star) in possession of a map to a gold mine that lesbian dance-hall owner Marsha Jordan plans to steal. The German version had a new score by Walter Baumgartner and was called **Django Nudo und die lüsternen Mädchen von Porno Hill**.

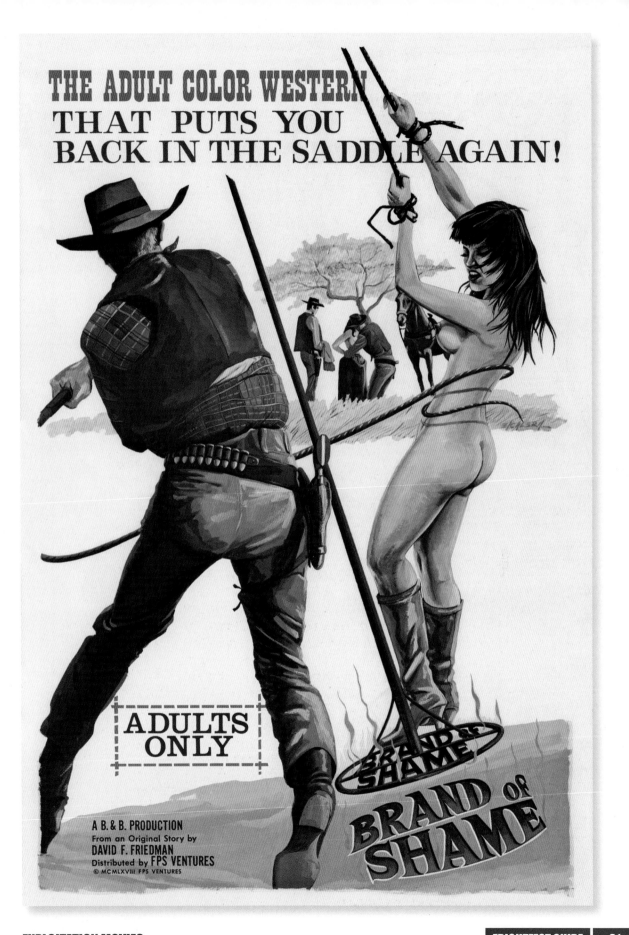

BRIDES OF BLOOD

USA/Philippines, 1968
Director: Gerardo de Leon, Eddie Romero. Producer: Eddie Romero.
Screenplay: Cesar Amigo.
Cast: John Ashley, Kent Taylor, Mario Montenegro, Beverly Hills [Beverly Powers],
Eva Darren, Oscar Keesee.

In 1959 two key figures of the future Filipino fantasy genre combined to create **Terror Is a Man** (1959) starring Francis Lederer, fresh from **The Return of Dracula** (1958), as mad Doctor Girard attempting manimal experiments in **Island of Lost Souls** (1932) tradition. They were director Gerardo de Leon and producer Eddie Romero, who literally had the Asian horror market to themselves with such titles as **Curse of the Vampires** (1970) and **Beast of the Yellow Night** (1971). They also turned the basic concept of **Terror Is a Man** into the 'Blood Island' trilogy starring American teen idol and **Beach Party** regular John Ashley. The first of these was **Brides of Blood**, in which a scientist, his wanton wife and a Peace Corps volunteer arrive at a Pacific island to research the flora and fauna and help the natives. They soon discover radiation is causing strange mutations and the natives have taken to sacrificing their maidens to a hideous monster. At drive-in screenings, female patrons were given free plastic wedding rings to wear. **Mad Doctor of Blood Island** (1969) and **Beast of Blood** (1971) complete the trilogy even though their storylines have little to do with each other.

KITTEN IN THE CAGE

USA, 1968
Director: Richard MacLeod. Producer: Richard MacLeod.
Cast: Miriam Eliot, John Durnham, Tony Warren, June Morgan [June Roberts], Guido Conte, Richard Woods.

Not everyone can be a director. But so many have tried. Especially when they think the craft doesn't matter as the punters only want to see tits and ass anyway. That's why so many sexploiters from the Golden Age look dragged through a hedge backwards, have non-existent editing, dreadful dubbing, or narration to jettison that expense altogether. You can hear their question echo down through the ages, "Well, how hard can it be to point a camera anyway?" Some got away with it, just, like Michael and Roberta Findlay, Doris Wishman and Harrison Marks. Others rose to the top because they showed a modicum of understanding the medium, like Joe Sarno and S.F. Brownrigg. Masters of their art like Russ Meyer were the jewels in a tarnished crown. Then there are people like Richard MacLeod, who tried to assemble oddments here and short ends there into a movie with some cohesive narrative with dire results. There can be no other explanation for this patience–testing affair, detailing an asylum runaway chased by mobsters, the authorities and lesbian go-go girls because she knows where a stash of valuable gems is hidden, being a hopeless confusion of nudity, naughtiness and noir.

the OFFICE PARTY

The funniest, **Wickedest Orgy Ever Filmed!**

Wild SEXetaries

Swinging Stenos

Lustful Executives

THE OFFICE PARTY

USA, 1968
Director: Ron Scott. Producer: Whit Boyd, Ludwig Moner.
Screenplay: William E. Hamelman. Cinematography: Ludwig Moner.
Cast: Byron Lord, Judy Farr, Larry Tanner, Michelle Michelle, Dianne Davis, Jimmie Raye.

Producer Whit Boyd and his repertory company go at it again in this routine sexploiter directed by Ron Scott (**Party Girls**, 1969) starring every actor who has ever appeared in his budget output including Byron Lord, Judy Farr, Michelle Michelle, Larry Tanner, Dianne Davis, Jimmie Raye, etc. This time they play the staff of the Harris Company, whose only business seems to be pleasure. Rather than actually work there's a frenzy of sexual activity at every level from the top echelons of management through the stenographers' pool to the switchboard operators, the supply room and the janitor's basement. Doesn't matter if you're the boss or the lowly office boy, it's how to succeed in business without really working but screwing. As in every Boyd bonkbuster, it ends in a free-for-all orgy that looks great in the trailer and on the ever-evocative poster, but in reality fails to deliver on every promise. Along with this one, Boyd's Texas-based company Crescent International Pictures also distributed **Scarlet Negligee** and **Sand of Ecstasy** in 1968, the same year President Richard Nixon appeared on 'Rowan and Martin's Laugh-In', 'Hawaii Five-O' began airing on CBS and The Beatles topped the charts with 'Hey Jude'. No wonder no one was interested.

SUBURBAN PAGANS

USA, 1968
Director: Shannon Carse [William Rotsler]. Producer: Shannon Carse [William Rotsler]. Screenplay: Shannon Carse [William Rotsler]. Cinematography: Sam Rayven.
Cast: James Brand, Cara Peters, Kathy Williams, Christine Thomas, Karen Richards, Carole Sanders [Marsha Jordan].

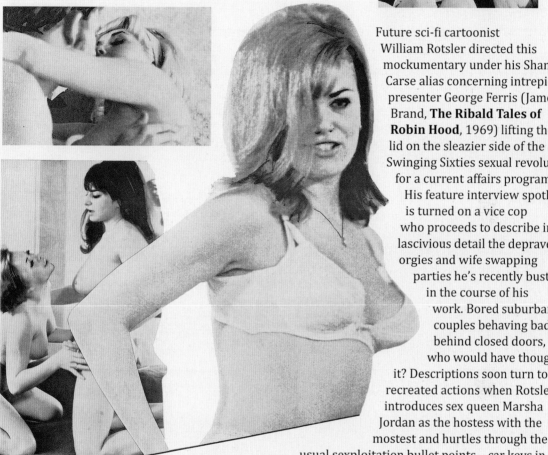

Future sci-fi cartoonist William Rotsler directed this mockumentary under his Shannon Carse alias concerning intrepid TV presenter George Ferris (James Brand, **The Ribald Tales of Robin Hood**, 1969) lifting the lid on the sleazier side of the Swinging Sixties sexual revolution for a current affairs programme. His feature interview spotlight is turned on a vice cop who proceeds to describe in lascivious detail the depraved orgies and wife swapping parties he's recently busted in the course of his work. Bored suburban couples behaving badly behind closed doors, who would have thought it? Descriptions soon turn to recreated actions when Rotsler introduces sex queen Marsha Jordan as the hostess with the mostest and hurtles through the usual sexploitation bullet points – car keys in a pile, embarrassed topless dancing, strip poker, overweight husbands moving in for some dry humping on the lounge carpet, antiseptic shower scenes, lesbian fumblings and hot tub threesomes. Cara Peters from Russ Meyer's **Good Morning and Goodbye!** (1967) puts her ample bosom to use once more in a solo go-go dance. It's yet more lurid voyeurism from the Rotsler canon, also including **Street of a Thousand Pleasures** (1972), **She Did What He Wanted** (1971) and **Midnight Hard** (1971).

A BOXOFFICE INTERNATIONAL PICTURE

SUBURBAN ROULETTE

SUBURBAN ROULETTE

USA, 1968
Director: Herschell Gordon Lewis. Producer: Herschell Gordon Lewis.
Screenplay: James Thomas, Sheldon Seymour [Herschell Gordon Lewis].
Music: Sheldon Seymour [Herschell Gordon Lewis]. Cinematography: Roy Collodi.
Cast: Elizabeth Wilkinson, Ben Moore, Ione Rolnick, Thomas Wood [William Kerwin],
Vicki Miles [Allison Louise Downe], Tony McCabe.

Veteran grindhouser Herschell Gordon Lewis had been there and done that by 1966 after changing the drive-in horror landscape with his gore trilogy of **Blood Feast** (1963), **Two Thousand Maniacs!** (1964) and **Color Me Blood Red** (1965). Looking for other suitable avenues of exploitation he divined the Swinging Sixties were changing attitudes so quickly and radically that social issues had to be the Next Big Thing. The Pill, Abortion, Free Love, Women's Liberation and Wife Swapping became the subjects of four softcore movies Lewis made during 1966-68. The first to be executive produced by David Chudnow (**Kwaheri: Vanishing Africa**, 1964) was this tale of the Fisher family moving into what appears to be a suburban neighbourhood of model respectability. Before long though the staid family are boozing it up and promiscuously bedding complete strangers on a wife-swapping party circuit where flesh takes the place of money at the roulette wheel. Containing no real nudity of note, little sexual pay-off aside from some bisexual innuendo and groping, plus endless jealous arguing, this sex in suburbia opus is strictly dullsville once past the split-level credits and lounge theme song by The Faded Blue – "Let's swap partners, Here's the game, **Suburban Roulette**"!

Get An Eyeful Of What Goes On Behind The Keyholes Of Suburbia!

starring:
ELIZABETH WILKINSON
BEN MOORE
IONE ROLNICK
VICKIE MILES
TONY McCABE
THOMAS WOOD

produced by DAVID CHUDNOW
directed by HERSCHELL GORDON LEWIS
released by ARGENT FILM PRODUCTIONS, INC.

Who's Your Partner
For The Evening?

WATCH THE BIRDIE...DIE!

USA, 1968
Director: Don Doyle. Producer: Jacques Descent. Screenplay:
Peter John. Music: John Bath. Cinematography: Jacques Descent.
Cast: Angela Carnon, Dennis Maloney, Donna Bradley [Julie
Conners], Honor Lawrence, Ron South, Lynn Lyons.

Here's what the real 'Mad Men' of Madison Avenue got up to after the
Summer of Love deconstructed politics, music, creativity and sexual
inhibitions. Playgirl Cheryl Darwin (Angela Carnon, **Guess What
Happened to Count Dracula?**, 1970), the mistress of Bill Sheridan
(Ron South), seduces Tom Bender (Dennis Maloney), head of a high-flying
advertising agency. Her goal is to become the 'Body Lotion Girl' of the
agency's latest mega-account. Although their marriage is a loveless
one of convenience, Bill's conniving lesbian wife Paula (Honor
Lawrence) is on a power trip. So she gets the commission
to take the photographs for the advertising campaign
in order to destroy her husband's relationship
with the ambitious social climber. First on the
agenda is to seduce Cheryl into some hot girl-
on-girl action during the steamy shooting
session. By the time Bill learns of his wife's
duplicitous intentions, Cheryl has already
succumbed to Paula's advances. In a final
act of desperation Bill guns down both
women in the studio and commits suicide.
Director Don Doyle's only other movie was
an obscure adaptation of the Ed Wood Jr.
Vietnamese whorehouse novel 'Mama's
Diary' titled **Operation
Redlight** (1969) and
starring the **Plan 9
from Outer Space**
(1959) man
himself.

ADULTS ONLY!

EXPERIENCE FEEL-A-VISION !

THE STAR OF THIS PICTURE IS "YOU"

YOU

USA, 1968
Director: Paul Hunt.
Producer: Paul Hunt, Bob Cresse.
Screenplay: R.G. Vicry [Ronald Víctor García].
Cinematography: H.P. Edwards [Paul Hunt].
Cast: Natasha Shore, Leisha Kai, Linda Reese, Joseph P. Phillips, Carolyn Ornsby, Shelley Williams.

From the pressbook: "For the first time in the history of exploitation films we, the producers, guarantee Your audience will experience every pleasurable sensation as the star. Through new camera techniques never before attempted we are able to put Your audience on the edge of their seats, gasping for breath... for as a chef samples his culinary arts, Your audience will savour each moment of erotic pleasure through FEEL-A-VISION. Your audience will boast that in one night they were able to whip a Young girl to her masochistic climax... feel the warmth of a Young female hitchhiker's gratitude for giving her a ride... answer a voyeur's plea to endure his Young wife's sensuous desires... be sucked into a back alley profession they only dreamed existed... be pulled into a religion that requires a witness to an act of awareness by two Young female believers and finally to participate with them in the most bizarre rite of depravity... take pictures of a would be starlet in a celebrated model studio and for a few dollars more get exactly what they want... get anything they wanted from a Young Mexican girl in trouble with the police in return for helping her escape..."

Why should Bogart Peter Stuyvesant go to war and kill strangers, when the pickings are better in his own bedroom?

JAMES H. NICHOLSON & SAMUEL Z. ARKOFF present The FOUR LEAF production

ANGEL, ANGEL, DOWN WE GO

STARRING
JENNIFER JONES
JORDAN CHRISTOPHER · CO-STARRING **HOLLY NEAR** · **LOU RAWLS** · CHARLES AIDMAN DAVEY DAVISON AND **RODDY McDOWALL** AS 'SANTORO'
COLOR BY MOVIELAB
WRITTEN BY ROBERT THOM · PRODUCED BY JEROME F. KATZMAN · EXECUTIVE PRODUCER SAM KATZMAN · DIRECTED BY ROBERT THOM · SONGS WRITTEN BY BARRY MANN AND CYNTHIA WEIL · An AMERICAN INTERNATIONAL Picture
©1969 American International Pictures, Inc.

ANGEL, ANGEL, DOWN WE GO

USA, 1969
Director: Robert Thom. Producer: Jerome F. Katzman. Screenplay: Robert Thom. Music: Fred Karger, Barry Mann, Cynthia Weil. Cinematography: John F. Warren.
Cast: Jennifer Jones, Jordan Christopher, Roddy McDowall, Holly Near, Lou Rawls, Charles Aidman.

In the 1960s, ageing Hollywood divas like Bette Davis, Joan Crawford and Olivia De Havilland headed to horror to revive their careers in **What Ever Happened to Baby Jane?** (1962) and **Lady in a Cage** (1964). But many fading stars, while appalled at that trend, thought nothing of riding the second nostalgia wave into drug-fuelled mod fantasies. Lana Turner took **The Big Cube** (1969), Carol Channing went **Skidoo** (1968), Ava Gardner was **Tam Lin** (1971) and Jennifer Jones starred in this sick slice of Hollywood decadence, meeting her maker after skydiving with a faulty parachute. Jordan Christopher plays the Jim Morrison-type pop star Bogart, demi-god lead singer with The Wild Ones (the band features Roddy McDowall and Lou Rawls!), who **Teorama**-style beds an heiress, seduces her mother and turns the father gay, accompanied by an array of terrible Barry Mann and Cynthia Weil songs. 'Hey Hey Hey And A Hi Ho' and 'The Fat Song' prime examples. A high camp concoction written and directed by genre guru Robert Thom, fresh from the acid fascism of **Wild in the Streets** (1968), after it flopped it was re-titled **Cult of the Damned** to cash in on the Charles Manson gang's murder of Sharon Tate.

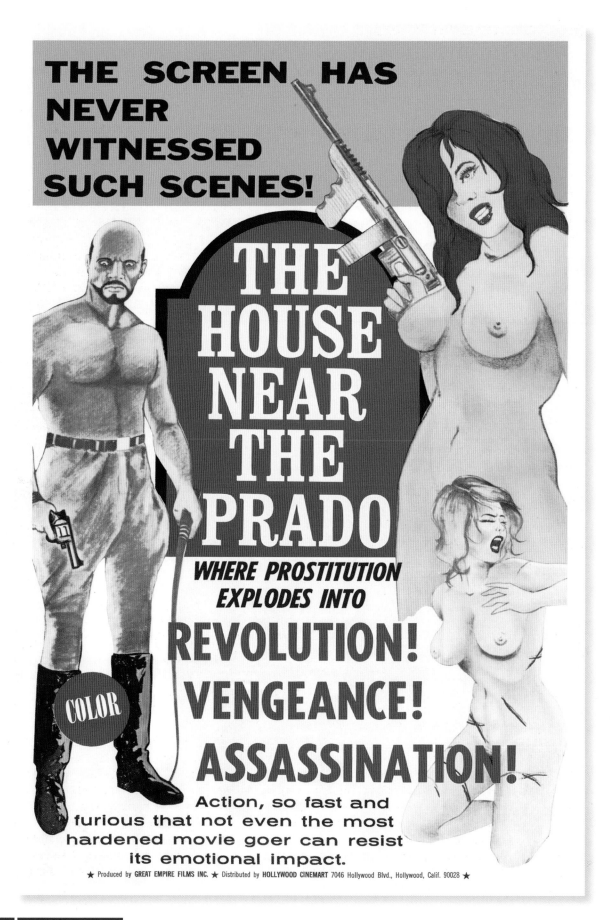

THE HOUSE NEAR THE PRADO

USA, 1969
Director: Jean Van Hearn. Producer: Jean Van Hearn. Screenplay: Jean Van Hearn. Music: Jaime Mendoza-Nava.
Cast: Julia Blackburn, Marlin Marin, Marsha Jordan, Guy Anthony, Charles Napier.

The Prado is the main Spanish national art museum, located in central Madrid. Were 42nd Street habitués supposed to know that reference back in the late Sixties? Doubtful. But writer/producer/director Jean Van Hearn obviously thought he should add a bit of cultural shading to this 'roughie' Spanish Civil War tale of armed hookers, sadistic military leaders and bloody revolution. Inept and sleazy as Hearn's other works – **Nymphs (Anonymous)** (1968) and **Love Me Like I Do** (1970) – at least it starred two of the best names in the exploitation business, Marsha Jordan, then the current Queen of Softcore sinema, and Charles Napier, the future King of B Movie Character Actors. It was Hearn's Napier double-bill, **The House Near the Prado** and **The Hanging of Jake Ellis** (1969), that caught the eye of director Russ Meyer who quickly cast the granite-like square-jawed, menacing hard-ass for the ground-breaking full-frontal 'pickle shot' in **Cherry, Harry & Raquel!** (1969). Napier would subsequently appear in **Beyond the Valley of the Dolls** (1970), **The Seven Minutes** (1971) and **Supervixens** (1975) for the big-breast-fixated Meyer. Where **The House Near the Prado** title proved an off-putting liability, the alternate **Diary of a Madam** one was quickly substituted.

HOUSE OF THE RED DRAGON

USA, 1969
Director: John Donne. Producer: Charles H. Leonard.
Cinematography: Louis Jennings.
Cast: Suzie Wong, Geraldine Kaye, Mason Bakman [John Vincent], Diane Hansen, Tai Hamilton.

Alice in Acidland (1969) director John Donne must have been on LSD when he concocted this strangely belated mix of **The World of Suzie Wong** (1960) and **The Terror of the Tongs** (1961). 1890: stowaway Suzie Wong arrives in San Francisco to find herself in the middle of the Tong wars and witness to a runaway slave girl murder. Finding work peddling opium at the Mandarin Club, owned by a distant uncle who heads the Red Dragon Tong, she has to continually avoid his sexual overtures. With the Tong wars escalating over internecine grievances, the police contact Chang, leader of the rival Black Scorpions, for help in averting mass slaughter and assign a special agent to destroy the Red Dragons. When her uncle discovers Suzie was a witness to the dockside murder, he sends her to his Den of Pleasure to train as a Singsong Girl. There her teacher falls in love with her as he schools her in the art of lovemaking and they formulate plans to get her immigration papers and open a respectable House of Pleasure. Bogus as this history lesson was, a clip appeared in **American Sexual Revolution** (1971) to illustrate Yellow Peril vice rackets.

WILD BEYOND BELIEF!

SATAN'S SADISTS

USA, 1969
Director: Al Adamson. Producer: Al Adamson.
Screenplay: Dennis Wayne [Greydon Clark]. Music: Harley Hatcher.
Cinematography: Gary Graver, Vilmos Zsigmond [uncredited].
Cast: Russ Tamblyn, Scott Brady, Kent Taylor, John 'Bud' Cardos,
Robert Dix, Gary Kent.

Shot at the Spahn Ranch, the Manson Family residence – hence the gratuitous allying to that shocking tragedy. The Satans, an outlaw biker gang led by badass Anchor (**West Side Story**, 1961, dancer Russ Tamblyn on the comeback trail), go on a killing spree and head for the Mojave Desert to silence witnesses to their crime. Considered one of trashmeister Al Adamson's best movies, it was written by future genre director Greydon Clark, who also played the role of Acid. Clark met Adamson in 1967 after an actress in his Hollywood acting class introduced them both. Adamson gave Clark a bit part in **The Fakers**, released after **Satan's Sadists** had become a worldwide hit, as **Hell's Bloody Devils** in 1970. Cementing their relationship further, Adamson offered Clark the chance to adapt a short western story he owned into an ABC TV movie. The final script was well received and former MGM star Robert Taylor agreed to appear but just prior to shooting in Spain in 1968 he died of cancer and the project was put in turnaround. However, word travelled about the script and a financier approached them to produce something for $50,000 – **Satan's Sadists** being the result.

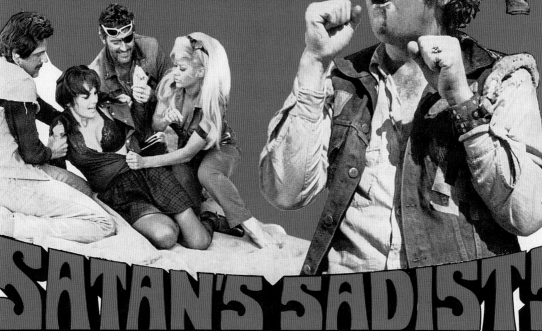

THE SCAVENGERS

USA, 1969
Director: R.L. Frost [Lee Frost]. Producer: R.W. Cresse [Bob Cresse], Wes Bishop [uncredited].
Screenplay: R.W. Cresse [Bob Cresse]. Music: Lee Frost, Paul Hunt. Cinematography: Robert Maxwell.
Cast: Jonathon Bliss [John Bliss], Maria Lease, Michael Dikova, Roda Spain, James E. McLarty,
Jody Berry.

Of the many grindhouse directors who shot to fame during the 1960s, R. Lee Frost (born David Kayne) is one of the versatile best. His "fine calibre" talents (as the poster of **Love Camp 7**, his 1969 disasterpiece, screamed!) graced **The Defilers** (1965), **Hot Spur** (1968) and many other infamous titles. Known for his dextrous camera, he was the person all distributors wanted to spice up their European imports with racy sex inserts: **London in the Raw** (1964) and **Witchcraft '70** just two foreign films benefitting. Interestingly, Frost was hired to direct **Race with the Devil** (1975) starring Peter Fonda, but jittery Fox producers freaked out at his faster-than-lightning shooting methods and fired him. It's impossible to talk about Frost's career without mentioning ex-carny writer/producer Bob Cresse. Together they formed a formidable team and made some of the sleaziest shockers ever – **Love Is a Four Letter Word** (1966), **Mondo Bizarro** (1966) – and this adult post Civil War western packed with rape, murder and slow-motion violence. Although Frost's riposte to Sam Peckinpah's **The Wild Bunch**, the movie failed dismally, despite a lavish souvenir brochure on sale in the foyer, and it was quickly repackaged as **The Grabbers**, only to flop again.

EASTMAN COLOR
FOR
ADULTS

STARRING
JONATHAN BLISS · MARIA LEASE · MICHAEL DIKOVA · RODA SPAIN · R. W. CRESSE · R. L. FROST · R. W. CRESSE
PRODUCED BY   DIRECTED BY   ORIGINAL STORY BY

THE SIDEHACKERS

USA, 1969
Director: Gus Trikonis. Producer: Ross Hagen. Screenplay: Tony Houston.
Music: Mike Curb, Jerry Styner. Cinematography: Jon Hall.
Cast: Ross Hagen, Diane McBain, Michael Pataki, Claire Polan, Richard Merrifield, Goldie Hawn.

From one of the all-time great exploitation companies, Crown International, comes one of their stupidest. Everyone remembers sidehacking, the newest thrill in racing circa 1969, right? Apparently it originated in Germany when some extreme motorcyclists decided the sport would be more exciting if they added a passenger platform for a dangerous-looking balancing element. Anyway, when ace sidehacker Rommel ('Daktari' star Ross Hagen) gives Paisley (Claire Polan, Mrs. Hagen) the cold shoulder, she tells exhibition rider boyfriend J.C. (exploitation stalwart Michael Pataki) he raped her. So J.C.'s gang beat Rommel up and kill his fiancée Rita (Diane McBain). When Rommel recovers he

naturally goes on a revenge rampage that ends very badly indeed. Originally titled **Five the Hard Way**, veteran matinee idol Jon Hall (**Arabian Nights**, 1942, and **Cobra Woman**, 1944, both co-starring Maria Montez) executive produced, and according to the press book invented the 'Fantascope' system, which put the audience in the middle of the action so they'd feel the dust and danger. It was just another widescreen format to anyone with any technical sense though. Director Gus Trikonis was a Shark in **West Side Story** (1961) and married one of the film's extras, a certain Goldie Hawn.

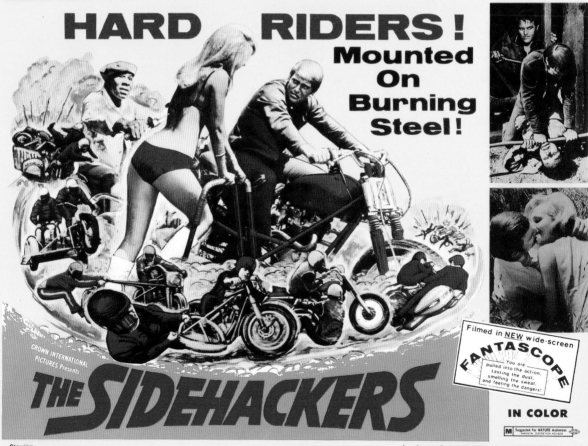

THEIR FORM is HUMAN BUT THEY HAVE CROSSED OVER... Is this sex after death?

the WITCHMAKER

THE ANSATE CROSS ......
SYMBOL OF LIFE, LOVE AND DEATH

WAS DEATH ONLY THE BEGINNING?

HOW DID THEY SATISFY THEIR WEIRD DESIRES?

M Suggested for MATURE AUDIENCES (parental discretion advised)

THE WITCHMAKER In terrifying Technicolor – Techniscope
STARRING ANTHONY EISLEY · THORDIS BRANDT · ALVY MOORE
AND JOHN LODGE as LUTHER the BERSERK
Executive Producer L.Q.JONES Written, Produced & Directed by WILLIAM O. BROWN ·
A Las Cruces–Arrow Production From Excelsior Distributing Company

THE WITCHMAKER

USA, 1969
Director: William O. Brown. Producer: William O. Brown. Screenplay: William O. Brown. Music: Jaime Mendoza-Nava. Cinematography: John Arthur Morrill. Cast: Anthony Eisley, Thordis Brandt, Alvy Moore, John Lodge, Shelby Grant, Larry Vincent.

While not in the same league as their **Brotherhood of Satan** (1971) or **A Boy and His Dog** (1975), the Alvy Moore/L.Q. Jones production team made this credible horror effort, also known as **The Legend of Witch Hollow**. 'Green Acres' sit-com regular Moore plays psychic researcher Dr. Ralph Hayes on a Louisiana swampland investigation into the murders of eight women. Buxom Thordis Brandt plays Anastasia, the 'sensitive' ancestor of a witch worshipped by local Satanist Luther the Berserk (John Lodge) and his blood-drinking coven. Could Anastasia be their thirteenth acolyte? Complete with daft dance routine during the black magic ritual party, low-budget horror hunk Anthony Eisley as the hero, three former 'Playboy' playmates and 'Fright Night' TV horror host Seymour, under the name Larry Vincent, in the role of Amos Coffin, this was a slow but solid supernatural shocker. Later, when paired with Ted V. Mikels's **The Corpse Grinders** (1971), the double bill entered the grindhouse circuit with a 'Certificate of Assurance' gimmick. Being of sound mind and body you had to sign the document – all numbered 23601 – before entering the theatre to indemnify the owners should you suffer a coronary, insanity or death watching the 'terrifying' attraction.

AFRICA EROTICA

USA, © 1969, first public screening 1970
Director: Zygmunt Sulistrowski. Producer: Zygmunt Sulistrowski.
Screenplay: Jordan Arthur Deutsch. Music: Moacir Santos, Enrico
Simonetti, Zygmunt Sulistrowski. Cinematography: Sebastiano Celeste,
Herbert V. Theis.
Cast: Darr Poran [Zygmunt Sulistrowski], Carrie Rochelle, Alice Marie.

Polish filmmaker Zygmunt Sulistrowski was a trailblazer of the
softcore faux documentary adventure. His pioneering format was
simple: take a sexy model to an exotic location, cobble together a
story and, *voila*, lush erotica designed for fast grindhouse play-off.
Naked Amazon (1955) and **The Virgin of the Beaches** (1976)
were two of his more famous titles. Just Jaeckin's **Emmanuelle**
(1974) would become the Gold
Standard for this particular genre of

genitalia globetrotting, but five years earlier Sulistrowski took an Amphicar
up the Nile with his most bonkers version ever. Photographer Darr Poran
(the director himself) bumps into complete stranger Carrie Rochelle on the
street and asks if she'll fly to Africa with him for a photo shoot. Naturally
she instantly agrees and after stock footage of wildebeests, baboons and
elephants, they wind up in Tanzania and Uganda where Carrie gets her
kit off, fights a snake determined to squeeze her to death and reminisces
about the time she was brutally raped as a teenager. Those flashbacks to
extra footage shot with French porn actors Brigitte Lahaie, Maude Carolle,
Guy Royer and Richard Lemieuvre in 1976 resulted in a 'new film', released
in 1977 as **Frissons Africains** in France and **Africa Excitation** in Italy.

BIGFOOT

USA, © 1969, first public screening 1970
Director: Robert F. Slatzer. Producer: Anthony Cardoza. Screenplay: Robert F. Slatzer, James Gordon White.
Music: Richard A. Podolor. Cinematography: Wilson S. Hong.
Cast: John Carradine, Joi Lansing, Chris Mitchum, Lindsay Crosby, Doodles Weaver, Haji.

Purportedly shot in undisclosed mountain wilderness locations where
the actual yeti creature of American Pacific Northwest rural legend was
alleged to have been sighted, this ridiculous adventure about the sub-
human Missing Link kidnapping women for breeding purposes might be
the worst Bigfoot movie ever. Yes, even in the crowded field of **Bog** (1979),
The Legend of Boggy Creek (1972), **Shriek of the Mutilated** (1974), **The
Curse of Bigfoot** (1975), **Sasquatch: The Legend of Bigfoot** (1976) and
Snowbeast (1977) to name just a scant few. Horror icon John Carradine
wants to capture the beast for vulgar sideshow exhibition while a student
biker gang (led by Chris Mitchum, star Robert's son and Lindsay Crosby,
crooner Bing's likewise) riding imported motorcycles (Harleys being
too expensive for this poverty row production) rush to the rescue of the
Sasquatch-menaced model Joi Lansing. Laugh-out-loud scenes include the
'King of the Woods' – i.e. skinny stuntman in a ratty gorilla suit – battling a
real bear, light relief Doodles Weaver's schtick consistently tanking, the inept dynamite lighting climax,
Carradine's hilarious variation on the **King Kong** (1933) line "It was beauty that killed the beast" and
Russ Meyer buxom favourite Haji in a bikini being used as Bigfoot bait.

COOL IT, BABY!

Brutally Clashing Head on in a Fury of Blood and Burning Rubber!

GOD FORGIVES...
THE BLACK ANGELS *DON'T!*

a portrait of the family.

A MERRICK INTERNATIONAL FILM STARRING

DES ROBERTS   **JOHN KING III**

LINDA JACKSON

CO-STARRING CLANCY SYRKO · BEVERLY GARDNER · JAMES WHITWORTH

BLACK ANGELS

COLOR BY MOVIE LAB

PRODUCED AND DIRECTED BY LAURENCE MERRICK

RESTRICTED
Under 17 requires accompanying
Parent or Adult Guardian

BLACK ANGELS

USA, 1970

Director: Laurence Merrick. Producer: Leo Rivers [Louie Lawless]. Screenplay: Laurence Merrick.
Music: Morgan Cavett. Cinematography: Laurence Merrick, Jack Beckett [uncredited].
Cast: Des Roberts, John King III, Linda Jackson, James Young-El, Clancy Syrko, Beverly Gardner.

Laurence Merrick ran an acting studio in Los Angeles and very enterprisingly used his students (some being ex-GIs on career-generating government grants) in experience-building projects that could also make some cash on the side. So he directed the first – and last – Blaxploitation biker picture about a war between black and white motorcycle gangs. The Choppers, a real all-black Hells Angels troupe, and Satan's Serpents, an all-white faction led by Chainer (Des Roberts) who while tough on the outside is all for racial diversity. "Any beef we have with the Choppers is about territory, not colour", he says before the Serpents get infiltrated by a member of the Choppers passing for white. The Black Angels of the title actually refer to a couple of ineffectual white cops who Merrick cuts to every so often to break up the monotony of barbiturate-induced sex and uppers-fuelled violence. Merrick, who was eventually shot by a stalker in 1977, insisted his actors never change their clothes during the 14-day shoot at the Paramount Ranch. This, together with employing the authentic Choppers, was supposed to imbue the proceedings with a down-and-dirty realism that would give the rapes, stabbings, highway chasing and ravine jumping a dramatic lift. It didn't.

BLOOD MANIA

USA, 1970
Director: Robert Vincent O'Neil. Producer: Chris Marconi, Peter Carpenter. Screenplay: Toby Sacher, Tony Crechales. Music: Don Vincent. Cinematography: Bob Maxwell, Gary Graver.
Cast: Peter Carpenter, Maria de Aragon, Vicki Peters, Reagan Wilson, Jacqueline Dalya, Eric Allison.

If it's a Crown in comes with a frown! Or that's what most punters thought whenever they saw that company's coronet logo. The same corporation who foisted **The Hellcats** (1968) and **Nightmare in Wax** (1969) amongst numerous others on an unsuspecting grindhouse audience also did the same with this talky murder thriller from **The Psycho Lover** (1970) director Robert Vincent O'Neil. Basically Maria de Aragon (from **The Cremators**, 1972), decides to bump off her rich, sick father Eric Allison (who went on to star in John Landis's **Schlock**, 1973) so she can help her doctor boyfriend Peter

Carpenter (also the co-writer) pay off a blackmailer who knows about his back street abortionist past. Job done, but the inheritance goes to her sister Vicki Peters instead. So the duplicitous duo must formulate yet another murder plan. Shoddily filmed throughout, with only a few Mario Bava-esque lighting changes and a splatter death by candelabra punctuating the tedium, the 'shocking climax' alluded to on the grabby poster of the day is merely a perfunctory jump cut. A marginally better come-on than the original "Intense Terror Warning! We Cannot Be Responsible If You Never Sleep Again!" No mention of sleeping during the performance though!

THE CAPTIVES

USA, 1970
Director: Carl Borcht [Lee Frost]. Producer: B.T. København
[Armand Atamian]. Cinematography: E.R. Frederiksen.
Cast: Brigit Krøyer, Karl Hansen [Ray Sebastian], Orla Nsu,
Emil Kjaerum, Leif Betheas, Annelise Detts [Annette Michael].

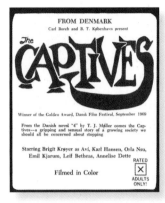

The second of three sniff-of-a-shoestring budgeted, non-sync-sound softcore quickies (**Ride Hard, Ride Wild**, 1970, and **Slaves in Cages**, 1971, the consecutive others) that super-sleaze director Lee Frost (under his pseudonym Carl Borcht) and producer Armand Atamian made using short-end film scraps and passed off as Danish productions through their Phoenix International Films, although shot in California. To further complete the grifting illusion fake Danish names disguised the American cast and certain posters advertised the facts it was "Based on the Danish novel '4' by T.J. Moller" and had won a "Gold Award" at the Dansk Film Festival in September 1969. The cautionary tale has a wealthy industrialist and his wife travelling through Denmark stopping to give a young girl a lift and then getting abducted by her gang to become their sexual playthings for the night. The pressbook stated, "Carl Borcht moves his cast expertly through a story that on occasion seems almost stylized and unreal, which only heightens by contrast the scenes concerning human sex. The film has a message far greater than 'don't stop for hitchhikers'. Denmark is the first country in the world to legalize pornography. Perhaps through that the generation depicted here could be possible".

THE CHRISTINE JORGENSEN STORY

USA, 1970
Director: Irving Rapper. Producer: Edward Small. Screenplay: Robert E. Kent, Ellis St. Joseph.
Music: Paul Sawtell, Bert Shefter. Cinematography: Jacques R. Marquette.
Cast: John Hansen, Quinn Redeker, John W. Himes, Ellen Clark, Rod McCary, Will Kuluva.

Entertainer and famous transsexual Christine Jorgensen was born George William Jorgensen, Jr., 1926, in the Bronx. In the early 1950s, she made headlines for having a sex change in Denmark from man to woman. At an early age, Jorgensen became aware of feeling like a woman trapped inside a man's body and made the gender reassignment decision after being drafted into the army and endlessly ridiculed for not appearing masculine enough. In 1953 the faux Danish Girl told her life story to 'American Weekly' magazine but it wasn't until 1969 she agreed to let it become a United Artists biopic. But under the direction of Irving Rapper, famous for his 1940s Bette Davis melodramas, and starring newcomer John Hansen, who as Christine looked like a truck driver in drag, the film was an old-fashioned camp disaster. Every single sanctimonious moment is wrong-headed in Rapper's cringe-inducing claptrap: George bullied for playing with dolls rather than footballs, George cowering bayoneting soldier dummies, George's distaste at being hit on by a homosexual executive, George desperately trying hetero action with a prostitute, Christine falling chastely in love with a journalist. A box-office failure from day one, even the grindhouse crowd hated this po-faced anachronism.

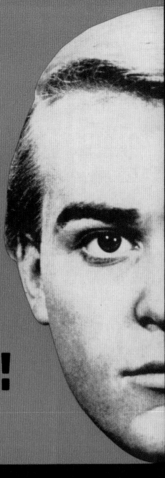

THE FIRST MAN TO BECOME A WOMAN!

EDWARD SMALL
presents

"THE *Christine* JORGENSEN STORY" X

introducing
JOHN HANSEN

Screenplay by
ROBERT E. KENT and ELLIS ST. JOSEPH

Based on the book by
CHRISTINE JORGENSEN

Directed by IRVING RAPPER · Produced by EDWARD SMALL   COLOUR By Deluxe **United Artists**

THE FAMILY

Italy/France, 1970
Director: Sergio Sollima. Producer: Arrigo Colombo,
Giorgio Papi. Screenplay: Sauro Scavolini, Gianfranco
Calligarich, Lina Wertmüller, Sergio Sollima.
Music: Ennio Morricone. Cinematography: Aldo Tonti.
Cast: Charles Bronson, Jill Ireland, Michel Constantin,
Telly Savalas, Umberto Orsini, George Savalas.

Thanks to **Once Upon a Time in the West** (1968)
and **Guns for San Sebastian** (1968) weather-beaten
tough guy Charles Bronson was the No.1 box office
draw in Europe as the 1970s dawned. This crime
adventure was shot in New Orleans but produced
in Italy, where Bronson was known as Il Brutto/
The Brute. Although he didn't know it at the time
Spaghetti Western/Eurospy director Sergio Sollima,
working from a script by future art-house director
Lina Wertmüller, captured Bronson just as he was
phasing out of his macho action man career in the
likes of **The Magnificent
Seven** (1960) and **The
Dirty Dozen** (1967) and
gaining a harder edge and

minimal acting style that soon exploded into global megastardom with Michael
Winner's controversial vigilante drama **Death Wish** (1974). **The Family**, aka
Violent City, provided Bronson with what would prove to be his archetypal
role – an independent criminal with a conscience that elevates him from the
rest of the underworld, a wronged man with few words seeking justifiable
revenge letting his actions speak for him. Here Bronson is a semi-retired hitman set-up by his girlfriend, played by Bronson's real-life wife and frequent
co-star Jill Ireland, to kill pre-'Kojak' crime boss Telly Savalas.

FLESH FEAST

USA, © 1969, first public screening 1970
Director: Brad F. Grinter. Producer: Veronica Lake, Brad F. Grinter. Screenplay: Thomas B. Casey, Brad F. Grinter.
Cinematography: Thomas B. Casey.
Cast: Veronica Lake, Phil Philbin, Doug Foster, Craig McConnel, Harry Kerwin, Chris Martell.

1940s sex siren Veronica Lake ('The Peek-a-Boo Girl'), star of the classic **Sullivan's Travels** (1941)
and **The Blue Dahlia** (1946) dragged herself out of alcohol-induced retirement to co-produce this
pitiful shocker. Other middle-aged stars like Bette Davis, Joan Crawford and Shelley Winters were axing
psychological problems in an assortment of chillers from **What Ever Happened to Baby Jane?** (1962)
to **Whoever Slew Auntie Roo?** (1972), why shouldn't she grab a piece of the lady killer action? So off
she went to Miami Beach to headline this Brad F. Grinter cheapie (he directed **Blood Freak**, 1972) as
Dr. Elaine Frederick, a mad scientist and concentration camp survivor carrying out youth restoration
experiments. Using flesh-eating maggots (Grinter raised real ones in garbage cans to save on budget)
to get rid of the old skin tissue, Elaine is asked by crazed neo-Nazis to work on a very special elderly
patient. That turns out to be Adolf Hitler, whom his Hispanic acolytes want to rebuild the Third Reich.
Something Elaine is not going to let happen as she turns the war criminal over to her cannibal swarm.
This gruesome abomination was Lake's swansong. She died three years later a hopeless drunk.

FROM EAR TO EAR

France, 1970
Director: Louis Soulanes. Producer: C. Léon-Dufour. Screenplay: Louis Soulanes. Music: Claude Capra. Cinematography: Albert Susterre.
Cast: Nicole Debonne, Robert Lombard, Solange Pradel, Liliane Bert, Danielle Argence, Jean Gemin.

One of the more arresting posters to grace 42nd Street, thanks to its full-on imagery and day-glo colouring, masked the sordid French sex thriller **Les cousines/The Cousins** based on Fletcher D. Benson's novel 'The Perverse Women's Night'. Directed by Louis Soulanes (a prolific screenwriter/ cinematographer), this twisted slab of erotic Eurosleaze gained notoriety for undergoing extensive cuts to appease the MPAA, yet still receiving an X rating. What could be that salacious to warrant even the tone being certified? Elisa (Nicole Debonne, Max Pecas's **Her and She and Him**, 1970) lives with her mute, wheelchair-bound sister Josine, blonde cousin Lucile (Solange Pradel, Jean Rollin's **The Rape of the Vampire**, 1968) and mother in a French country villa. When Elisa isn't canoodling with dykey Lucille, or banging her hunky boyfriend on the side, she's torturing and humiliating Josine by hitting her, fondling her breasts and blaring out music from a transistor radio she straps to her wheelchair. With their parents away one weekend Elisa and Lucile throw a party that gets out of hand, resulting in a drunken death. After disposing of the corpse, they worry Josine saw everything, and decide to kill her too. But there's something they don't know...

THE
SHOCK ENDING
OF ALL TIME!

**FROM
EAR
TO
EAR**

a JERRY GROSS
presentation

YOU MIGHT LIVE WITH AN *ALCOHOLIC !*
OR YOU MIGHT LIVE WITH A *DOPE ADDICT !*

BUT NOT

A Habit
Whispered
About...

A Habit
Practiced
by Strange
Women...

HIS WIFE'S HABIT

USA, 1970
Director: Joy N. Houck Jr. Producer: Albert J. Salzer. Screenplay: Joy N. Houck Jr., Albert J. Salzer, Robert A. Weaver. Music: Norma Green, Jim Helms, Gary Le Mel. Cinematography: Robert A. Weaver.
Cast: Georgine Darcy, Marcus J. Grapes, Christina Hart, David Gelpi, Michael Anthony, Gerald McRaney.

What's a son to do when his father owns over 200 movie theatres in Texas and Georgia and is desperate for exploitable down home product? Make it himself of course, which is exactly what Joy N. Houck Jr. did through his father's Howco International banner. Junior's first effort was the daft murder shocker **Night of Bloody Horror** (1969), originally put on a double bill with this one, also shot on location in New Orleans, under the title **Women and Bloody Terror**. When Senior had milked the dual programme for all it was worth, and noting that contemporary publications like 'Castle of Frankenstein' had named **Women and Bloody Terror** one of the worst movies ever made, he split the bill up, and sent it out on the distant grindhouse circuit with a more sexed up moniker. Essentially it was a pitiful riff on the stalking scenario; Lauren Worthington (Georgine Darcy, Miss Torso in **Rear Window**, 1954) is the promiscuous wife sleeping with everyone she meets, including her daughter's boyfriend, who gets terrorized by a brutish motel parking attendant and his psychotic friend. After killing her latest lover, the two maniacs continue harassing Laura until both die in a mundane police shoot-out.

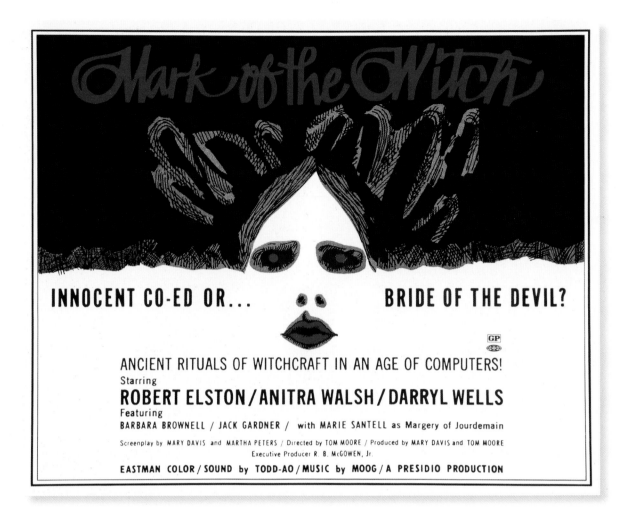

INNOCENT CO-ED OR...   BRIDE OF THE DEVIL?

ANCIENT RITUALS OF WITCHCRAFT IN AN AGE OF COMPUTERS!
Starring
ROBERT ELSTON / ANITRA WALSH / DARRYL WELLS
Featuring
BARBARA BROWNELL / JACK GARDNER / with MARIE SANTELL as Margery of Jourdemain

Screenplay by MARY DAVIS and MARTHA PETERS / Directed by TOM MOORE / Produced by MARY DAVIS and TOM MOORE
Executive Producer R. B. McGOWEN, Jr.

EASTMAN COLOR / SOUND by TODD-AO / MUSIC by MOOG / A PRESIDIO PRODUCTION

MARK OF THE WITCH

USA, 1970
Director: Tom Moore. Producer: Mary Davis, Tom Moore. Screenplay: Mary Davis, Martha Peters.
Music: Whitey Thomas. Cinematography: Robert E. Bethard.
Cast: Robert Elston, Anitra Walsh, Darryl Wells, Jack Gardner, Barbara Brownell, Marie Santell.

Everybody has to start somewhere. So if Tom Moore, the future director of the long-running Broadway hit musical 'Grease', had to gain experience with this bargain basement rip-off of Mario Bava's **Black Sunday** (1960) it would be churlish to complain. **Mark of the Witch** introduces the concept of regional exploitation filmmaking. Many exhibitors got tired of paying the Forty Thieves for their cheap products, essentially money for old rope. So they would often get together, create their own purple prose title, write a very basic script, employ local stagehands and theatre people and cast actors culled from amateur dramatic societies. They would then make the movie and release it using the 'four walling' method – saturation play in one particular area so there was no choice but to see it for the local population. Such was the case with this Dallas, Texas, shot horror reviving the old chiller chestnut of a witch cursing the town she's killed in being reincarnated to take revenge on the descendants responsible for her persecution. With lots of talk, very little action, weak murders, virtually no horror to speak of and an excruciating theme hymn, regional grindhouse garbage doesn't get much worse than this.

MARSHA, THE EROTIC HOUSEWIFE

USA, 1970
Director: Don Davis. Screenplay: Jason Hunter.
Music: Chet Moore, Jim Moore.
Cinematography: Wayne Carter.
Cast: Marsha Jordan, Ann Myers [Ann Perry], Mark
Edwards [Edward Blessington], Christine Murray
[Luanne Roberts], Leslie Morgan, Roger Gentry.

Marsha Jordan ruled late '60s and early '70s
Sinema. The Queen of Softcore was born Carolyn
Marcel Jordan in Alabama and grew up in a
Catholic convent thanks to her strict religious parents. But the Delta Airlines ex-stewardess soon got
discovered while vacationing in Los Angeles, her sexy girl-next-door looks, blonde hair, shapely figure and
down-to-earth demeanour considered the perfect image for Adults Only movies. She played everything
from Lady Godiva in **Lady Godiva Rides Again** (1969) to **The Divorcee** (1969), stopping off to win horror
fan hearts as one of Robert Quarry's
bloodsucker brides in the cult classic
Count Yorga, Vampire (1970).
Given the name-in-the-title honour
by regular director Don Davis, this
is one of Jordan's best, in which she
plays Marsha Bannister who learns
of her new husband's lengthy affair
with another woman. Her first desire
is for revenge through promiscuous
affairs with any man she can lay her
hands on. Then, with the help of her
lifelong friend, she ultimately realizes
this path can only lead to disaster and
what she really wants is to save her
marriage. How she does this is witty,
practical and surprising, complete
with the explicit backdrop her legion
of male fans demanded.

THE PSYCHO LOVER

USA, 1970
Director: Robert Vincent O'Neil. Producer:
Robert Vincent O'Neil, William Rowland.
Screenplay: Robert Vincent O'Neil. Music:
Norma Green, Jim Helms, Gary Le Mel.
Cinematography: Robert Maxwell.
Cast: Lawrence Montaigne, Jo Anne
Meredith, Elizabeth Plumb, Frank Cuva,
John Vincent, Sharon Cook.

KILL! KILL! KILL!
KILL! KILL! KILL!
KILL! KILL! KILL!

The voice...
The voice was there...
Always there...
Driving him to
perform acts...
Brutal acts...
Against women
he wanted to love.

No question, this twisted thriller is **Blood Mania** (1970) and
Wonder Women (1973) director Robert Vincent O'Neil's
finest hour. Marco is a maniac with mommy issues suspected
of carrying out a series of strangulations with nylon stockings.
Mad psychiatrist Kenneth Alden (US TV drama staple Lawrence
Montaigne) knows he's the culprit for sure as the patient has
confessed all on his couch. But rather than turn Marco into the
police, he devises a cunning plan to kill the wife who is refusing
to divorce him. For his sexy mistress saw **The Manchurian
Candidate** (1962) and all her talk about the brainwashing
plot in that John Frankenheimer directed classic fires
his dark imagination. So he hypnotizes Marco into
committing what he thinks will be the perfect crime –
except the wife isn't going to succumb quite as easily as
he thought. Watch out for that faulty TV set! With tense
stalking sequences, impressive lighting and camerawork,
a bombastically appropriate score, plus songs from Gary
Le Mel and Ginger Blake (horror's Bacharach and David),
fine thesping from the headliners (Jo Anne Meredith shines
as the resentful wife) and a shocking multiple murder climax

THE
PSYCHO
LOVER

A shocking story...
A more shocking ending!

every exploitation target is hit in this taut nerve-shredding minor gem, also known as **Psycho Killer**.

THE BIG DOLL HOUSE

USA/Philippines, 1971
Director: Jack Hill. Producer: Jane Schaffer, Cirio H. Santiago [uncredited].
Screenplay: Don Spencer. Music: Hall Daniels. Cinematography: Fred Conde.
Cast: Judy Brown, Roberta Collins, Pam Grier, Brooke Mills, Pat Woodell, Sid Haig.

Director Jack Hill's Filipino-filmed broads-behind-bars flick was the top-grossing movie for producer Roger
Corman's New World Pictures in his distribution label's inaugural year. Made for $150,000, it took over
$10 million at the box-office thanks to endless summer playoff at America's drive-ins and grindhouses.
Exploitation royalty because it set in stone many of the conventions the WIP genre still adheres to, it's
a heady combo of random violence, a little skin, crisp pace and Blaxploitation Queen Pam Grier stealing
every scene she's in as the lesbian prostitute. The future icon was worth every penny of the $500 a
week she was paid to headline the guilty pleasure. Sentenced to 99 years hard labour for the murder of
her gay playboy husband, Judy Brown is imprisoned with five hard cases, all junkies, pyromaniacs and
revolutionaries. When not involved in working under the tropical sun, catfights, mud wrestling, shower
soaping and cockroach racing, the inmates endure various tortures overseen by a hooded inquisitor. Enter
sleazy Sid Haig, who peddles food and booze to the jungle jail, using it as a cover to smuggle in contraband.
He ends up helping the convicts break out and joining the revolt raging outside the bamboo walls.

EXPLOITATION MOVIES

Big Doll House

Their bodies
were caged,
but not
their desires.

They would
do anything
for a man—
or to him.

Metro-Goldwyn-Mayer Presents "Big Doll House" · Starring Judy Brown · Roberta Collins · Pam Gr i er
Brooke Mills · Pat Woodell · Sig Haig · Produced by Jane Schaffer · Screenplay by Don Spencer
Directed by Jack Hill · A New World Pictures Release · Color by Deluxe   MGM

THE BROTHERHOOD OF SATAN

USA, 1971
Director: Bernard McEveety. Producer: L.Q. Jones, Alvy Moore.
Screenplay: William Welch. Music: Jaime Mendoza-Nava.
Cinematography: John Arthur Morrill.
Cast: Strother Martin, L.Q. Jones, Charles Bateman, Ahna Capri,
Charles Robinson, Alvy Moore.

Just prior to directing, producing and writing **A Boy and His Dog** (1975), one of the keynote sci-fi independents of its era, L.Q. Jones (Justice Ellis McQueen Jr., he adopted the character name from his first acting job, **Battle Cry**, 1955), produced and starred in this beloved banner horror with co-producer partner/actor Alvy Moore. They play the sheriff and his simple-minded deputy respectively, who must stand up to the title coven driven by old age to trade their decrepit bodies for new ones. Strother Martin has his best role since **Cool Hand Luke** (1967) as the chief warlock honing in on local children for a secret soul-swap ceremony in US TV series director Bernard McEveety's effectively eerie Satanic Panic. First the witches must dispose of the annoyingly protective parents of their juvenile targets, and they do this by having the youngsters' toys adopt destructive powers. The eye-catching opening sequence has a toy tank suddenly transforming into its full-size counterpart and demolishing all in its path except the cabal's objective. When the brotherhood kidnap Charles Bateman's daughter, the last child needed for the transformation ritual of thirteen, it's a race against time that, in keeping for the era, ends badly.

A demon-spirit of madness and murder holds a California town in the grip of terror.

CAGED MEN

Canada, 1971
Director: Ed Forsyth. Producer: Avron M. Slutker.
Screenplay: Ed Forsyth, Jerry Thomas. Music: Allan Alper.
Cinematography: Peter Reusch.
Cast: Ross Stephenson, Maureen McGill, Richard Gishler,
Jeremy Hart, Edward Blessington, Don MacQuarrie.

Women In Prison films were an exploitation mainstay.
Men In Prison movies were rare and if this Canadian
eye-roller is anything to go by it's hardly surprising.
While not as horrendously homophobic as **Fortune
and Men's Eyes,** made the same year, this naïve drama
posits a view so outmoded even for its era, that all gays
are women trapped in male bodies. Ridiculously dumb
Elliot Markham (Ross Stephenson) wants to impress his
two-timing girlfriend Sherri (Maureen McGill), so he
agrees to become the getaway driver in a bank robbery.
Unfortunately, when the heist goes wrong Sherri turns
him in and he's sentenced to two years in jail where
criminal psycho Evans (Jeremy Hart) intends to make
him his prison bitch. Originally titled **I'm Going to Get
You... Elliot Boy**, then the more heterosexually slanted
Caged Men Plus One Woman before it was abridged
to appeal to **The Boys in the Band** (1970) brigade, every male prison cliché is present and correct –
shower ogling, drag queen tormenting, sadistic wardens corrupting, lip-smacking corporal punishment
dispensing, cell block rioting, inmates protesting they are only gay during their stay... Tawdry trash with
no redeeming features, the reason it was quickly off-loaded to red light district play.

CHROME AND HOT LEATHER

USA, 1971
Director: Lee Frost. Producer: Wes Bishop.
Screenplay: Michael Allen Haynes, David Neibel, Don
Tait. Music: Porter Jordan. Cinematography: Lee Frost.
Cast: William Smith, Tony Young, Michael Haynes,
Peter Brown, Marvin Gaye, Cherie Moor [Cheryl Ladd].

Yet another trash classic from **Love Camp 7**
(1969) exploitation auteur Lee Frost. By the
early 1970s the Hells Angels biker genre was
seriously on the wane – in fact AIP only released
one more, **The Dirt Gang** (1972), after this. So it
was no wonder the Harley Davidson rebel formula
was spiced up here with gung-ho attitude straight out of John Wayne's legendary paean to patriotism
The Green Berets (1968). Sergeant Mitch heads home after a gruelling tour of duty in Vietnam. He's
engaged to the beautiful Kathy (Cherie Moor, soon to become Cheryl Ladd) and is ready to settle

down to safe civilian life. Unfortunately, while out for
a drive with her best friend, Kathy is harassed by the
Wizards, a tough biker gang led by T.J. (genre staple
William Smith), resulting in a fatal car crash. So Mitch,
along with a few of his army buddies (one being Tamla
Motown superstar Marvin Gaye making his dramatic
movie debut), set out to take full artillery, mortar and
tear-gas revenge on the motorcycle maniacs who ruined
his future. While not the best of the biker bunch, Frost
sends up the genre as he neatly hews to its tropes.

CUT-THROATS NINE

Spain, 1971
Director: Joaquín Luis Romero Marchent. Screenplay:
Joaquín Romero Hernández, Santiago Moncada. Music:
Carmelo A. Bernaola. Cinematography: Luis Cuadrado.
Cast: Robert Hundar [Claudio Undari], Emma Cohen,
Alberto Dalbés, Antonio Iranzo, Manuel Tejada,
Ricardo Díaz.

Want to know where Quentin Tarantino got **The Hateful Eight** (2015)? Look no further than Joaquín
Luis Romero Marchent's Paella Western, originally titled **Condenados a vivir/Condemned to Live**.
Produced just as the vogue for violent westerns was dying out, but the nihilistic horror market was
burgeoning, Sergeant Claudio Undari/Robert Hundar (Marchent's **100.000 dollari per Lassiter/
One Hundred Thousand Dollars for Lassiter**, 1966 star), and his daughter Emma Cohen (**Horror
Rises from the Tomb**, 1973) are escorting a gang of degenerate prisoners shackled together with gold
chains through snowy mountains on their way to execution. Ambushed by bandits, the motley crew
must progress on foot, but soon the criminals rebel, burn the Sergeant to a crisp, rape the daughter and
squabble incessantly about how the gold will eventually be divided. Extra gore was inserted into the
final print on the insistence of the American distributors, who also gave prospective patrons 'Terror
Masks' so they could shield their eyes from the added throat-slashing, eviscerations and eyeball-
shooting. Co-scripted by a Spanish master of the horror genre, Santiago Moncada – **Macabre** (1969),
Mario Bava's **Hatchet for the Honeymoon** (1970), **The Fourth Victim** (1971), **They're Coming to Get
You** (1972) and the sublime **The Bell of Hell** (1973).

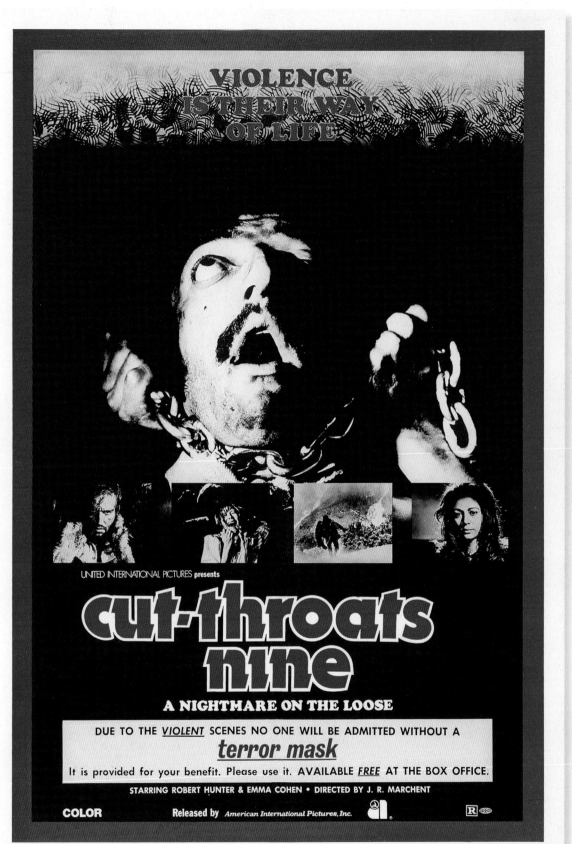

DIARY OF A RAPE

Sweden, 1971
Director: Gustav Wiklund. Producer: Ingemar Ejve, Gustav Wiklund. Screenplay: Gustav Wiklund, Tony Forsberg. Music: Berndt Egerbladh, Ralph Lundsten. Cinematography: Tony Forsberg. Cast: Christina Lindberg, Heinz Hopf, Björn Adelly, Siv Ericks, Janne Carlsson, Birgitta Molin.

Rape as a word loomed large in many sexploitation posters during the heyday of the genre. Just like the exhortation Orgy it created instant sensation and acted as forbidden encouragement in the target voyeur audience. Also released in the States as **The Depraved**, this film actually was the Swedish import **Exposed** before distributor Group 1 International (which would become a major horror player in the late 1970s with **Mansion of the Doomed**, 1976, and **Meatcleaver Massacre**, 1977) controversially re-titled it **Diary of a Rape**. One of the early Scandinavian movies that launched nubile starlet Christina Lindberg on the erotica circuit with **Maid in Sweden** (1971), **The Swinging Co-Eds** (1972) and **Sex and Fury** (1973) before reaching its zenith with **They Call Her One Eye** (1973), this was noted Finnish actor Gustav Wiklund's break into the directing field. Symptomatic of its time, teetering on art-house by trying to blend the notion of free love with darker pretensions while still providing the lip-smacking sexual fantasy elements, Lindberg plays a promiscuous Swedish teenager torn between an older, sadistic lover who turns blackmailer, and her naïve schoolboy crush. There's drugs, wild parties, bondage and the rape fantasy that saw this sophisticated sexploiter banned in 36 or 27 countries depending on which copywriter you believed.

THE HARD RIDE

USA, © 1970, first public screening 1971
Director: Burt Topper. Producer: Charles Hanawalt. Screenplay: Burt
Topper. Music: Harley Hatcher. Cinematography: Robert Sparks.
Cast: Robert Fuller, Sherry Bain, Tony Russel, Marshall Reed, Biff Elliot,
William Bonner.

Burt Topper was working as a roofer in Beverly Hills when
someone asked the handsome labourer if he was interested in
being in the movies. A contract actor for a brief period – he tested
for **Hiawatha** (1952) but lost to Vince Edwards – he decided to
gamble on himself as a director, raised $12,000, and helmed the
desert war drama **Hell Squad** (1958), released by exploitation
marvels American International Pictures. The company liked
being in business with Topper, so he was put in overall charge of
AIP theatrical film production. Particularly fond of the Hells Angels
genre, he wrote and directed this one about discharged marine Phil (Robert Fuller), just home from
Vietnam, being bequeathed a motorcycle nicknamed Baby by a dead buddy. But things get messy when
the bike comes with waitress girlfriend Sheryl (Sherry Bain) attached and a promise to rival Indian
gang-leader Big Red (Tony Russel) that he rides his friend's chopper at his funeral. Between punctures,
punch-ups and Civil War clichés upturned into biker tropes, Righteous Brother Bill Medley sings 'Swing
Low, Sweet Chariot', Junction sing 'Falling in Love with Baby' and Bluewater the rest of the material
penned by **Satan's Sadists** (1969) composer Harley Hatcher.

THE JESUS TRIP

USA, 1971
Director: Russ Mayberry.
Producer: Joseph Feury.
Screenplay: Dick Poston.
Music: Bernardo Segall.
Cinematography: Flemming Olsen.
Cast: Tippy Walker; Robert Porter,
Billy Green Bush, Diana Ivarson,
Virgil Frye, Carmen Argenziano.

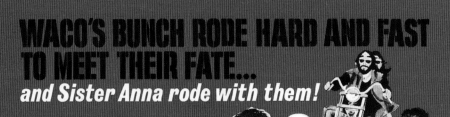

WACO'S BUNCH RODE HARD AND FAST TO MEET THEIR FATE...
and Sister Anna rode with them!

IN THEIR FLIGHT TO FREEDOM THEY BECAME
THE RAVAGED
Their fate was decided in the middle of a desolate desert!

EVE MEYER PRESENTS
A JOSEPH FEURY/SAUL BRANDMAN PRODUCTION
Starring TIPPY WALKER · ROBERT PORTER · BILLY "GREEN" BUSH Co-starring DIANA IVARSON
VIRGIL FRYE · CARMEN ARGENZIANO · WALLY STRAUSS .... Executive Producer SAUL BRANDMAN
Produced by JOSEPH FEURY · Written by RICHARD POSTON · Directed by RUSS MAYBERRY
PG COLOR Released by EMCO FILMS INC

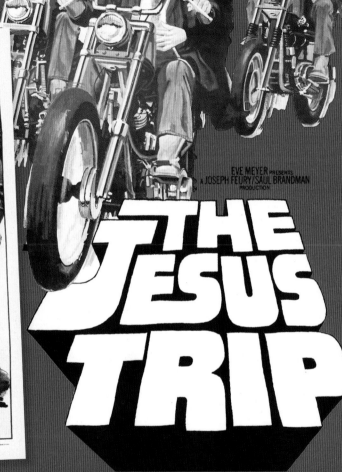

EVE MEYER PRESENTS
A JOSEPH FEURY/SAUL BRANDMAN
PRODUCTION

THE JESUS TRIP

In between helming episodes of such notable American TV series fare as 'The Monkees', 'The Flying Nun', 'I Dream of Jeannie', 'The Brady Bunch', Ironside' and 'Dallas', director Russ Mayberry directed one of the best-worst Hells Angels flicks. Throwing religion and blasphemy into the usual Harley and Hot Leather mix, this cheesy rider has Robert Porter playing Waco, whose gang hides out in a desert convent when the police discover heroin stashed in their motorbike handlebars. Arizona state trooper Tarboro (Billy Green Bush) starts hunting them down after they kidnap nun Anna (Tippy Walker). But Waco's gang are really innocent of the crime and soon, not only is Tarboro in hot pursuit, but also the real villains of the piece in a helicopter. Everybody ends up in a church where Waco's mob destroys the stash to prove they are innocent. Tarboro shoots a couple of them, because they're roadkill scum, and there has to be a few deaths in such a movie anyway. Completely out of the blue Anna falls in love with Waco and decides to renounce Christ and leave her religious life behind to become a motorcycle mama. Also released by Emco as **The Ravaged**, this is brutal, camp and hilarious in equal measures.

THE PINK ANGELS

USA, 1971
Director: Lawrence Brown [Larry G. Brown].
Producer: Edward Atkinson, Mas Kamatani. Screenplay:
Margaret McPherson. Cinematography: Michael Neyman.
Cast: John Alderman, Tom Basham, Henry Olek, Bruce
Kimball, Michael Pataki, Dan Haggerty.

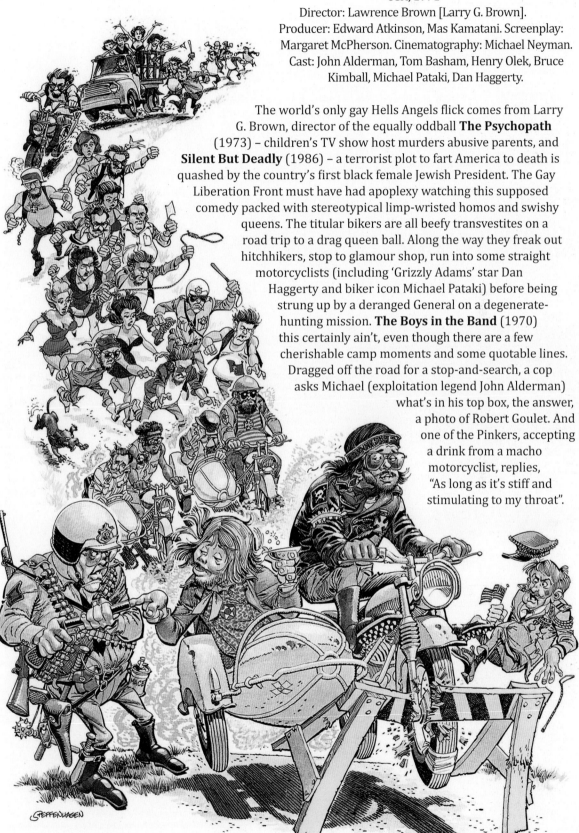

The world's only gay Hells Angels flick comes from Larry G. Brown, director of the equally oddball **The Psychopath** (1973) – children's TV show host murders abusive parents, and **Silent But Deadly** (1986) – a terrorist plot to fart America to death is quashed by the country's first black female Jewish President. The Gay Liberation Front must have had apoplexy watching this supposed comedy packed with stereotypical limp-wristed homos and swishy queens. The titular bikers are all beefy transvestites on a road trip to a drag queen ball. Along the way they freak out hitchhikers, stop to glamour shop, run into some straight motorcyclists (including 'Grizzly Adams' star Dan Haggerty and biker icon Michael Pataki) before being strung up by a deranged General on a degenerate-hunting mission. **The Boys in the Band** (1970) this certainly ain't, even though there are a few cherishable camp moments and some quotable lines. Dragged off the road for a stop-and-search, a cop asks Michael (exploitation legend John Alderman) what's in his top box, the answer, a photo of Robert Goulet. And one of the Pinkers, accepting a drink from a macho motorcyclist, replies, "As long as it's stiff and stimulating to my throat".

AFTER SHE FINISHED WITH THE MEN... SHE STARTED IN ON THE BOYS!

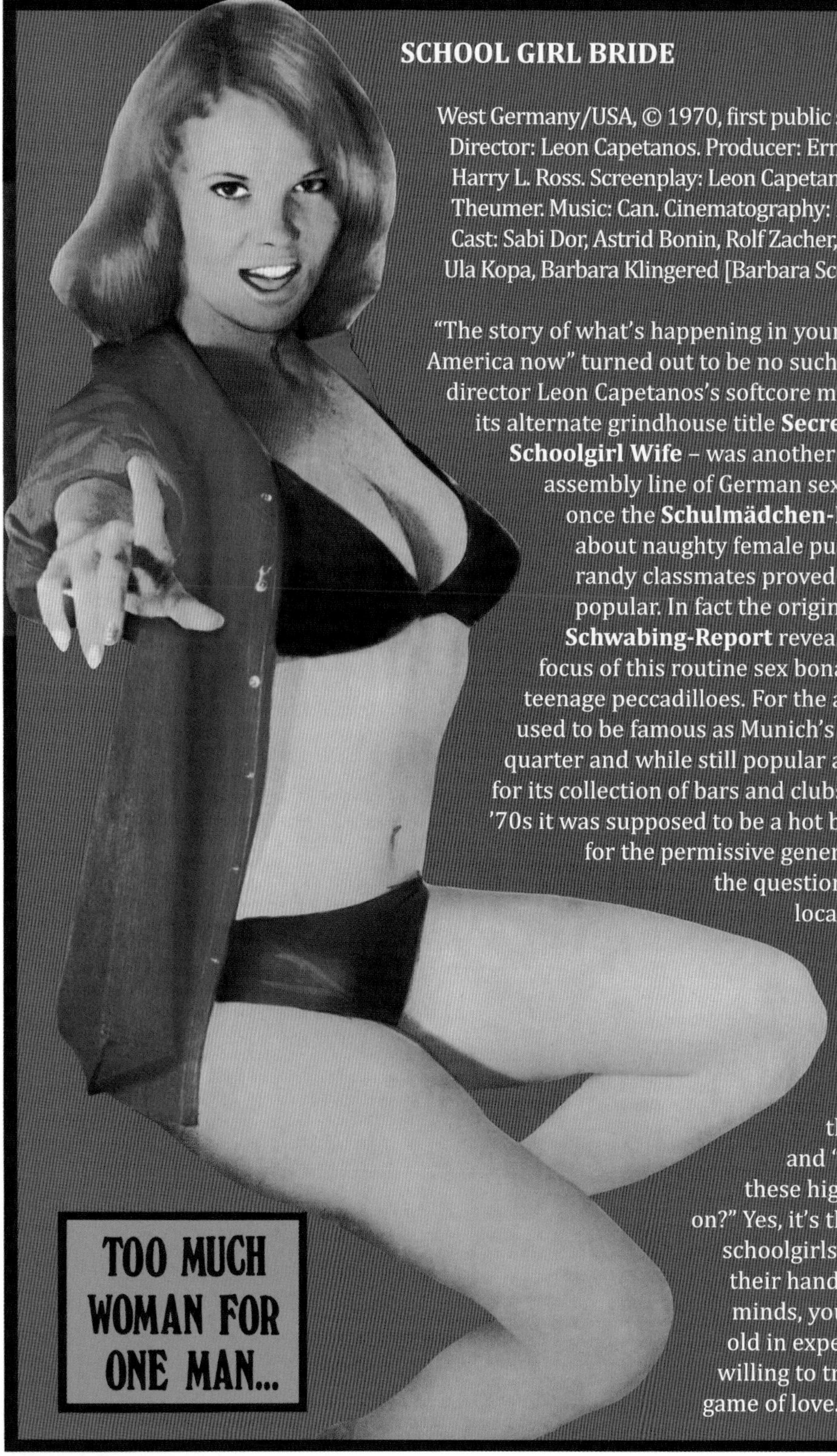

SCHOOL GIRL BRIDE

West Germany/USA, © 1970, first public screening 1971
Director: Leon Capetanos. Producer: Ernst R. von Theumer,
Harry L. Ross. Screenplay: Leon Capetanos, Ernst R. von
Theumer. Music: Can. Cinematography: Klaus König.
Cast: Sabi Dor, Astrid Bonin, Rolf Zacher, Hartmut Solinger,
Ula Kopa, Barbara Klingered [Barbara Scott].

"The story of what's happening in your city all over
America now" turned out to be no such thing. For
director Leon Capetanos's softcore mockumentary –
its alternate grindhouse title **Secret Life of a
Schoolgirl Wife** – was another in the long
assembly line of German sexploiters made
once the **Schulmädchen-Report** series
about naughty female pupils and their
randy classmates proved perennially
popular. In fact the original title **Cream –
Schwabing-Report** reveals the narrow
focus of this routine sex bonanza of assorted
teenage peccadilloes. For the area of Schwabing
used to be famous as Munich's bohemian
quarter and while still popular among tourists
for its collection of bars and clubs, back in the
'70s it was supposed to be a hot bed of free love
for the permissive generation. Some of
the questions posed to the
locals here are "Why
do some teenage
girls decide to
marry rather
than just go
steady?", "Why
do the boys call
them superchicks?"
and "What turns
these high school girls
on?" Yes, it's the story of bored
schoolgirls with time on
their hands and sex on their
minds, young in body but
old in experience and always
willing to try variations in the
game of love.

TOO MUCH WOMAN FOR ONE MAN...

EXPLOITATION MOVIES

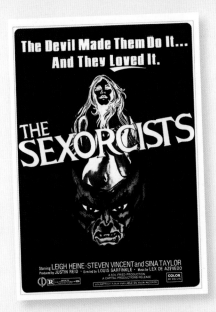

The Devil Made Them Do It...
And They **Loved** It.

THE
SEXORCISTS

Starring LEIGH HEINE · STEVEN VINCENT and SINA TAYLOR
Produced by JUSTIN REID · Directed by LOUIS GARFINKLE · Music by LEX DE AZEVEDO

THE SEXORCISTS

USA, 1971
Director: Louis Garfinkle. Producer: Justin Reid. Screenplay: Louis Garfinkle. Music: Lex de Azevedo. Cinematography: Robert Eberlein. Cast: Sonja Dunson, Branch Halford, Leigh Heine, Charlotte Mathieu, Sina Taylor, Steve Vincent.

Group therapy encounter sessions where you could find yourself were all the rage in flower powered Hollywood and the subject matter would inveigle its way into such mainstream releases as **Bob & Carol & Ted & Alice** (1969) and **The Harrad Experiment** (1973). Independent producers also saw gold in them thar' cheap thrills and jumped on the bandwagon with **The Single Girls** (1973) and this loser, the only film directed by Louis Garfinkle, producer of **I Bury the Living** (1958) and writer of **The Doberman Gang** (1972). It concerned a sex therapist putting eight applicants through erotic rituals at his Californian 'health resort'. Under the title **Beautiful People** it flopped. But two years later Garfinkle took it off the shelf and repackaged it with a catchy new title after the massive success of William Friedkin's horror blockbuster **The Exorcist** (1973), which became the most shocked about movie of the year. Rip-offs were coming from all directions – Germany's **Magdalena, Possessed By the Devil** (1974), Italy's **House of Exorcism** (1974), Turkey's **Seytan** (1974) – but none dared do what Garfinkle did. He used the exact Friedkin approved font from the Warner Bros. press book, and at the same angle, for the re-release poster.

SIMON, KING OF THE WITCHES

USA, 1971
Director: Bruce Kessler. Producer: David Hammond.
Screenplay: Robert Phippeny. Music: Stu Phillips.
Cinematography: David L. Butler.
Cast: Andrew Prine, Brenda Scott, George Paulsin,
Norman Burton, Gerald York, Ultra Violet.

Past its sell-by-date even as it was being shot, this
counterculture character study masquerading
as a horror movie – one hallucinogenic poster
screamed 'Groovy' – is a trippy mix of flower
power, Black Magic and narcotics. It came from
executive producer Joe Solomon, a specialist in
offbeat movies revolving around social misfits. Here, that outsider is bearded Andrew Prine (**Grizzly**,
1976), a warlock living in a Los Angeles storm drain, making a living casting spells for the wealthy

Hollywood 'In Crowd'. The main thrust of the confusing plot
had Simon Sinestrari, believing he's the reincarnation of a great
magician, using his powers to foil an unscrupulous drug squad
cop trying to frame him on a heroin rap. After killing the crooked
law enforcer by stepping into his magic mirror, he discovers
the city Commissioner actually runs the drug trade. When his
pill-popping addict girlfriend (Brenda Scott, Prine's ex-wife)
dies, Simon helps the fuzz bust the pushers in high places but
is murdered with his ceremonial dagger by crazed junkies for
his trouble. Although very much a product of its time – sloppy
psychedelic visuals, tame sex rituals, Andy Warhol Superstar Ultra
Violet playing a Satanist – it still hits the far out freak-fest spot.

SIX WOMEN

USA, 1971
Director: Michael Bennett. Producer: Ed De Priest, Kirdy
Stevens. Screenplay: Mikel Angel. Cinematography: Ron Garcia.
Cast: Mikel Angel, Marsha Jordan, James Sweeney, Erik Stern,
Antoinette Maynard, Sandy Dempsey.

This ultra-cheap western was the only movie directed by
future **The Serpent and the Rainbow** (1988) production
manager Michael Bennett. Headman Charley (Mikel Angel,
a Blaxploitation biker fixture in **Angels Die Hard**, 1970,
The Hard Ride, 1971, and **The Black Six**, 1973, who also
wrote the script), must keep the unruly hellcats in line

en route from Santa Fe to an all-male prison in Sonora, nicknamed "The Pit", and isn't shy about using
his bullwhip to ensure a peaceful journey. Softcore sexpot Marsha Jordan is one of the magnificent six
alongside **And When She Was Bad...** (1973) star Lyllah Torena/Lila Larue, Linda McDowell (**The Adult
Version of Jekyll & Hide**, 1972), Sandy Dempsey (**The Maltese Asparagus**, 1970), and Maria Arnold,
who appeared in 15 sexploitation movies in 1971 alone, including **The Flanders and Alcott Report on
Sexual Response**. The sextet – accent on the sex – is completed by Antoinette Maynard (**One Million
AC/DC**, 1969) who anchors the main set piece in the entire nude, bad and ugly affair. She plays Mexican
spitfire Dolores, who escapes but is recaptured by Charley, tied to a tree by her wrists, stripped to the
waist and mercilessly flogged as the remaining wild bunch watch in warning.

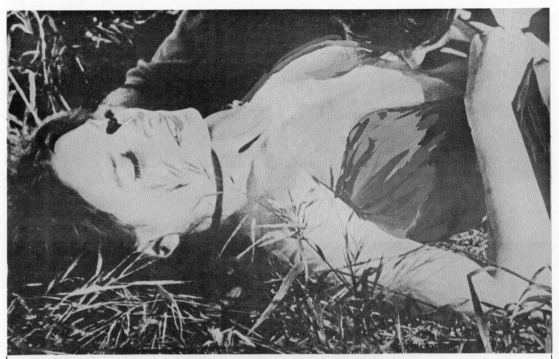

SIX HELLCATS RAMRODDED FROM SANTA FE
TO AN ALL MALE PRISON IN SONORA
--CALLED THE PIT!

EDWARD DePREIST Presents

RATED
X

SIX WOMEN

Starring
MIKEL ANGEL · MARSHA JORDAN · LILA RUE · JAMES SWEENEY

Produced by
EDWARD DePREIST

Directed by
MIKE BENNET · RELEASED BY ADPIX **EASTMANCOLOR**

PRINTED IN USA   CENTRAL LITHOGRAPH
LOS ANGELES   213-749-8898

WOMEN IN CAGES

THE VELVET VAMPIRE

USA, 1971
Director: Stephanie Rothman. Producer: Charles S. Swartz. Screenplay: Maurice Jules, Charles S. Swartz, Stephanie Rothman. Music: Clancy B. Grass III, Roger Dollarhide. Cinematography: Daniel Lacambre.
Cast: Michael Blodgett, Sherry Miles, Celeste Yarnall, Gene Shane, Jerry Daniels, Sandy Ward.

After learning the ropes as director Curtis Harrington's associate producer on **Voyage to the Prehistoric Planet** (1965) and **Queen of Blood** (1966), Stephanie Rothman was hired by maverick Roger Corman alongside Jack Hill (**Spider Baby**, 1967) to incorporate footage from a troubled Yugoslavian film he had bought cheaply into another cobbled together production. Liking what he saw in the final result, **Blood Bath** (1966), Corman let Rothman loose on this hippie blood-sucker that stood hoary vampire clichés on their counter-culture head. Dune buggy loving Diane LeFanu (Celeste Yarnall, star of **Eve**, 1968) tempts uptight Sherry Miles and Michael Blodgett (**Beyond the Valley of the Dolls**, 1970) to her Mojave Desert pad, after introduction by art gallery owner Carl Stoker (Gene Shane from **Werewolves on Wheels,** 1971). There they are seduced by psychedelic dreams and uninhibited sex to leave their establishment repressions behind and become pleasure seekers in dangerous undead Diane's netherworld. In the unusual finale Diane meets her doom on the streets of LA when forced to shed the clothing protecting her from the sun. Despite feminist hopes, Rothman never did amount to anything special, with only **Terminal Island** (1973) of further note in her short credit list.

WOMEN IN CAGES

USA/Philippines, 1971
Director: Gerardo de Leon. Producer: Ben Balatbat, Cirio H. Santiago [uncredited], Roger Corman [uncredited]. Screenplay: James H. Watkins, David R. Osterhout. Cinematography: Felipe Sacdalan.
Cast: Judy Brown, Roberta Collins, Jennifer Gan, Pam Grier, Bernard Bonnine, Charles Davis [Charlie Davao].

Director Jack Hill's Filipino-filmed broads-behind-bars flick **The Big Doll House** (1971) was the top-grosser for producer Roger Corman's New World Pictures in his distribution label's inaugural year. Made for $150,000 it established every Women In Prison convention the genre still adheres to and took over $10 million at the box-office. This was the cash-in follow-up, which unusually made even more money thanks to now-established Blaxploitation star Pam Grier turning in a superb performance as sadistic lesbian prison matron Alabama, a character name Quentin Tarantino would use in homage in his **True Romance** (1993) script. She makes life hell for Jennifer Gan (**Naked Angels**, 1969) in her own private torture chamber after the naïve American has been set-up by her drug-dealing boyfriend. So Gan convinces cellmate staples Roberta Collins and Judy Brown to jungle escape. Perfunctory direction from Gerardo de Leon, veteran of **Mad Doctor of Blood Island** (1969) infamy, aside this is the one to see to understand why Grier became such an icon for uttering such dialogue as "Never have pity. This game is called survival. Let's see how well you can play it. I was strung-out on smack at ten and worked the streets when I was twelve".

He may be a
stranger...
a friend...
or the quiet
guy who lives
next door.

It really happened
Based on a true story

The
Zodiac
Killer

THE ZODIAC KILLER

USA, 1971
Director: Tom Hanson. Producer: Tom Hanson. Screenplay: Ray Cantrell,
Manny Cardoza. Cinematography: Robert Birchall, Wilson Hong.
Cast: Hal Reed, Bob Jones, Ray Lynch, Tom Pittman, Mary Darrington,
Frank Sanabek.

Before David Fincher tackled the same subject in **Zodiac** (2007), there was
this version of the murderous events surrounding the North California serial
killer who slaughtered seven victims between December 1968 and October 1969.
The killer's identity still remains unknown but that didn't stop Tom Hanson (also director of the 1972
smuggling caper **A Ton of Grass Goes to Pot**) ruminating on the case including the series of taunting
letters detailing the minutiae of the crimes sent to the local Bay Area press containing mind-bending
cryptograms. Fincher's film was based on Robert Graysmith's acclaimed bestselling book, Hanson's
on a co-written script by Ray Cantrell, star of **The Hellcats** (1968) and **Bigfoot** (1970)! Two possible
suspects are offered up for analysis: a hard-drinking trucker going through vindictive divorce issues
and a milquetoast mailman whose fury erupts if anyone moans about his delivery service. Neither
convincing candidates. Supposedly created in order to prick the conscience of the actual killer so he'd
turn himself in, or prompt those witnesses too scared to come forward – comment cards were placed
in each theatre so they could write down their suspicions – this depressing experience is the worst
combination of nasty exploitation and realistic true-crime drama.

THE ADULT VERSION OF JEKYLL & HIDE

USA, © 1971, first public screening 1972
Director: L. Ray Monde [Lee Raymond]. Producer: B. Ron Eliot [Byron
Mabe], David F. Friedman [uncredited]. Screenplay: Robert Birch.
Music: William Loos [William Loose], William Allen Castleman.
Cast: Jennifer Brooks [Laurie Rose], Rene Bond, Jane Tsentas, Linda
York, Jack Buddliner [John Barnum], Harry Schwartz [Norman Fields].

A year after Hammer produced **Dr. Jekyll & Sister Hyde**, in which
the obsessive physician changed gender in his experimental
quest for the elixir of life, Forty Thief *par excellence* David F.
Friedman silently and uncredited executive produced a similar
version loaded with softcore nudity, male full-frontals, kinky
sex and whiplash violence. Doubtless Robert Louis Stevenson
was spinning in his grave with the extreme makeover given his
classic horror story by United Airlines pilot-turned-director Lee
Raymond (as L. Ray Monde), also responsible for the same year's
Love Thy Neighbor and His Wife. In this shoddy, barely audible
retelling, shot in Victorian California with all the care of an Andy Milligan 'gore blimey' epic,

Dr. Chris Leeder (Jack Buddliner aka John Barnum) finds
the medical notebook of one Dr. Jekyll while scouring
antiques stores with his fiancée Cynthia (Laurie Rose aka
Jennifer Brooks). Finding the key formula, he's compelled
to drink the resulting potion, and his personality splits
into the voluptuously leggy blonde Miss Hyde (Jane
Tsentas) with murderous seduction and castration solely
in mind. It's when Miss Hyde sets her lesbian sights on
Cynthia that Jekyll has to turn equally nasty himself. Porn
star Rene Bond plays Jekyll's secretary Debby.

starring **TAB HUNTER** · co-starring CHERIE LATIMER · NADYNE TURNEY · ISABEL JEWELL · LINDA LEIDER · ROBERTA COLLINS
produced by TAMARA ASSEYEV · Written and Directed by CURTIS HANSON · A TAMARA ASSEYEV-CURTIS HANSON PRODUCTION
[M] METROCOLOR · A NEW WORLD RELEASE

THE AROUSERS

USA, © 1971, first public screening 1972
Director: Curtis Hanson. Producer: Tamara Asseyev. Screenplay:
Curtis Hanson. Music: Charles Bernstein. Cinematography: Daniel
Lacambre, Edmund Anderson.
Cast: Tab Hunter, Cherie Latimer, Nadyne Turney, Isabel Jewell,
Linda Leider, Rory Guy [Angus Scrimm].

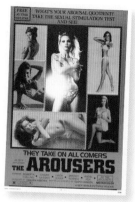

Sweet Kill was a suspense horror produced by Tamara Asseyev, who would hit the big time later with **Big Wednesday** (1978) and **Norma Rae** (1979). Written and directed by Curtis Hanson, whose star would also ascend with **The Bedroom Window** (1987), **The Hand That Rocks the Cradle** (1992) and the Oscar-winning **L.A. Confidential** (1997), it was reviewed as "a milestone in Tab Hunter's career", and "in the tradition of **Psycho** (1960)" by the Los Angeles Times. Unfortunately this unnerving and creepy shocker about a sexually dysfunctional Californian gym teacher killing girls failing to stimulate him – something going back to watching his mother undress while hidden in a closet – was a total flop. So producer Roger Corman, who had distributed it under his New World Pictures banner, asked Hanson to shoot extra nude scenes over a weekend to sex the movie up even more. Under the title **The Arousers** and with the addition of a free foyer sex-drive test, Corman sent the movie out on the grindhouse circuit again. It didn't help and Hunter had to wait for John Waters' **Polyester** (1981) before successfully reinventing his post teen idol persona. Future **Phantasm** (1979) star Angus Scrimm, billed as Rory Guy, cameos.

THE BIG BIRD CAGE

USA/Philippines, 1972
Director: Jack Hill. Producer: Jane Schaffer, Cirio H. Santiago
[uncredited]. Screenplay: Jack Hill. Music: William Loose, William
A. Castleman. Cinematography: Philip Sacdalan.
Cast: Pam Grier, Anitra Ford, Candice Roman, Sid Haig, Carol
Speed, Karen McKevic.

The follow-up to **The Big Doll House** (1971), which was also written and directed by Jack Hill, did exactly what all Women In Prison movies successfully did – gender swap the traditional penitentiary clichés. Here WIP doyenne Pam Grier is sent to infiltrate a Banana Republic's prison camp, known as the Big Bird Cage in reference to the sugar mill dominating the compound, in order to recruit women who won't mind servicing the sexual needs of revolutionary leader Django's (exploitation great Sid Haig) rebel forces. Played more for laughs with mud fights, catfights, gang fights, fire fights, every sort of fight, homosexuality, lesbianism, lard rub-downs and nude jungle romps, it's less a Filipino version of **The Great Escape** (1963) than great escapism. Profitably released by Roger Corman's New World Pictures the exploiter extraordinaire said, "It had a little bit of sex, a little bit of violence and a great deal of humour. That was the key. They were sold in the advertising to a large extent on the basis of sex and violence. But when you saw the films, there wasn't that much sex and violence in them. They were just very funny and the audiences were delighted to find them so."

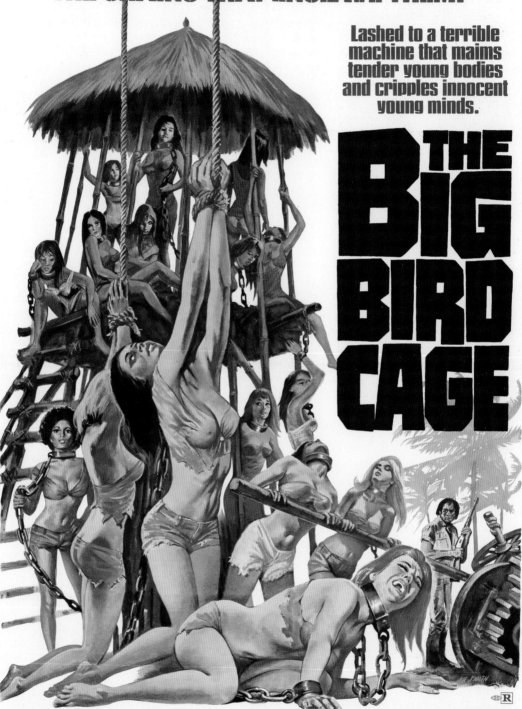

WOMEN SO HOT WITH DESIRE THEY MELT THE CHAINS THAT ENSLAVE THEM!

Lashed to a terrible machine that maims tender young bodies and cripples innocent young minds.

THE BIG BIRD CAGE

MEN WHO ARE ONLY HALF MEN AND WOMEN WHO ARE MORE THAN ALL WOMAN

METROCOLOR starring PAM GRIER · ANITRA FORD · CANDICE ROMAN · CAROL SPEED and SID HAIG
produced by Jane Schaffer · written and directed by Jack Hill · A New World Pictures Release

EXPLOITATION MOVIES

FRIGHTFEST GUIDE 127

FROM THE SUN COME THE FIRE-PEOPLE TO INCINERATE ALL MANKIND!

The CREMATORS

GREAT BALLS OF FIRE:
SCORCHING!
RAVAGING!
ENGULFING!

THE CAPTIVE FEMALE

USA, 1972
Director: Marc B. Ray. Producer: Alan Roberts.
Screenplay: Larry Alexander, Marc B. Ray.
Music: Rockwell. Cinematography: Stephen H. Burum.
Cast: Fred Holbert, Leigh Mitchell, Robert Knox, Ron Bastone,
Suzette Hamilton, Rory Guy [Angus Scrimm].

One grade Z flick, two campaigns to monetize its lame cheesiness for separate markets. Under the title **Scream Bloody Murder**, Marc B. Ray's amateur hour horror was "Filmed in violent vision and gory color!" and free

blindfolds were given out to viewers to cover their eyes because it was so horrifying to watch. Many did consider it unwatchable in fact and found the blindfolds a blessing. The second campaign, re-titled **The Captive Female**, was aimed at the roughie crowd and accented the plot's third act in its bondage design. Disturbed Matthew (Fred Holbert) mangles his hand while running over his father with a thresher. Given a hook prosthetic he returns home from the lunatic asylum and goes on a killing spree again, hacking up his new stepfather with an axe and bashing his mother's head in. On the run he picks up a cheap hooker (Leigh Mitchell, who also plays Matthew's mom to further underline the **Psycho**, 1960, allegory), pretends he's a wealthy landowner, kills the owners of a mansion and ties her up to the bed for the depressingly drawn-out conclusion. Complete with crazily distorted camera hallucinations, a cameo by Angus (**Phantasm**, 1979) Scrimm and two further titles, **Matthew** and **Claw of Terror**.

THE CREMATORS

USA, 1972
Director: Harry Essex. Producer: Harry Essex. Screenplay: Harry Essex. Music: Albert Glasser.
Cinematography: Robert Caramico.
Cast: Maria de Aragon, Marvin Howard, Eric Allison, Mason Caulfield, R.N. Bullard, Cecil Reddick.

On the one positive hand this opus was adapted from the Julian C. May (as Judith Ditky) story 'The Dune Rollers' from the December 1951 edition of 'Astounding Science Fiction' magazine and directed by Harry Essex, scripter of the classic '50s creature features **It Came from Outer Space** (1953) and **Creature from the Black Lagoon** (1954). On the other far more negative one May's first published offering had already received a poor adaptation in the 'Tales of Tomorrow' television series, cost the paltry sum of $40,000, and Essex had just helmed the direct to TV disaster **Octaman** (1971). Not great credentials to replicate the exciting-looking poster mayhem depicting an intergalactic fireball landing on Earth to roll over human beings reducing them to flesh ash. Can hapless Dr. Thorne stop it scorching the entire world? Picked up by Roger Corman's New World Pictures for a song, there was no way this alien abomination couldn't fail to make money based on its minimal outlay. And this led to **Star Wars** (1977)? For two people, yes: star Maria de Aragon played Greedo in the George Lucas original, while Doug Beswick's ingenious optical effects got him a job on **The Empire Strikes Back** (1980).

There's no place to hide when THE DEAD ARE ALIVE!

NATIONAL GENERAL PICTURES Presents

ALEX CORD · SAMANTHA EGGAR · JOHN MARLEY | THE DEAD ARE ALIVE

HORST FRANK and with NADJA TILLER Written by LUCIO BATTISTRADA and ARMANDO CRISPINO

Produced by MONDIAL TE. FI.   Directed by ARMANDO CRISPINO   Technicolor® Ⓖ A NATIONAL GENERAL PICTURES RELEASE

THE DEAD ARE ALIVE

Yugoslavia/Italy/West Germany, © 1971, first public screening 1972
Director: Armando Crispino. Screenplay: Armando Crispino, Lucio Battistrada.
Music: Riz Ortolani. Cinematography: Erico Menczer.
Cast: Alex Cord, Samantha Eggar, John Marley, Horst Frank, Enzo Tarascio, Enzo Cerusico.

The US title for **L'etrusco uccide ancora/The Etruscan Kills Again** suggests a zombie slant but Living Dead lovers were in for shock when it turned out to be a macabre murder mystery in the Giallo vein. A series of gory killings seem to have been committed by Tuchulka, an Etruscan demon god. Alcoholic mental case archaeologist Alex Cord (**Inn of the Damned**, 1975) is blamed for wandering around the ancient ruins and reviving a curse, and attracts police interest because he suffers blackouts and has no alibis. As Cord tries to rekindle his relationship with ex-wife Samantha Eggar (**The Brood**, 1979), now married to tyrannical conductor John Marley (**The Godfather**, 1972), the death toll rises until the modern-day maniac's identity is revealed in an amphitheatre with Verdi's 'Requiem' blaring out. Director Armando Crispino's Spoleto-set thriller captures precisely the Italian Film Industry psyche of the time. What clearly started its pre-production life as a supernatural chiller swerves into Giallo territory solely because Dario Argento's sterling output was raking in the cash. Absurdly fake as it is, this half-baked horror parades a gleeful array of over-excited obsessives and sadistic misfits to enjoy. Crispino's other Giallo, **Macchie solari/Autopsy** (1975) fell equally short.

THE DIRT GANG

USA, © 1971, first public screening 1972
Director: Jerry Jameson. Producer: Joseph E. Bishop, Art Jacobs [Arthur A. Jacobs]. Screenplay: William Mercer, Michael C. Healy. Music: The Harvest. Cinematography: Howard A. Anderson Jr.
Cast: Paul Carr, Michael Pataki, Lee De Broux, Jon Shank, Nancy Harris, T.J. Escott.

He'll get a face full of bloody tread marks and a 250 lb. dirt bike right where he doesn't need it.

By the time 1972 rolled around the Hells Angels genre had pretty much fizzled out. So there had to be an extra layer to any movie daring to pass off the standard drug-fuelled biker rebels without a cause vs. douche-bag authority tropes. Exploiters *par excellence* American International Pictures thought they had another marketable plot wrinkle in this dreadful last gasp, directed by Jerry Jameson who graduated to the big-time with such blockbusters as **Airport '77** (1977) and **Raise the Titanic** (1980) before heading back to series television where he originally made his name. The anti-heroes here weren't straddling Harleys or wearing cut-off denim jackets; their vehicles were off-road dirt bikes and their duds of choice helmets and leather pants.

These 'outlaws' terrorise a film crew shooting in the desert, with rape of the female crew uppermost in their addled minds. With the usual 1970s style of over-heated acting and grungy cinematography, it provided yet another opportunity for top exploitation character actor Michael Pataki to strut his stuff. Best known for his roles in **Grave of the Vampire** (1972), **The Bat People** (1974) and **Dracula's Dog/Zoltan, Hound of Dracula** (1977), Pataki always added extra shading to every part he played.

EVIL COME EVIL GO

USA, 1972
Director: Walt Davis. Producer: Robert C. Chinn. Screenplay: Walt Davis.
Music: Dan Goodman, Jim Wingert. Cinematography: Manuel S. Conde.
Cast: Cleo O'Hara, Sandra Henderson, Jane Louise, Rick Cassidy, Margot
Devletian, Chesley Noone [Chesley Noon].

Sleazy, off-the-wall cine-scum doesn't come any more distasteful or disarming than this technically inept grindhouse cheapie from director Walt Davis (**Ride a Cock Horse**, 1973). Sister Sarah Jane Butler is a prim and proper Singing Nun type who travels the country with her guitar and street preaches against the evils of sex and sin. To make her church-going point she picks up disgusting johns in local bars, takes them to no-tell motels and slaughters them tired H.G. Lewis fashion. But there's more. Sarah Jane goes to Hollywood, where she's given shelter by lesbian Penny who initiates her in the delights of Sapphic love, with the least erotic groping session in history. In return the good Sister makes Penny a fully paid up member of her 'Sacred Order of the Sisters of Complete Subjugation'. The two gal pals then proceed to sing hymns at more immoral men to cleanse their souls before butchering them to save "all the sweet, innocent girls from their stinking, sweaty bodies". But there's even more. The country and western singalong theme: "Will you strike with your blade, till they've all finally paid, Sarah Jane, Sarah Jane, Sister Sarah you're insane." 'Son of a Preacherman' it ain't!

X WARNING UNSUITABLE FOR PERSONS UNDER 18 YEARS OF AGE

No man is safe from the "Preacherwoman" –
She's a Man-Hating, Hymn-Humming Hell Cat!

FEMALE CONVICT SCORPION: JAILHOUSE 41

Japan, 1972
Director: Shunya Itô.
Producer: Kineo Yoshimine.
Screenplay: Shunya Itô, Fumio Kônami,
Hirô Matsuda. Music: Shunsuke Kikuchi.
Cinematography: Masao Shimizu.
Cast: Meiko Kaji, Fumio Watanabe,
Yukie Kagawa, Kayoko Shiraishi,
Eiko Yanami, Hiroko Isayama.

The second in the four-part series of Women In Prison films adapted from Toru Shinohara's edgy manga perfectly sums up cross-party fandom where grindhouse meets art-house and neither side feels short-changed. Meiko Kaji, made famous by her roles in the **Stray Cat Rock** (1970-71) series and future **Lady Snowblood** (1973) icon, stars as ruthless avenger Matsu, nicknamed Scorpion by hardened fellow inmates at Jailhouse 41. Serving out the solitary confinement sentence meted out in the previous instalment, **Joshû 701-gô: Sasori** (1972) for disfiguring the now one-eyed warden, Matsu is continuously hosed down, gang-raped and abused by the sadistic prison guards. But after escaping with six other female convicts, the men who wronged her had better watch out. For she intends to humiliate her fair share of male authority figures while ensuring her bestial rapists are stripped, beaten and emasculated. With little dialogue and little nudity but copious violence and surreal hallucinations all beautifully filmed, director Shunya Itô makes female empowerment an important part of the exploitation smorgasbord to create a poetic trash aesthetic that's an exquisite eyeful of visual virtuosity. Clearly an influence on Quentin Tarantino's **Kill Bill** (2003/4) duo, this is a masterpiece from Japan's infamous Toei Studios.

GARDEN OF THE DEAD

USA, 1972
Director: John Hayes. Producer: H.A. Milton [Daniel Cady]. Screenplay: Jack Matcha. Music: Jaime Mendoza-Nava [uncredited]. Cinematography: Paul Hipp. Cast: Phil Kenneally, Duncan McLeod, John Dullaghan, John Dennis, Susan Charney, Lee Frost.

This **Night of the Living Dead** (1968) inspired low-budgeter has prison inmates getting high sniffing the experimental formaldehyde they are being forced to manufacture. Stoned out of their minds, the convicts plan a great escape but are shot and killed by the guards and buried in hastily dug graves. But needing their formaldehyde fix, they rise from the dead to take revenge on the sadistic wardens with hoes and sharp rakes. It introduces us to the career of director John (Patrick) Hayes, who drew the attention of horror fans thanks to a run of quirky quickie '70s terrors including **Dream No Evil** (1970), **Grave of the Vampire** (1972) and **End of the World** (1977). A journeyman through the US exploitation industry, Hayes made 'roughies' – **Help Wanted Female** (1968) and **Sweet Trash** (1970), cheapo action – **The Cut-Throats** (1969), and sleazy crime thrillers – **Mama's Dirty Girls** (1974) before skidding into bargain basement video porn in the 1980s. Beginning his show business career as an actor before turning to directing industrial training films, around 1965 Hayes formed Clover Films with his best friend Daniel Cady, and it was under this banner he produced **Garden/Grave/Tomb of the Dead**, guest-starring notorious director Lee Frost.

MILLENIUM PRODUCTIONS PRESENTS

GARDEN OF THE DEAD

POOR ALBERT & LITTLE ANNIE

USA, 1972
Director: Paul Leder. Producer: Leon Roth. Screenplay: William W. Norton. Music: Herschel Burke Gilbert.
Cinematography: William Swenning.
Cast: Zooey Hall, Geri Reischl, Joanne Moore Jordan, Greg Mullavey, Marlene Tracy, Frank Whiteman.

Flopping under this original title, director Paul Leder (the 3D **Ape**, 1976) was given one of the best exploitation monikers of all time, **I Dismember Mama**. 'Boxoffice' magazine, the exhibitor bible at the time, raved about this cheapskate slasher, saying it had real high-grossing potential for theatre owners seeking sensationalist fare. The branded 'up-chuck cup' giveaway apparently the puke-green icing on the cake. But it wasn't to be, under any title or configuration – the most desperate a "Frenzy of Blood!" double bill with the Spanish import **The Blood Spattered Bride** (1972). Perhaps the subject matter, even considering the less-watchful ethics of the era, proved off-putting to most horror hounds. For it was about a mother-fixated deranged youth (Zooey Hall, from the 1971 gay shocker **Fortune and Men's Eyes**) sublimating his murderous Oedipal passions with the pure and innocent nine-year-old daughter of her housekeeper. If his sexual urges took over during the night and the soft porn movies hidden in his room can't suffice, he heads to the streets to stalk women with loose morals. Luckily the bunch of idiot cops finally cotton on and chase him to a mannequin warehouse where he jumps out of a window to his death.

ROMAL PRODUCTIONS
presents
Poor Albert & Little Annie

THESE WOMEN TRUSTED ALBERT... they shouldn't have!

THE NURSE
She deprived him of his only pleasure.

THE NIGHT LADY
She wanted money — he wanted love.

THE HOUSEKEEPER
She was dead the minute she opened the door.

ANNIE
The child woman he wanted to marry, not kill.

THE SLASHER... IS THE SEX MANIAC

Italy, 1972
Director: Roberto Bianchi Montero. Producer: Eugenio Florimonte. Screenplay: Luigi Angelo, Italo Fasan, Roberto Bianchi Montero. Music: Giorgio Gaslini. Cinematography: Fausto Rossi.
Cast: Farley Granger, Sylva Koscina, Silvano Tranquilli, Femi Benussi, Susan Scott [Nieves Navarro].

Or **So Sweet, So Dead** and **Rivelazioni di un maniaco sessuale al capo dell squadra mobile** ('Revelations of a Sex Maniac by the Head of the Flying Squad') to give director Roberto Bianchi Montero's well-structured Giallo its alternative export and original Italian titles. Cop Farley Granger is hunting the Avenger, a knife-wielding murderer targeting unfaithful wives of prominent men. Uncovering the killer's identity, he sets a trap in which his own deceitful spouse will be the black-clad assassin's final victim. Populated with a pleasing array of Giallo stars – Sylva Koscina, Femi Benussi, Susan Scott – and underscored by Giorgio Gaslini's sublime thriller themes, the lurid US title, above average nudity quotient, blatant bloodshed and tacky subplots about necrophilia, this tense and surprising addition to the genre is a true guilty pleasure. After doing the 42nd Street horror circuit, unscrupulous distributor William Mishkin repackaged and re-edited it for the porno trail as **Penetration** – "The Ultimate X-Crime" – adding hardcore inserts from Kim Pope, Marc Stevens, Harry Reems and Tina Russell, rendering it virtually incomprehensible. In the early 1960s Montero had a good run of success with the Mondo movies **Sexy Nudo** (1963), **Africa Sexy** (1963) and **Mondo Balordo** (1964).

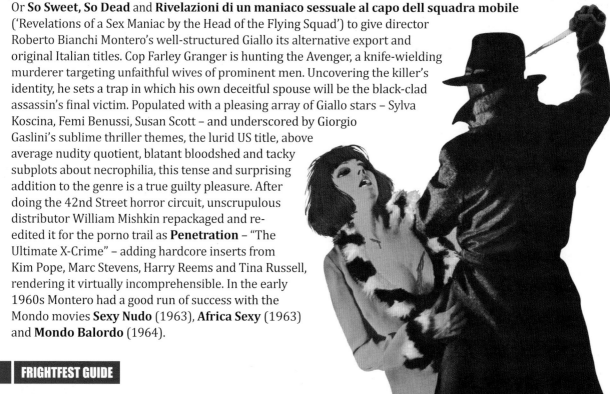

SLEAZY RIDER

USA, 1972
Director: Roger Gentry. Producer: Marland Proctor. Screenplay: Roger Gentry. Cinematography: Rod Williamson. Cast: Jody Bishop, Jim Gentry [Roger Gentry], Penny Boran, Starlyn Simone, Becky Pearlman [Becky Sharpe].

Billed as 'second shirtless miner' in John Hayes' cowboy brothel western **Fandango** (1970) under his acting alias Jim Gentry, it was as Roger Gentry the former 1950s Texas footballer signed his directing career. This was Gentry's debut feature and there are no prizes for guessing what the main source of inspiration was for the title. Dennis Hopper's **Easy Rider** had been released four years prior but such was the impact it had on mainstream culture and the Hollywood mindset in general, its ripple effects were still being felt all through the independent film arena. But whereas Hopper's hip low budget mantra for the drop out generation touched a mystic nerve, Gentry's 60-minute long patience-tester was a crude sexploitation biker flick that deserves its obscurity. Gentry cast himself as Sam the Sheriff who, after assaulting a Hells Angels' old lady, finds the whole gang invading his home for some sexual humiliation, rape and orgiastic behaviour with his entire family. In his first and – not surprisingly – only film credit Jody Bishop stars as leader of the pack Fry. Gentry doesn't stint on the full-frontal nudity or simulated masturbation in this lurid trashfest from executive producer Armand Atamian, star of **The Animal** (1968).

ARMAND
ATAMIAN
presents

JODY
BISHOP in...

Sleazy Rider

IN **COLOR**

The curse that begins with a kiss.

She's got it.

STIGMA

USA, 1972
Director: David E. Durston. Producer: Charles B. Moss Jr. Screenplay: David E. Durston. Music: Jacques Urbont.
Cinematography: Robert M. Baldwin.
Cast: Philip Michael Thomas, Harlan Cary Poe, Josie Johnson, Peter Clune, William Magerman, Connie Van Ess.

On the surface David E. Durston's **I Drink Your Blood** (1970) and this heavy-handed combo of Blaxploitation and sex hygiene picture might seem poles apart. But the former concerns a group of hippies who arrive at backwoods community, slip an old man some LSD, and in revenge are fed rabies-infected meat pies. **Stigma** continues those themes albeit in STD terms. Dr. Calvin Crosse (Philip Michael Thomas before he was 'Miami Vice' famous) is a black doctor just out of medical school who moves to a small, isolated New England coastal town to set up a medical practice. In this bigoted community syphilis is running rampant and destroying the lives of the locals. Aided by friendly Vietnam veteran Bill Waco (Harlan Cary Poe), Crosse discovers the cause of the epidemic is none other than the Sheriff's daughter (Josie Johnson) who congenitally acquired the infection in the womb. Now grown up and contagious, she's been having group sex with the teen population in order to pay back her old man for his past marital infidelities. Complete with quick cuts of actual VD victims, it ends with her fervently kissing her father to re-infect him with the guilty source of her condition.

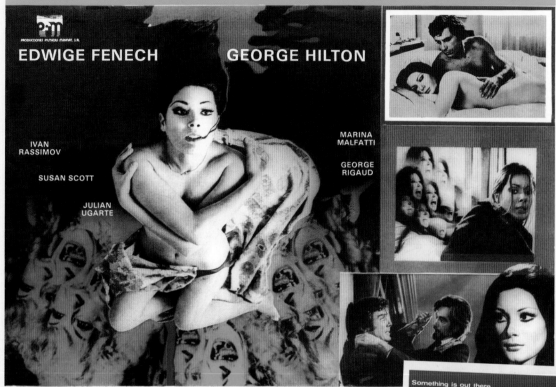

THEY'RE COMING TO GET YOU

Italy/Spain, 1972
Director: Sergio Martino. Producer: Mino Loy, Luciano Martino.
Screenplay: Ernesto Gastaldi, Sauro Scavolini. Music: Bruno Nicolai.
Cinematography: Giancarlo Ferrando, Miguel Fernández Mila.
Cast: George Hilton, Edwige Fenech, Ivan Rassimov, Julian Ugarte,
Susan Scott [Nieves Navarro], Maria Cumani Quasimodo.

A bevy of gorgeous Eurostarlets, led by the undisputed Queen of Italian
B movies Edwige Fenech, grace director Sergio Martino's fetching giallo/
horror hybrid. Shot around London's Putney Bridge and incorporating
elements of **Rosemary's Baby** (1968) and **Repulsion** (1965) into its
spaghetti shocker tropes, Fenech plays Jane, an attractive woman
suffering from terrible nightmares relating back to the childhood
trauma of seeing her mother murdered. Prey to persecution mania, her husband advises she consult a

psychiatrist to work through fears of a mysterious stranger trying to kill her. Then her new neighbour
Mary (Susan Scott/Nieves Navarro) offers to cure her phobias via Devil worshipping black magic orgies.
Is it all a delusion or unpleasant reality? Bog-standard Agatha Christie lurks under all the frenetic style,
nightmarish imagery (a fish-eye lens used to make the kinky Satanic sequences suitably hallucinatory)
and stalking suspense, yet as woman-in-peril movies go, this is one of the best from the era. Originally
titled **Tutti i colori del buio/All the Colors of the Dark**, director Martino scored in every genre he
tackled; Giallo proper **Excite Me** (1972), slasher **Torso** (1973), cannibal adventure **Prisoner of the
Cannibal God** (1978) and monster fantasy **Island of the Fishmen/Screamers** (1979).

VOODOO HEARTBEAT

USA, 1972
Director: Charles Nizet. Producer: Ray Molina. Screenplay: Charles Nizet.
Cast: Ray Molina, Philip Ahn, Ern Dugo, Forrest Duke, Ebby Rhodes, Mike Zapata.

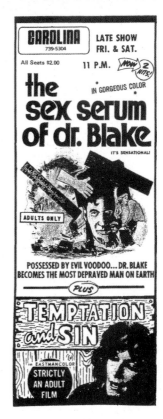

Top Secret information has leaked to Oriental spies that American scientists have found a youth serum in the African jungles. Red China needs the elixir to keep its leader Mao Tse Tung in power forever. But after a bungled heist by Chinese commandos, the serum falls into the hands of Dr. Blake (producer Ray Molina) who turns into a fanged beast

craving for blood when he ingests it. Shot on location in Las Vegas by Charles Nizet, director of the Amazon fantasy **Slaves of Love** (1969), this weird and wonderfully awful Dracula hybrid should have been shot at dawn. But unlike its loony central vampire character who turns to ash after being shot by cops, it remained on the grindhouse circuit for years, also under **The Sex Serum of Dr. Blake** title. Molina's sideburns, suit and tie, the hokey torture scenes depicting arm and ear butchering and the Vegas Strip strutting buxom bikini-clad beauties add a bottom of the barrel charm to the garish proceedings. Gimmick suggestions? Pass out bottles of sugared water as 'youth serum' and employ a young man to carry a sign claiming he's 162 years old but has kept his looks because of it.

BLOOD ORGY OF THE SHE-DEVILS

USA, © 1972, first public screening 1973
Director: Ted V. Mikels. Producer: Ted V. Mikels. Screenplay: Ted V. Mikels. Music: Carl Zittrer.
Cinematography: Anthony Salinas.
Cast: Lila Zaborin, Victor Izay, Tom Pace, Leslie McRae, William Bagdad, Ray Myles.

The Astro-Zombies 'auteur' Ted V. Mikels earned a justifiable reputation in independent horror circles more for his eccentric lifestyle sharing a Californian castle with seven women than any talent for filmmaking. None of his movies are any good – from **I Crossed the Color Line** (1965) and **The Girl**

in Gold Boots (1968) to **The Corpse Grinders** (1971) and **The Doll Squad** (1974). This horror tour de farce is more famous for American newspapers refusing to advertise its full title, something Mikels made sure got used in subsequent exploitation campaigns. The plot is something to do with witch queen Mara (Lila Zaborin) leading her Californian coven of acolytes, or as she puts it "My wolfpack of voluptuous virgins", in ritual sacrifices of male victims. The Black Arts, American Indian spirits materialising during a séance (Zaborin is hilarious speaking in tongues), past life reincarnation and witchcraft flashbacks – unfortunately the budget didn't stretch to a medieval wardrobe as the polyester pants attest – this is rock bottom rubbish. But it ends hilariously with a fake bat being thrown on burning coals to release Mara's evil, shown as a poor translucent superimposition of a vaporous form floating upwards in a raging, screaming death.

A TERRIFYING, SCREAMING PLUNGE TO
THE DEPTHS OF HELL!

TED V. MIKELS
presents

BLOOD ORGY
OF THE
SHE-DEVILS

THE CANDY SNATCHERS

USA, 1973
Director: Guerdon Trueblood. Producer: Bryan Gindoff. Screenplay: Bryan Gindoff.
Music: Robert Drasnin. Cinematography: Robert Maxwell.
Cast: Tiffany Bolling, Ben Piazza, Susan Sennett, Brad David, Vince Martorano,
Bonnie Boland.

"Was a piece of Candy worth a fortune in diamonds?" This minor grindhouse gem is a surprisingly gripping slice of vintage sleaze packing a powerful final punch. Tiffany Bolling, exploitation's 'It' girl for a brief period (see also **Wicked, Wicked**, 1973, and **Kingdom of the Spiders**, 1977), stars as the self-centred Jessie, who devises the daring kidnap and live burial of the 16-year-old daughter of diamond dealer Avery Phillips (Ben Piazza). But the simple plan, inspired by a TV drama Jessie watched, and carried out with her psycho brother Alan (Brad David) and dimwit Eddie (Vince Martorano) goes horribly wrong when Avery refuses to pay the ransom. What the kidnappers don't know is that Candy is Avery's stepdaughter, and he only married her drunken wealthy mother for the money. So Candy's death will make him rich and accelerate his own plan to head to Brazil with his mistress. As the abductors quarrel, and Avery digs his own money-grubbing heels in, it turns out Candy's burial was witnessed by a mute boy desperate to reveal her whereabouts... Just as shocking as the downbeat ending? The theme song 'Money is the Root of All Happiness' sung by Kerry Chater.

THE CAULDRON OF DEATH

Spain/Italy, 1973
Director: Tulio Demicheli. Producer: José G. Maesso. Screenplay: Santiago Moncada, José G. Maesso, Mario Di Nardo. Music: Nando De Luca.
Cinematography: Francisco Fraile.
Cast: Christopher Mitchum, Barbara Bouchet, Arthur Kennedy, Manuel Zarzo, Malisa Longo, Eduardo Fajardo.

Hollywood legend Robert Mitchum's second son Christopher got his first star billing in this ultra-violent example of the Poliziotteschi genre. Although he had a second-string career in America appearing in **Chisum** (1970), **Bigfoot** (1970), and **Big Jake** (1971), Christopher's decision to head to Europe for **Summertime Killer** (1972) began a boom period for the youthful blond. After getting a karate black belt in 1973, Argentine director Armando Bartolomé Demichelli/Tulio Demicheli cast him as Ricco (the film's original title) in this Spanish/Italian co-production featuring popular Euro-starlets Barbara Bouchet and Malisa Longo. Released from prison after a two-year sentence, Ricco finds out his father was murdered by godfather

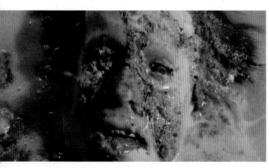

Don Vito (Arthur Kennedy). Worse, the mob boss has also nabbed his girlfriend Rosa (Longo). So with counterfeiter's daughter Scilla (Bouchet) at his side, mean machine Ricco karate chops his way to a bag of cash belonging to Vito, precipitating an all-out vendetta. Also known as **Ricco the Mean Machine** and **Heavy Dues**, the title used for its 1979 US release was **The Cauldron of Death**, which refers to the infamous *sine qua non* sequence in the catalogue of bloody cruelty where a victim has his genitals sliced off and shoved in his mouth before being dissolved in an acid tank.

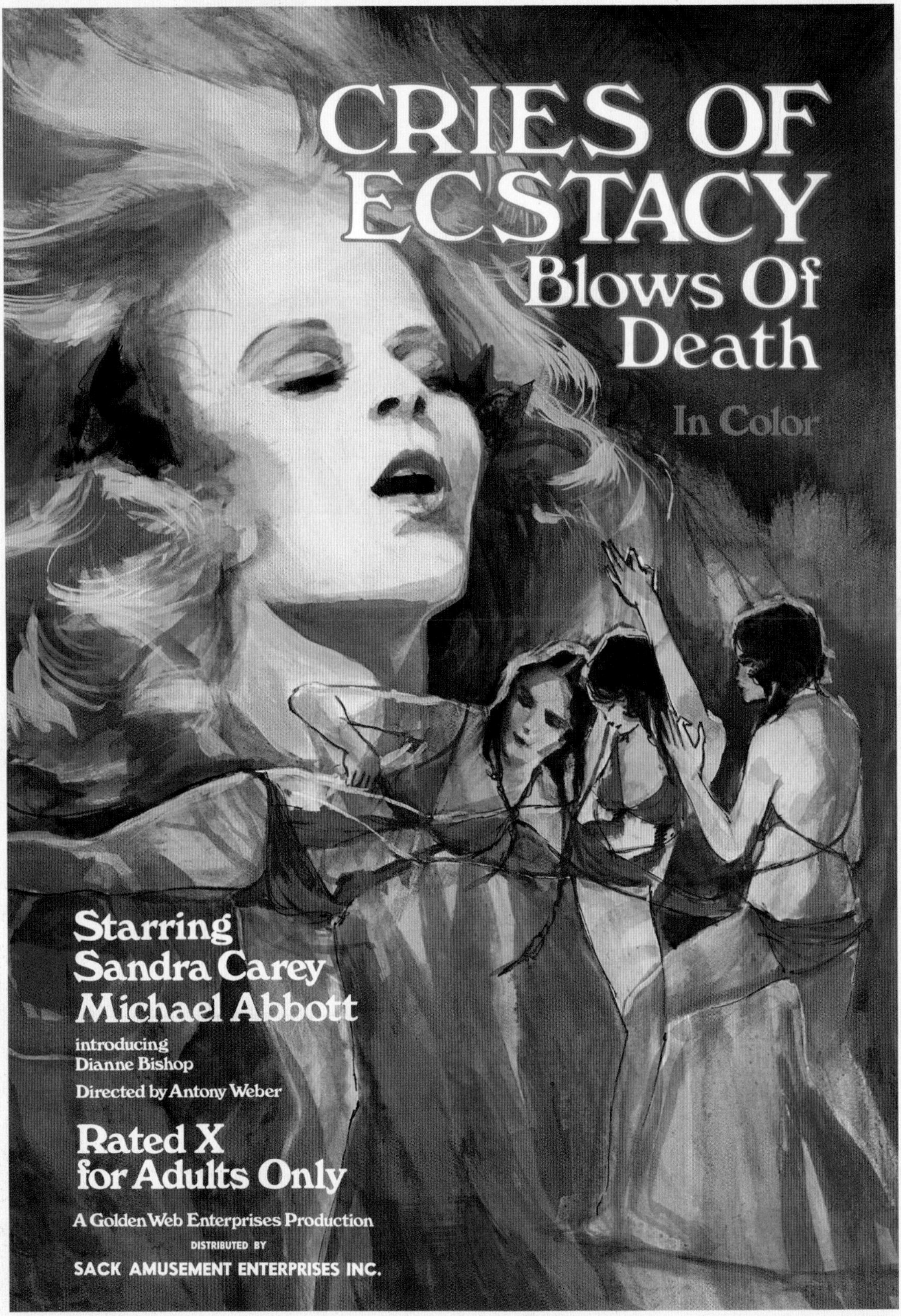

CRIES OF ECSTACY
Blows Of Death

In Color

Starring
Sandra Carey
Michael Abbott
introducing
Dianne Bishop
Directed by Antony Weber

Rated X
for Adults Only

A Golden Web Enterprises Production
DISTRIBUTED BY
SACK AMUSEMENT ENTERPRISES INC.

THE CHAPERONE

USA, 1973
Director: Jaacov Jaacovi [Jourdan Alexander].
Producer: Jaacov Jaacovi [Jourdan Alexander].
Screenplay: Svetlana, Jaacov Jaacovi [Jourdan
Alexander]. Music: John Jones. Cinematography:
Jaacov Jaacovi [Jourdan Alexander].
Cast: Sandy Dempsey, Walter Roland Moore,
Paula Lane, John Tull, Sandy Carey, Doug Senior.

Before he changed his name to Jourdan
Alexander to direct a welter of hardcore
pornography including **Little Orphan
Dusty** (1978), **Sex Wish** (1992), **Kiss Is a
Rebel with a Cause** (1993) and **Junkyard
Anal** (1994), Jaacov (pronounced Jack-
Off?) Jaacovi helmed a couple of starter
sexploiters, the adult western **A Fistful of
44s** (1971) and this violence-laced thriller
starring two heavyweight Sex Queens
named Sandy – Dempsey (**The Playmates**,
1973, who died a year after filming it) and
Carey (**Deep Jaws**, 1976). Ever since Wes
Craven's landmark **The Last House on
the Left** (1972) had gouged a huge chunk
of money from the drive-in circuit with
its "To Avoid Fainting, Keep Repeating, It's Only a Movie ...Only a Movie" strap-line ('borrowed' from
the Herschell Gordon Lewis **Color Me Blood Red** 1965 campaign), canny producers were looking to
emulate its success with copycat storylines. Hence babysitter Marsha (Dempsey) ends up facing a group
of switchblade-wielding thugs with rape and murder on their minds in this unsavoury sex shocker
scripted by Jaacovi and his **Little Orphan Dusty** actress Svetlana Mishoff/Marsh, who would soon turn
director herself with **800 Fantasy Lane** (1979), **Panty Raid** (1984) and **Miami Spice** (1986).

CRIES OF ECSTACY, BLOWS OF DEATH

USA, 1973
Director: Antony Weber. Producer: Antony Weber. Cinematography: John C. Stevens.
Cast: Sandy Carey, Michael Abbott, John Martin, Dianne Bishop, Sherri Mason, Uschi Digard.

2062: A Sparse Oddity. One hundred years after Earth's decimation by Cold War nuclear attack, an
underground generation have grown up with heightened sex drives. Now they live in colour-coded
plastic bubbles furnished with purified air and water. Leaving your pink, yellow or green transparent
environment without permission means death. But that hasn't stopped a bunch of renegade bikers,
sporting gas masks and bows and arrows, roaming the wastelands on a rape and pillage mission.
The resulting sex and violence actions of which is the main thrust of this incredibly rare post-apocalyptic
sexploiter featuring two die-hard sex queens – Amazonian Russ Meyer staple Uschi Digard and **The
Wanton Nymph** (1972) Sandy Carey – amongst the bevy of fly-by-night glamour mag beauties. The
narrator opens with the untrue disclosure that director Antony Weber's feeble fable will focus on the
"ecstasy rather than the despair" of this futuristic landscape and proceeds to highlight nude chess games,
Zardoz (1974) inspired skimpy costumes and orgies while gradually ramping up the karate 'blows
of death'. This one's famous for the Italian version, **Sesso delirio**, splicing in extra newsreel bombing
footage and scenes from George A. Romero's **The Crazies** (1973) to beef up the sci-fi content.

DIARY OF A STEWARDESS

USA, 1973
Director: William de Diego. Producer: Carlos Tobalina.
Music: William S. Baker.
Cast: unknown

Forget the movie – a drab mile high club, sexy trolley
dolly, randy pilot jet-lagged affair – this Carlos Tobalina
produced sexploiter was one of very few to have a pop
single released to tie in with its 42nd Street premiere.
Bob Grabeau sang the smooth and silky theme song –
opening lyrics "Though to some she's just a stewardess,
she is like a bird in search of happiness" – the flipside
was 'Fasten Your Seatbelts' (what else?), and he was
1950s famous for mimicking the voice of superstar
Nat King Cole. Grabeau performed the romantic ballad
'Bella Notte' for the record album of Walt Disney's
Lady and the Tramp (1955) and also collaborated
with composers Sammy Fain, Jule Styne, Nelson Riddle
and Dimitri Tiomkin on various film projects. Released
by Segue Records, the A side was co-written by the
legendary Buddy Feyne, the first person to sing the classic song 'Stardust' on TV, and praised for his
swinging hep-cat lyrics in the biggest hipster hits of the 1930/40s including 'Tuxedo Junction' and 'After
Hours'. Feyne also wrote the original theme song lyrics for the Blaxploitation classic **Dolemite** (1975)
that all-round creator and star Rudy Ray Moore re-jigged into his own signature entrance hymn.

THE DIRTY DOLLS

USA, 1973
Director: Godfrey Daniels [Stu Segall]. Producer: Edward E.
Paramore [Harold Lime]. Screenplay: Godfrey Daniels [Stu Segall].
Cinematography: Gary Graver.
Cast: John Alderman, Denise Drake, Sharon Kelly [Colleen
Brennan], Chris Schwarzer, Cyndee Summers, C.D. LeFleure
[George 'Buck' Flower].

A second feature that played the sleaze environs of Times
Square consistently during the 1970s, this softcore roughie
has unstable psycho Johnny Feral (John Alderman, **The Pink Angels**, 1971) running a criminal gang
of four teenage sluts, one being his younger sister Dee Dee (Denise Drake). After successfully pulling a
daring bar robbery, Johnny thinks his mini-skirt mob is ready for the big-time and forces them to carry
out a diamond heist. Unfortunately they bring back with the loot
two witnesses as hostages, much to Johnny's displeasure – until the
girls organise an orgy to take his mind off the fact their fence has
backed out of the deal. But when the male courier prisoner starts
getting cosy with Dee Dee in the hope she'll set him free, Johnny kills
the other one when she too tries to escape. Realising her brother is
going too far, Dee Dee confronts him, and in a fury Johnny rapes her
relentlessly. Totally embarrassed by enjoying the incest, Dee Dee
steals a gun, unchains the courier and shoots them both to freedom.
Shot in a few days in the glare of bad lighting, with a threadbare
script and hilarious dialogue, it's a down and dirty shame!

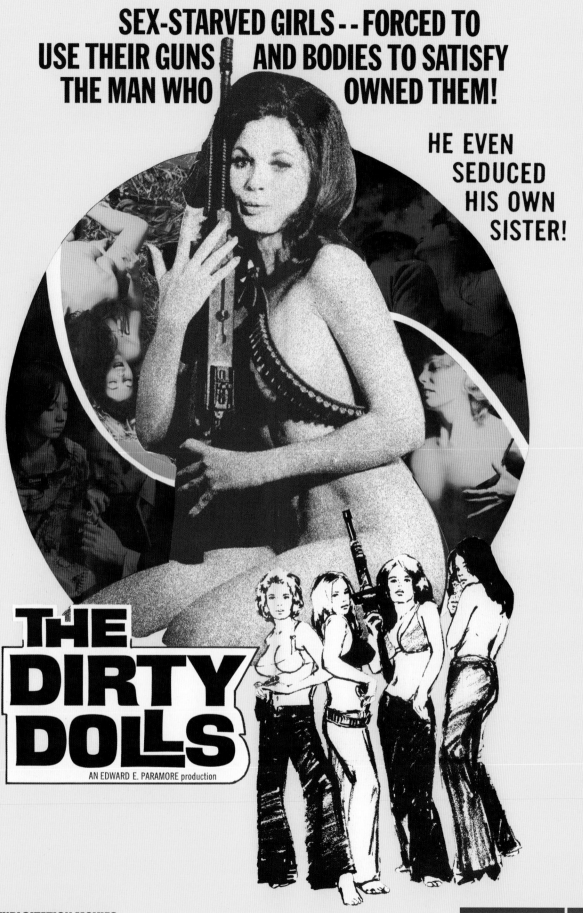

SEX-STARVED GIRLS -- FORCED TO
USE THEIR GUNS AND BODIES TO SATISFY
THE MAN WHO OWNED THEM!

HE EVEN
SEDUCED
HIS OWN
SISTER!

THE DIRTY DOLLS

AN EDWARD E. PARAMORE production

THE NEWEST EDGAR ALLAN POE
HORROR-SUSPENSE THRILLER !

"THIS IS A REALLY BIG ONE . . .
A BRILLIANT, FAST MOVING SHOCKER . . .
IT'S TERRIFIC!"
Cinema Magazine

DR. TARR'S
TORTURE
DUNGEON

GROUP 1 presents EDGAR ALLAN POE'S "DR. TARR'S TORTURE DUNGEON"
starring CLAUDE BROOK · ELLEN SHERMAN · MARTIN LASALLE and ROBERT DUMONT
directed by   produced by   written by
JOHN L. MOCTEZUMA   ROBERT VISKIN and J.G. ELSTER   CHARLES ILLESCAS
BLAZING COLOR   A GROUP 1 RELEASE

DR. TARR'S TORTURE DUNGEON

Mexico, © 1972, first public screening 1973
Director: Juan López Moctezuma. Producer: Roberto Viskin. Screenplay: Carlos Illescas, Juan López Moctezuma.
Music: Nacho Méndez. Cinematography: Rafael Corkidi.
Cast: Claudio Brook, Arthur Hansel, Ellen Sherman, Martin LaSalle, David Silva, Pancho Córdova.

During Mexico's turbulent 1960s Juan López Moctezuma became a key figure in popular culture for creating a long-running radio jazz programme and hosting a late-night TV showcase for silent era horror movies. Failing to break into the film industry, despite a few minor acting roles, he turned his attention to the avant-garde theatre movement that was making great creative leaps forward. Via this work he met Alejandro Jodorowsky and assisted his symbiotic colleague in the production of **Fando y Lis** (1968) and the landmark Midnight Movie **El Topo** (1970). That association and experience was all he needed to make his step into film directing, his debut feature being this astute blurring of surrealism and horror under the title **The Mansion of Madness**. The entire plot is essentially summarized in the first few minutes; reporter Gaston LeBlanc (Arthur Hansel) is visiting France to write a story on the asylum run by Dr. Maillard (Mexican superstar Claudio Brook) and his innovative methods for treating the insane. But when he arrives the lunatics have taken over the asylum in this astonishingly visual version of Edgar Allan Poe's 'The System of Dr. Tarr and Professor Fether' staged as a carnival **Marat/Sade** (1967).

THE FEMALE BUTCHER

Spain/Italy, © 1972, first public screening 1973
Director: Jorge Grau. Screenplay: Jorge Grau, Juan Tébar, Sandro Continenza. Music: Carlo Savina. Cinematography: Fernando Arribas.
Cast: Lucia Bosé, Espartaco Santoni, Ewa Aulin, Ana Fara, Silvano Tranquilli, Lola Gaos.

Former film critic Jorge Grau was wondering how to enter the lucrative world of exploitation horror and, after studying the profits made by Hammer's **Countess Dracula** (1970), realized he too could forge something out of the legend of Erzebeth/ Elizabeth Bathory, the 17th century Hungarian noblewoman who thought bathing in virgin blood would keep her eternally young. So with Lucia Bosé, Miss Italy 1947, as the Countess,

and with **Candy** (1968) sexpot Ewa Aulin as an innkeeper's daughter, he helmed this supernaturally enhanced version. Opening with a ritual exhumation of a suspected vampire who is then officially given a public decapitation, it is hoped the rash of blood-draining murders afflicting the local maiden population will end. No such luck as Bathory's husband commits suicide but returns in undead form to keep his wife supplied with the fresh blood she craves. Beautifully shot, with atmosphere to spare, Grau pulls back from the gore, obviously storing all that up for his next feature **The Living Dead at Manchester Morgue/Don't Open the Window** (1974). Filmed as **Ceremonia sangrieta/Blood Ceremony**, it was first seen in the US as **The Legend of Blood Castle** and then re-released in 1979 as **The Female Butcher** with a terrific come-on campaign.

FRUSTRATED WIVES

UK, 1973
Director: Arnold Louis Miller. Producer: Arnold Louis Miller, Sheila Miller. Screenplay: Alan Paz. Music: De Wolfe. Cinematography: Tony Leggo.
Cast: Hilary Lebow [Hilary Farr], Claire Gordon, Amber Kammer, Kim Alexander, Tristan Rogers, Gordon Whiting.

Many leading figures of the British sexploitation business had music hall backgrounds due to variety theatre dealing in prurient material. Harrison Marks and Pete Walker began their careers as stand-up comedians and Arnold Louis Miller was the nephew of Nat Mills, one half of the celebrity knockabout act Nat Mills and Bobby. In a career spanning a quarter of a century, Miller worked as a director, producer and writer and is best known for the exploiters he made in association with the companies Compton and Tigon. Initially working in the 'harmful' comics industry with 'Tales from the Crypt', when this business folded he moved into glamour magazines, joining forces with Stanley Long to produce the girlie rag 'Photo Studio' and shooting 8mm 'nudie' shorts released under their Stag Films banner. Miller's first film to gain a cinema release was the **Nudist Memories** (1961) short, followed by **Nudes of the World** (1961) and the Mondo exposés **West End Jungle** (1961), **London in the Raw** (1964) and **Primitive London** (1965). After producing the famous horrors **The Sorcerers** (1967), **The Blood Beast Terror** (1967) and the classic **Witchfinder General** (1968), he directed his last movie, this fag-end rural sex saga, aka **Sex Farm**.

'GATOR BAIT

USA, © 1972, first public screening 1973
Director: Ferd Sebastian, Beverly Sebastian. Producer: Ferd Sebastian, Beverly Sebastian. Screenplay: Beverly Sebastian. Music: Ferd Sebastian. Cinematography: Ferd Sebastian.
Cast: Claudia Jennings, Sam Gilman, Clyde Ventura, Bill Thurman, Ben Sebastian, Janit Baldwin.

John Boorman's **Deliverance** (1972) was the reason for the existence of this tale of lust and murder in the Louisiana bayou from husband and wife team Beverly and Ferd Sebastian. A swamp-set sweaty-sex Hixploitationer, it stars the late, great Playmate-tuned-action-starlet Claudia Jennings (**The Great Texas Dynamite Chase**, 1976, **Deathsport**, 1978, **Fast Company**, 1978). Our curvaceous heroine headlines as back water dweller Desiree Thibodeau, who poaches alligators to support her family. The corrupt Sheriff (Bill Thurman) wants her in jail, but local lads Billy Boy (Clyde Ventura) and Ben Bracken (Ben Sebastian, the directors' son) want her in their beds and devise a kidnap and rape plan of action. But when trigger-happy Billy kills Ben by accident during the fudged abduction, Billy tells Ben's kin that Desiree did it. The 'good ole boy' hunting party that's organised to take revenge leads to Desiree's sister Julie (Janit Baldwin) almost getting gang raped and then savagely killed. And when Desiree finds out, the hunters become the hunted in a violent comic strip that's both pacy and racy. The Sebastians made the semi sequel **Gatorbait II: Cajun Justice** in 1988, but female wrestler Jan Sebastian (the directors' daughter) was clearly no Jennings substitute.

'GATOR BAIT
HALF ANIMAL.. ALL WOMAN

Ginger's On To Something Big!

Now she takes on a beautiful evil woman out to blackmail an entire country... but Ginger has a few secret tricks of her own! And it's wilder and sexier than anything that ever turned you on before!

GIRLS ARE FOR LOVING

USA, 1973
Director: Don Schain. Producer: Ralph T. Desiderio. Screenplay: Don Schain.
Music: Bob Orpin. Cinematography: Howard Block.
Cast: Cheri Caffaro, Timothy Brown, Jocelyne Peters [Sheila Leighton],
Fred Vincent, Robert C. Jefferson, Rod Loomis.

For a nano-second in the early 1970s, Cheri Caffaro was a shining 42nd Street star of sexy action flicks thanks to a trashy trilogy of low rent, distaff James Bond adventures beginning with **Ginger** (1971), and continuing with **The Abductors** (1972). This was the third slapdash episode in the funky series directed by then husband Don Schain, in which Caffaro plays undercover government agent Ginger McAllister, assigned to bring a glamorous high-end insider trader trying to manipulate Asian-American markets to book. During the course of the deliciously seedy romp Caffaro (who won a 'Lifetime' magazine Brigitte Bardot lookalike contest in her teens) does a hokey striptease while singing an MOR torch song, gets tied up nude and tickled by feathers. Worse happens to Ginger's naked male captives; so they'll divulge Top Secret information each gets fitted with metal jockstraps for genital electrocution. Blaxploitation star and ex-pro ball player Timothy Brown (**Sweet Sugar**, 1972) plays Ginger's hunky CIA love interest with, it must be said, little interest. After this spotlight, Caffaro joined the Philippines-shot **Savage Sisters** (1974) ensemble and tried to do a 'Ginger' one last time in **Too Hot to Handle** (1976) before retiring to raise honeybees in Los Angeles.

THE HANGING WOMAN

Spain/Italy, 1973
Director: José Luis Merino.
Producer: Ramón Plana.
Screenplay: José Luis
Merino, Enrico Columbo.
Music: Francesco De Masi.
Cinematography:
Modesto Rizzolo.
Cast: Stan Cooper [Stelvio
Rosi], Maria Pia Conte, Dyanik
Zurakowska, Pasquale Basile,
Gérard Tichy, Paul Naschy.

Dracula the Terror of the Living Dead, **Return of the Zombies**, **Beyond the Living Dead** and **Bracula** were some alternative titles for this decent slice of Eurotrash directed by Spanish B movie hack José Luis Merino as **La orgía de los muertos**. Originally designed as another starring vehicle for Jacinto Molina under his Paul Naschy acting alias, the 'Christopher Lee of Madrid' realised too late he had a scheduling conflict so could only appear in a supporting role as Igor, a deranged necrophilic gravedigger, in this Victorian nonsense set in the Carpathian Mountains. There, sinister doctor Leon Droila (Gérard Tichy) is trying to harness Nebula Electricity to resurrect the dead. Into an eventful plot awash with cobwebbed crypts and secret passageways comes hero

FOR THE
SQUEAMISH
KEEP REPEATING
IT CAN'T BE TRUE
CAN'T BE TRUE
CAN'T BE TRUE
CAN'T BE TRUE
CAN'T BE TRUE

the
HANGING
WOMAN

Serge Chekov (Stan Cooper/Stelvio Rosi) for the reading of his uncle's will. He ends up grappling with Igor, decapitated by a knife wrenched from his own heart, as impressive looking zombies shamble around. The sole reason for its renamed drive-in existence rests on the potent success of the advertising campaign for **The Last House on the Left** (1972), the fittingly famous "To Avoid Fainting, Keep Repeating, It's Only a Movie" tag line used and amended here to "For the Squeamish..."

Meet ONE MAN'S FAMILY

REVEALED FOR THE FIRST TIME outside the courtroom -- the staggering details of the most hideously bizarre murders in the annals of crime **SURPRESSED UNTIL NOW** and **NOT PERMITTED** on TV, Radio or Family Newspapers!

TOLD IN THEIR OWN WORDS BY THE KILLERS THEMSELVES!

MANSON

A LAURENCE MERRICK FILM

MANSON

USA, 1973
Director: Robert Hendrickson, Laurence Merrick. Producer: Robert Hendrickson, Laurence Merrick. Screenplay: Joan Huntington. Music: Paul Watkins, Brooks Poston. Cinematography: Leo Rivers [Louie Lawless].
Cast: Charles Manson, Susan Atkins, Patricia Krenwinkel, Charles Watson, Robert Beausoleil, Linda Kasabian.

On January 25, 1971, Charles Manson was convicted on seven counts of murder and one of conspiracy to commit murder for his role in trying to start a race war with the bloody Sharon Tate and Leno and Rosemary LaBianca murders in Benedict Canyon, California, 1969. It was a crime that shocked the world, robbed **Rosemary's Baby** (1968) director Roman Polanski of his **Valley of the Dolls** (1967)/**Dance of the Vampires** (1967) actress wife, and caused wholesale panic among the Beverly Hills glitterati. Who incredibly nominated Laurence Merrick's documentary for an Academy Award, one imagines to broadcast their Chateau Marmont cocktail party collective grief abroad. Unfortunately, despite this exposé of life within the infamous Manson family being "told in their own words by the killers themselves", it's a complete snowjob, hence its quick move from sober arthouse release to sensation-seeking grindhouse playoff. Former cellmates of the Death Row ex-cult members reveal nothing of interest as grainy home movie footage of the family skinny-dipping, driving around in dune buggies and making Manson's coat is shown in endless split-screen, padded out further with lyrical song sections. Few details about the actual crux event stretches the material an awful long way indeed.

NIGGER LOVER

USA, 1973
Director: Greydon Clark. Producer: Alvin L. Fast. Screenplay: Greydon Clark, Alvin L. Fast. Music: Ed Cobb. Cinematography: Louis Horvath.
Cast: Greydon Clark, Tom Johnigarn, Jacqueline Cole, Bambi Allen, Aldo Ray, Jock Mahoney.

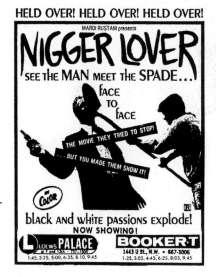

Grade Z movie actor Greydon Clark (**Satan's Sadists**, 1969) turned director with this provocatively titled race melodrama, filmed as **America the Beautiful**, that unsurprisingly got changed to **Tom**, **Mothers, Fathers and Lovers**, **The Bad Bunch** and **The Brothers**

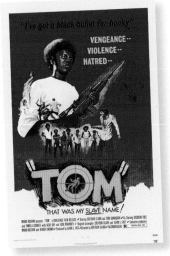

as it filtered through a varied distributor network. Executive produced by Mardi Rustam and co-written with Alvin L. Fast (who teamed again for Tobe Hooper's **Death Trap/Eaten Alive**, 1977), Clark cast himself as white Vietnam veteran Jim, who dutifully carries out the last wish of his African American war buddy blown to bits in combat. But while delivering the letter to his friend's father in the incendiary Watts area, he encounters hostility from his radical Black Power brother Tom (Tom Johnigarn, from **Sweet Jesus Preacherman**, 1973). Add into the cheap and cheerful mix Jim's love triangle with two hippie chicks (one played by Jacqueline Cole, Clark's wife, the other Bambi Allen, an Al Adamson casting favourite) and the two racist police detectives (played with unsettling fervour by Hollywood hacks Aldo Ray and Jock Mahoney) who Tom thinks Jim is in cahoots with. As per the genre the social message veneer was merely an excuse for gratuitous nudity and Blaxploitation bluster.

PETS

USA, 1973

Director: Raphael Nussbaum. Producer: Raphael Nussbaum, Mardi Rustam [uncredited]. Screenplay: Richard Reich, Raphael Nussbaum. Music: Jorge Del Barrio. Cinematography: Mark Rasmussen, Richard P. McCarty. Cast: Ed Bishop, Joan Blackman, Candy Rialson [Candice Rialson], Teri Guzmán, Bret Parker, Matt Green.

Originally an off-Broadway play written by Richard Reich and performed in May 1969 at the Provincetown Playhouse in Greenwich Village, 'Pets' comprised of three separate acts. The first was 'Baby with a Knife' about two lesbians, one of whom still likes a bit of hetero action, making a dangerous male burglar their live-in sex toy. 'Silver Grey Toy Poodle' had two sexy hitchhikers robbing an executive by the roadside and burglarising his home, taking his pet dog hostage. The third playlet was 'Pets' that had a raging chauvinist pig taking home his liberated date to put in his basement zoo of caged victims. 'Cue' magazine reviewed it thus: "Richard Reich is a playwright who has discovered a fascinating new toy – sadomasochism. So enthralled is he by the S&M mystique of discipline, power, sexual mastery and submission, torture and self-flagellation, that he has written no less than three one-acters in which people cage, whip, stab, and rape each other with gay abandon, all the while pontificating in language duller than an Abnormal Psych textbook". Undaunted, Reich allowed schlock producers Raphael Nussbaum and Mardi Rustam to combine the first two stories into the third main narrative with equally misogynistic, depressing results.

EXPLOITATION MOVIES

SHANGHAI LIL AND THE SUN LUCK KID

Hong Kong, 1973
Director: Yang Ching-Chen, Chu-Ko Ching-Yun. Producer: Run Run Shaw. Screenplay: Yang Ching-Chen.
Music: Chou Fu-Liang. Cinematography: Chuang Yan-Chien.
Cast: Shih Szu, Chin Han, Yee Yuen, Lung Fei, Cheng Fu-Hung, Han Su.

Kung Fu movies, Samurai sagas, Taekwondo epics, Ninja spectaculars and Karate pictures swept through the early 1970s in the aftermath of Bruce Lee's rise to global superstardom and sudden shocking death. The genre became the most prevalent form of action adventure the world over and as virtually twenty martial arts movies premiered every week in the Orient during this golden period, there was no product shortage for opportunistic distributors wanting to make a fast buck exploiting the bloody sword slashing, dirty tricks fighting and fascinating artistry. While Bruce Li, Bruce Le, Tommy Lee and Jackie Chan picked up where Bruce Lee left off, the distaff side rapidly came to the fore in the guise of Angela Mao, Polly Shang Kwan, Cheng Pei Pei, Kara Hui and Shih Szu. The latter Shaw Brothers leading lady might not have had the looks but she certainly had the moves, and found herself the star of this meaninglessly titled lowbrow head-kicker. Here she joins forces with a Sifu to evict his evil brother from the coal-mining town he's running with iron fists. Solid enough in the hand technique/lassoo department, such second rate items proved to be grindhouse lifeblood for a good five years.

THE MISTRESS OF THE MARTIAL ARTS!

THE SINGLE GIRLS

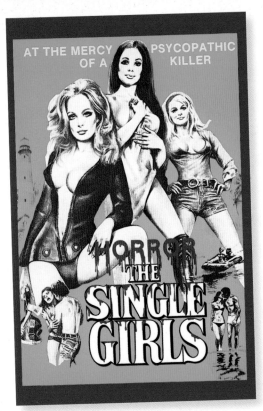

USA, 1973
Director: Ferd Sebastian, Beverly Sebastian. Producer: Ferd Sebastian, Beverly Sebastian. Screenplay: Ann Cawthorne, William Kerwin [uncredited]. Music: Bobby Hart, Danny Janssen. Cinematography: Ferd Sebastian.
Cast: Claudia Jennings, Jean Marie Ingels, Cheri Howell, Joan Prather, Greg Mullavey, Edward Blessington.

From infamous drive-in directors Ferd(inand) and Beverly Sebastian, who unleashed **The Hitchhikers** (1972) and **'Gator Bait** (1973) on an unsuspecting public, comes this sexed-up murder mystery in basic Agatha Christie drag. The usual nymphomaniacs, virgins, frigid housewives, nerds and jocks go to a Caribbean island retreat to find their inner liberated selves at the encounter group sessions run by a doctor well-versed in 1970s psycho-babble. Plenty of topless writhing later, shock horror, the guests start getting brutally killed off by a knife-wielding maniac. After the assassin is unmasked, and the hedonistic orgies dismissed as not the true swinger path to follow after all, marriage becomes the only viable option in this laugh a minute farrago that tries to be both sexually enlightened and demurely reactionary at the same time. The star of the show, as she was in many Sebastian attractions and other noted contemporary B movie fodder (**The Great Texas Dynamite Chase**, 1976, **Deathsport**, 1978), former 1970 'Playboy Playmate of the Year' Claudia Jennings lit up the screen. After paying her acting dues and narrowly missing out on replacing Kate Jackson in the 'Charlie's Angels' TV series, she sadly died in a 1979 car crash, her promise unfulfilled.

TENDER FLESH

USA, 1973
Director: Laurence Harvey. Producer: Jack Cushingham. Screenplay: Wallace C. Bennett, Jack Gross Jr. Music: Tony Camillo. Cinematography: Gerald Perry Finnerman.
Cast: Laurence Harvey, Joanna Pettet, Stuart Whitman, John Ireland, Meg Foster, Gloria LeRoy.

In some respects it was lucky that British movie icon Laurence Harvey died before he saw how badly his last film as director, producer and star was treated. A rather unbecoming swansong for the **Room at the Top** (1959) actor, he played a Korean War hero with a taste for human flesh, the result of having to eat three of his comrades after crashing on a deserted Pacific island. Now living as a reclusive photographer with his sister on Arrow Beach, California, a teenage hitchhiker stumbles on his cannibal secret wandering around his private property. But will the police believe her freezer menu stories? Briefly released by Warner Bros. as **Welcome to Arrow Beach**, the wholesale bad reviews caused them to withdraw and virtually disown it. Then the original production company, Brut, the fragrance people, ruthlessly cut it down – removing many of the endlessly talky dinner table scenes – leaving the grisly meat cleaver sequences to fend for themselves and launched it onto the grindhouse circuit under the exploitative **Tender Flesh** banner with a 'Warning' tag-line that was so in vogue at the time. It failed again and is now just a sad footnote in Harvey's glittering career.

YOU WON'T BELIEVE
WHAT'S BEHIND THE MEAT LOCKER DOOR !

A chilling story of cannibalism in the 20th century.

TENDER FLESH

WARNING:
What you will see when the girl opens the freezer door will be the most terrifying sight of your life! If you have a weak stomach, don't see this movie!

THE UNHOLY CONVENT

Italy/France/West Germany, 1973
Director: Domenico Paolella.
Producer: Tonino Cervi, Luggi Waldleitner [uncredited].
Screenplay: Domenico Paolella, Tonino Cervi.
Music: Piero Piccioni. Cinematography: Armando Nannuzzi.
Cast: Catherine Spaak, Suzy Kendall, Eleonora Giorgi, Martine Brochard,
Ann Odessa, Antonio Falsi.

This American re-titling of the Italian **Storia di una monaca di clausura/Story of a Cloistered Nun** is one of the better sacrilegious shockers in the Nunsploitation bracket and supposedly based on a true story. From the same producer, director and co-writers behind **Le monache di Sant'Arcangelo/The Nun and the Devil** (1973) – Antonio/Tonino Cervi and Domenica Paolella – here rich Carmela Simoni (excellent Eleonora Giorgi, seven years away from her signature role in Dario Argento's **Inferno**) is put into a nunnery after refusing an arranged marriage, preferring her peasant lover Giulio (Antonio Falsi) instead. Continually rebelling and being punished by her Mother Superior (Suzy Kendall, three years on from Argento's classic **The Bird with the Crystal Plumage**) she's befriended by lesbian nun Sister Elizabeth (German pop star Catherine Spaak, two years since Argento's **The Cat O'Nine Tails**) who helps her sneak out for clandestine trysts. But when she doesn't put out on the Sapphic front, and becomes pregnant, the love-crazed nun decides to eliminate her competition. More on the art-house cusp thanks to its bonkers **Spartacus** (1960) aspirations than all-out sleazy Nunsploitation, while the sex is mainly conducted off camera, the humiliation is full-on with naked whipping and enforced nave-to-altar floor licking.

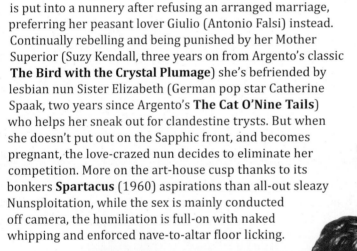

JERRY GROSS Presents "THE UNHOLY CONVENT"
Starring CATHERINE SPAAK · SUZY KENDALL · Directed by DOMENICO PAOLELLA

VICE SQUAD WOMEN

USA, 1973
Director: Al Fields. Producer: Al Fields. Screenplay: Al Fields.
Music: Richard LaSalle. Cinematography: William Foster.
Cast: Sonny Blaze, Robyn Whitting [Jacqueline Giroux],
Uschi Digard, Charla Hall, Jackie English, Richard Fullerton.

From director Al Fields, producer of the nudist
camp/Abominable Snowman horror **The
Beauties and the Beast** (1974), comes this tale
of the corruption running rampant in Any Town
U.S.A. As per the pressbook: "From the office of
the Mayor, to the Vice Cop on the beat, from the
Syndicate Boss to the lowly prostitute, EVERYONE
IS ON THE TAKE! You will see Councilman Thomas,
an 'honest' politician framed and drugged into posing
for lewd photographs, and Police Chief Wingate order
a 'contract' on one of his own men. Bottomless bars
and massage parlors are 'shaken down'. Criminals are
turned loose and the innocent are made guilty!" Phew!
Is this really the promised raw action certain to shock
the hardest viewer? If not there's always tart-with-
the-sensitive-heart Sonny Blaze, "Trapped in a world
of flesh, men's lust, and her own warped desires!" And
Robyn Whitting (who under her real name Jacqueline
Giroux appeared in **Slaughter's Big Rip-Off**, 1973) as the
teen wife of a rookie cop "Hungry for a love she could not
give!" Or Russ Meyer buxom favourite Uschi Digard as the
mistress of a syndicate boss "Who could turn on any man
and any woman (sometimes at the same time!)".

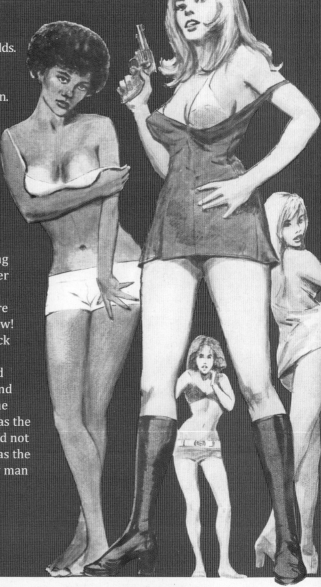

GUARANTEED THE MOST CONTROVERSIAL FILM EVER BASED ON SECRET POLICE REPORTS!

EACH GIRL A VICE SEXPERT

VICE SQUAD WOMEN

...ON THE TAKE, AND ON THE MAKE
...UNTIL THEY TOOK TOO MUCH!

BLACK AGENT LUCKY KING

USA, 1974
Director: Jack Bomay, Sal Watts. Producer: Sal Watts.
Screenplay: Sal Watts. Music: Jimmy Lewis.
Cinematography: Philip Caplan, Chuck Colwell.
Cast: Sal Watts, James Watts, Samaki Bennett, Claudia Russo,
Felice Kinchelow, Tito Fuentes.

Sal Watts hosted a Channel 20 TV talk show out of Oakland,
California. A massive movie fan he, like many of his fans
who called up to complain, loathed the current crop of
Blaxploitation fare and wanted something that truly reflected
African American culture. So he produced, co-scripted,
co-directed (with Jack Bomay), co-edited and starred in
Solomon King (the original title), shot entirely on location
in his hometown and around the Bay area. Former CIA
agent King intervenes in the political struggles of a small,
oil-rich Middle East country with
five commandos at his side, to wreak

vengeance for the assassination of exiled Princess Oneeba who had taken
refuge in his house. But Sal's plan to produce a quality motion picture that
made a major contribution to the Blaxploitation genre came unstuck when he
unveiled it to a sold out black-tie premiere crowd at the Paramount Theatre in
downtown Oakland. Everyone could see what an unexciting action caper it was,
full of insulting stereotypes, and loaded with snail-paced exposition. To cut his
losses Sal retitled it for fast grindhouse play-off but its only claim to lasting fame
remains the cameo from former baseball player Tito Fuentes, a good Sal pal.

BLACK HOOKER

USA, 1974
Director: Arthur Roberson. Producer: Joseph Holsen. Screenplay: Arthur Roberson.
Music: Art Freeman. Cinematography: Joseph Holsen.
Cast: Sandra Alexandra, Jeff Burton, Kathryn Jackson, Durey Mason, Teddy Quinn, Mary Reed.

Proving how desperate the Blaxploitation industry was when the genre seemed to be running out of

steam, look no further than this obscurity put out by multi-tasking Arthur
Roberson. He turned his existentialist play 'Street Sisters' into something so
endemically non-exploitative it couldn't be marketed to anyone, no matter
what demographic was targeted or what title was used, including **Black
Mama** and **Don't Leave Go My Hand**. A black prostitute, The Painted
Lady (none of the characters have names, just ciphers) gets pregnant and
leaves the white male offspring in the care of her parents, a kind old lady
and her stern minister husband (Jeff Burton, best known as the ill-fated
astronaut Dodge in **Planet of the Apes**, 1968). "Please love me Grandpa",
pleads the Young Boy to no avail as the old geezer is convinced nothing
good can come from any bastard born in such sordid circumstances.
Naturally trust issues become paramount to the Young Boy who dreams
of having a normal family but knows he can't settle down until he can talk
to his biological mother. Catatonically slow, clunky dialogue overdoing the
socio-political thrust of the piece and largely plot-free, this bored drive-in
audiences throughout the nation.

WHAT WOULD <u>YOU</u> DO IF YOUR MOTHER WAS A HOOKER?

she was
LOVABLE...

she was
MEAN...

DAMN
MEAN!

COLOR BY C.F.I.

®

BLACK HOOKER

CONFESSIONS OF A YOUNG AMERICAN HOUSEWIFE

USA, 1974
Director: Joe Sarno. Producer: Joe Sarno, Felix F. Voza [Phil Voza],
Tom Brumberger. Screenplay: Joe Sarno. Music: Jack Justis.
Cinematography: Stephen Colwell.
Cast: Rebecca Brooke [Mary Mendum], Jennifer Welles,
Chris Jordan, Eric Edwards, David Hausman, Lana Joyce.

"Your tits drive me out of my mind... I wanna pump my juice inside of you!" Okay, Joe Sarno's dialogue might often be laugh-out-loud lunatic, but with his direction he always managed to bring a certain sleekness and rose-tinted realism to his outrageous storylines, albeit of a melodramatic soap-opera kind. For that's where this celebrated auteur's main talent lay – taking typical Hollywood romantic plots and sexing them up with élan, nudity and taboo subject matters while always hewing to a moralistic denouement. This is one of Sarno's more compelling productions, gathering together for the first time a rep company of actors who would become famous for their Triple X exploits rather than this style of traditional softcore fare. Here, two couples are enjoying swapping relationships when mother pays a visit. There's Carole & Eddie & Anna & Pete, who all enjoy neighbourhood orgies, but when Carole's just widowed mother Jennifer (porn legend Jennifer Welles) arrives the foursome fears a carnal curtailment. But although initially shocked by their casual debauchment and adventurous promiscuity, hot cougar Jennifer soon joins in the fun until long-simmering incestuous tensions spring to the surface and her late-blooming sexual explorations come with a heavy emotional price tag.

DEL FONDO DEL MAR EMERGE
LA VIRGEN MORTAL DEJANDO
UNA ESTELA DE SANGRE Y HORROR

LA VIRGEN MORTAL

Director
NORMAN FOSTER

JOCK GAYNOR, LARRY WARD, DIANE McBAIN

IMPRESO EN MÉXICO POR

THE DEATHHEAD VIRGIN

USA/Philippines, © 1973, first public screening 1974
Director: Norman Foster. Producer: Ben Balatbat, John Garwood. Screenplay: Larry Ward, Jock Gaynor.
Music: Richard LaSalle. Cinematography: Fred Conde.
Cast: Jock Gaynor, Larry Ward, Diane McBain, Vic Diaz, Kim Ramos, Manny Ojeda.

Karate-kicking midgets! Papier-mache monsters! Buxom babes with blades! Filipino genre films of
the 1970s had it all in such filler from Manila as **Mad Doctor of Blood Island** (1968), **The Twilight
People** (1972), **Superbeast** (1972), **Night of the Cobra Woman** (1972), **Beyond Atlantis** (1973),
and the host of Women In Prison pictures cult producer Roger Corman made in those Pacific
islands. Boasting cheap labour, exotic scenery and non-existent health and safety regulations, the
Philippines was a dreamland for exploitation filmmakers whose barely legal productions incredibly
made it to sleaze pits around the globe. One schlock-wave was this poverty-stricken production
from indifferent director Norman Foster – whose credit suddenly flashes up after 15 minutes of the
movie unspooling – helmer of Disney's 'Davy Crockett' movies, the 'Zorro' TV series and the 'Batman'
cult show. It's a snail's-paced snoozer telling the legend of the last virgin princess of the Moro tribe
guarding the fortune in gold and jewels contained in a Spanish galleon sunk in 1850. Her spirit is
aroused when amateur treasure hunters Jock Gaynor and Larry Ward remove an ancient medallion
from around the neck of her submerged skeleton, causing her rebirth as a skull-masked naked
mermaid with a deadly harpoon.

DELINQUENT SCHOOLGIRLS

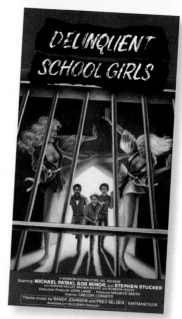

USA, 1974
Director: Gregory Corarito. Producer: Maurice Smith. Screenplay: Gregory
Corarito, John Lamb, Maurice Smith. Music: Randy Johnson, Fred Selden.
Cinematography: Louis Horvath.
Cast: Michael Pataki, Bob Minor, Stephen Stucker, Sharon Kelly, Brenda Miller,
George 'Buck' Flower.

Heard the one about the three mental patients who escape from the loony
bin and end up in a female detention centre? Oh, you have! Well, here's that
hoary story served up once again by trashmeister Gregory Corarito (**The
Sadistic Hypnotist**, 1969, **The Fabulous Bastard from Chicago**, 1969)
in the most inept, eye-opening and hilarious way possible. Exploitation's
pet villain Michael Pataki plays the most demented and incompetent
impressionist in history, soul brother stuntman Bob Minor the ever-horny
baseball-player rapist (his constant catchphrase – "This is the best lookin'
piece I've seen in a long time!") and Stephen Stucker (one of the first
actors to publicly declare his HIV status) the camply unbalanced gay fashion designer. On the run
from the State Asylum for the Criminally Insane, the trio of deviants stumble into the Oxford Corrective
Institute for Young Women, where the more unruly inmates have been refused leave for summer
vacation and are honing their late night karate and sports skills. Can our mad men evade the police and
the sexy campus students cast from the pool of well-known centrefold models in pin-up magazines?
Also known as **Carnal Madness**, this is packed with knock-about slapstick and borderline bad taste,
now that's lowbrow entertainment!

DERANGED

USA, 1974
Director: Jeff Gillen, Alan Ormsby. Producer: Tom Karr. Screenplay:
Alan Ormsby. Music: Carl Zittrer. Cinematography: Jack McGowan.
Cast: Roberts Blossom, Cosette Lee, Les Carlson, Robert Warner,
Marcia Diamond, Brian Sneagle.

A classic exploitation campaign for a classy production from
the creative trio of Bob Clark, Alan Ormsby and Jeff Gillen,
responsible for the apex of Canuxploitation horror, **Black
Christmas** (1974) as well as **Dead of Night** (1972) and **Children Shouldn't Play with Dead Things**
(1972). **Psycho** (1960) and **The Texas Chain Saw Massacre** (1974) were both partially based on the
exploits of real-life Wisconsin serial killer Ed Gein. But until Chuck Parello's **Ed Gein** (2000), this was
the shocker that came closest to the actual facts. The strangely named Roberts Blossom plays Ezra

Cobb, 'The Butcher of Woodside', who mummifies his mother's
body when she dies and then takes home other decomposing
corpses to keep her company before resorting to slaughter and
wearing the flayed skin of his victims. In an early assignment,
future special make-up effects genius Tom Savini created the
mummified corpses Ezra has placed around the family dinner
table. The only misstep taken by this shocker with a blackly
comic edge is the on-screen journalist narrator commenting on
the ramifications of every action. However Blossom is pitch-
perfect as the innocently twisted necrophile, the dread-laden
photography suitably atmospheric, with the snowy locations
imparting further layers of stark chilliness.

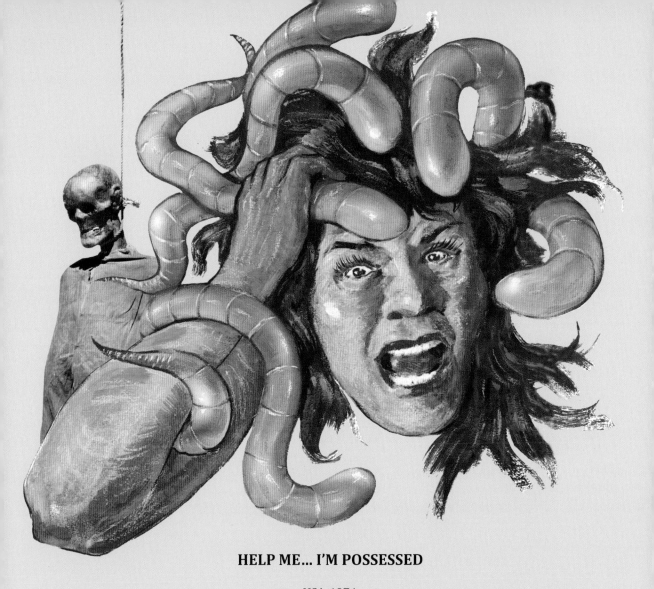

HELP ME... I'M POSSESSED

USA, 1974
Director: Charles Nizet. Producer: Charles Nizet. Screenplay: William Greer [Bill Greer], Deedy Peters.
Cinematography: Charles Nizet.
Cast: Bill Greer, Deedy Peters, Lynne Marta, Jim Dean, Tony Reese, Pierre Agostino.

Nevada-based hackmeister Charles Nizet gave up directing for 14 years after the dismal fate of this hastily thrown together cheapie shot in California's Bronson Canyon in 1974. But as the straight-to-video **Rescue Force** (1990) proved, he hadn't learnt anything during that inactive period. Or to be brutally honest, from his movies prior to the originally titled **The Possessed** (e.g. **Voodoo Heartbeat**, 1972). Dr. Arthur Blackwood (Bill Greer) manages a desert asylum where crazed inmates are kept in a typical exploitation basement with scantily clad women in chains and a hunchback assistant (Pierre Agostino, who as Peter Gold would appear in Enzo G. Castellari directed latter-day schlock). Blackwood's cure-all for madness is extreme torture, but those dying during such radical therapy have their legs chopped off to fit inside the job lot bought coffins. Meanwhile there's a monster running around outside terrorising everyone. Well, perhaps 'monster' is overstating the case, more like some red ribbons waved in front of an electric fan! With nothing depicted on screen to remotely connect it to **The Exorcist** (1973), the reason for its existence, or anything that makes proper sense, after a small drive-in release, this campy head-scratcher disappeared from view – just like Nizet.

THE SHOCKING. THE TERRIFYING. THE UNBELIEVABLE!

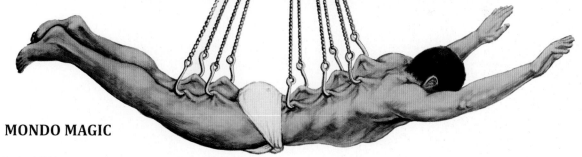

MONDO MAGIC

Italy, 1974
Director: Alfredo Castiglioni, Angelo Castiglioni, Guido Guerrasio. Screenplay: Alberto Moravia.
Cinematography: Alfredo Castiglioni, Angelo Castiglioni.
Cast: Mac Mauro Smith (narrator).

You'd never know it from the distributor hype but **Magia nuda/Naked Magic**, to give this high-class 'Mondo' its original title, is one of the least sensational the genre has produced. Part of a trilogy with **Secret Africa** (1969) and **Africa Ama** (1971) by Alfredo and Angelo Castiglioni, Milanese twins with a background in scientific research and archaeology, this opens with a boat cruising along the River Nile to the opening notes of 'Old Man River' before segueing into Zacar's 'Soleado', more famously known as the Christmas standard 'When a Child Is Born'. With its **Mondo Cane** copycat credentials in order we are treated to unusual tribal rituals practiced by the Dinka and Mundawi in Sudan, the Yanomamo in the Amazon jungle and various Philippine sects. From bathing in cow urine, drinking their blood and eating insects to stoning adulterous males, psychic surgery and circumcision festivals, all **Mondo** bases are covered by the Castiglionis, including the hilarious pogo-style warrior dance filmed in slow-motion to accent flapping sexual organs. Real shock value comes from the brutal animal slaughter shown – a giraffe and elephant sliced up by sharp spears – all in the name of preserving history for anthropological understanding of course.

MONDO MAGIC

MORE SHOCKING THAN "MONDO CANE"

THE MUTATIONS

UK, © 1973, first public screening 1974
Director: Jack Cardiff. Producer: Robert D. Weinbach.
Screenplay: Robert D. Weinbach, Edward Mann.
Music: Basil Kirchin. Cinematography: Paul Beeson.
Cast: Donald Pleasence, Tom Baker, Brad Harris, Julie Ege,
Michael Dunn, Scott Antony.

Jack Cardiff had an amazing career as a revered
cinematographer. From the stunning **Black Narcissus**
(1947) and **The Red Shoes** (1948) for Michael Powell
and Emeric Pressburger through Hitchcock (**Under
Capricorn**, 1949), Marilyn Monroe (**The Prince
and the Showgirl**, 1957) and Sylvester Stallone
(**Rambo: First Blood Part II**, 1985), his work was
extraordinary. Not so much when he turned director
for the Smell-O-Vision classic **Scent of Mystery** (1960), the Bond knockoff **The Liquidator** (1965)
and the Marianne Faithful pop-fart **The Girl on a Motorcycle** (1968). His final directing credit was for
this attempt to claw horror from the **Freaks** (1932) gene pool once more with crazy doctor Donald

Pleasence's theory that animal and plant life will eventually
combine to form a new species able to withstand climate and
environmental changes. Obviously he's experimenting to prove
this, aided by soon-to-be BBC TV 'Doctor Who' Tom Baker, the
deformed owner of a carnival freakshow hoping to be cured
of his ugliness. Baker's mutation was prosthetic whereas the
defects of Willie 'Popeye' Ingram, Esther 'Alligator Girl' Black,
Hugh 'Pretzel Boy' Baily and Felix 'Frog Boy' Duarte weren't.
Best scene? Sexpot Julie Ege menaced by her boyfriend turned
into a giant walking Venus Fly Trap.

NO RIG WAS TOO BIG FOR THEM TO HANDLE!

Double-clutchin'... gear-jammin' mamas who like a lot of hi-jackin' by day... a lot of heavy truckin' by night!

DİŞİ SOYGUNCULAR

CLAUDIA JENNINGS · LIEUX DRESSLER · DENNIS FIMPLE
JENNIFER BURTON · GENE DREW · PAUL CARR
Renkli Türkçe

TRUCK STOP WOMEN

USA, 1974
Director: Mark L. Lester. Producer: Mark L. Lester. Screenplay: Mark L. Lester, Paul Deason.
Music: Big Mack & The Truckstoppers. Cinematography: John Arthur Morrill.
Cast: Claudia Jennings, Lieux Dressler, Paul Carr, John Martino, Dennis Fimple, Gene Drew.

Mark L. Lester directed this exploitation masterpiece that won plaudits from critics and audiences around the world for treating sex, violence and sensationalism with self-aware love and affection. It put Lester on the commercial map and led to such eclectic entertainments as **Roller Boogie** (1979) with Linda Blair, **Class of 1984** (1982) with Michael J. Fox, Stephen King's **Firestarter** (1984) with Drew Barrymore, and **Commando** (1985) with Arnold Schwarzenegger. Having amassed credits on more than seventeen films, Lester founded and became President of American World Pictures in 1993, devoting himself to producing, directing and distributing films in the same genres he helped to popularize, like **Pterodactyl** (2005). This lip-smacking, violent, sleazy and high-camp affair is centred on a bloody turf war between mob hitman Smith (John Martino, **The Godfather**, 1972) and independent gun moll Anna (Lieux Dressler) over her prostitution and theft operation, HQ'd in a highway truck stop. Buxom daughter Rose (legendary Claudia Jennings in spitfire bimbo form) helps Anna run the best little whorehouse in New Mexico until Smith makes her an offer she can't refuse. Complete with a sub-Johnny Cash soundtrack and energetically eccentric performances, this manic pulp fiction represents one of Lester's finest hours.

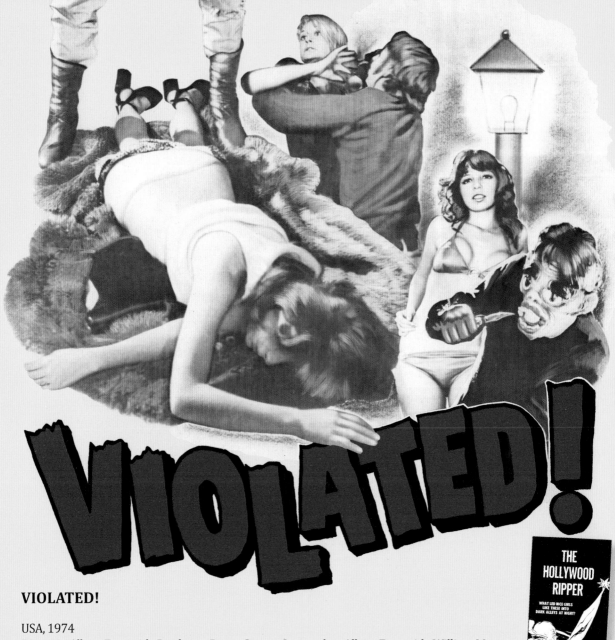

VIOLATED!

USA, 1974
Director: Albert Zugsmith. Producer: Roger Gentry. Screenplay: Albert Zugsmith, William Maron.
Cast: Rene Bond, Sandy Dempsey, Ric Lutze, Britt Mari, Susanne Suzan, Alta Christopher.

Famous for his classics of American cinema – Orson Welles's **Touch of Evil** (1958), Douglas
Sirk's **Written on the Wind** (1956), Jack Arnold's **The Incredible Shrinking Man** (1957)
– and his low-budget exploitation specialities such as **High School Confidential!** (1958),
Sex Kittens Go to College (1960) and **Confessions of an Opium Eater** (1962), producer and
screenwriter Albert Zugsmith ended his directing career with this tawdry rape revenge saga, also known
as **The Rapist** and re-released as **The Hollywood Ripper**. Scripter William Maron allegedly combed
through the police files of seventeen sadistic rapists in order to compose a true-to-life portrait of those
who carry out the heinous crime and the victims who suffer because of it. Hollywood is under siege by a
masked maniac terrorizing the city by raping and cutting swastika symbols into the flesh of young girls
before dumping their bruised and battered bodies unceremoniously into the gutters. The police have been
unable to catch this mad genius because his methods of entrapment are so varied and resourceful, so two
of his victims join forces to apprehend him instead. They set their psychological ambush, he bites, and
before long the fiendish monster is tied to a home made electric chair and blow-torched into confession.

THE ZEBRA KILLER

USA, 1974
Director: William Girdler. Producer: Gordon Cornell Layne, Mike Henry. Screenplay: William Girdler.
Music: Jerry Styner. Cinematography: William L. Asman.
Cast: Juanita Moore, Austin Stoker, Hugh Smith, James Pickett, Charles Kissinger, Valerie Rogers.

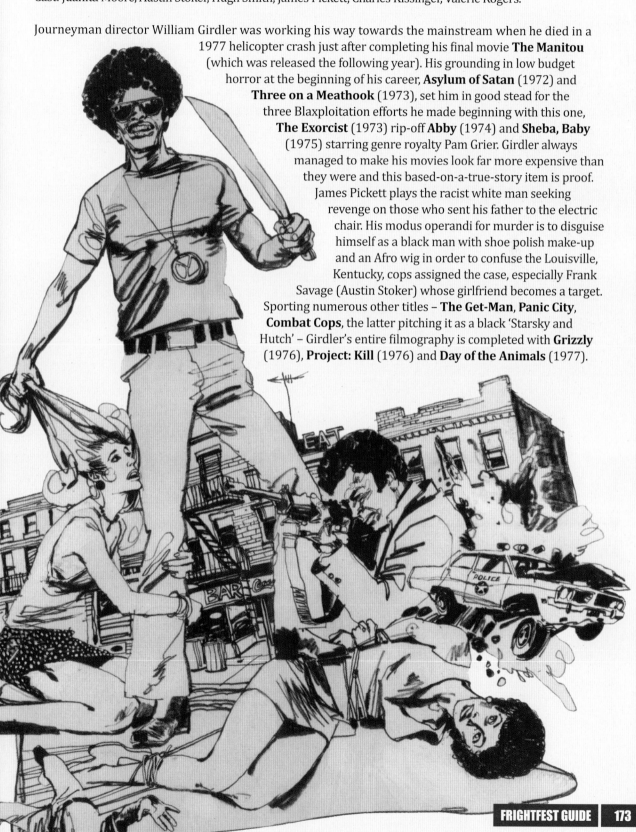

Journeyman director William Girdler was working his way towards the mainstream when he died in a 1977 helicopter crash just after completing his final movie **The Manitou** (which was released the following year). His grounding in low budget horror at the beginning of his career, **Asylum of Satan** (1972) and **Three on a Meathook** (1973), set him in good stead for the three Blaxploitation efforts he made beginning with this one, **The Exorcist** (1973) rip-off **Abby** (1974) and **Sheba, Baby** (1975) starring genre royalty Pam Grier. Girdler always managed to make his movies look far more expensive than they were and this based-on-a-true-story item is proof. James Pickett plays the racist white man seeking revenge on those who sent his father to the electric chair. His modus operandi for murder is to disguise himself as a black man with shoe polish make-up and an Afro wig in order to confuse the Louisville, Kentucky, cops assigned the case, especially Frank Savage (Austin Stoker) whose girlfriend becomes a target. Sporting numerous other titles – **The Get-Man**, **Panic City**, **Combat Cops**, the latter pitching it as a black 'Starsky and Hutch' – Girdler's entire filmography is completed with **Grizzly** (1976), **Project: Kill** (1976) and **Day of the Animals** (1977).

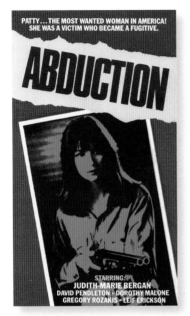

ABDUCTION

USA, 1975
Director: Joseph Zito. Producer: Kent E. Carroll. Screenplay: Kent E. Carroll.
Music: Ronald Frangipane, Al Steckler. Cinematography: João Fernandes.
Cast: Judith-Marie Bergan, David Pendleton, Gregory Rozakis, Leif Erickson,
Dorothy Malone, Lawrence Tierney.

Before giving the exploitation world two superior slashers, **The Prowler** (1981) and **Friday the 13th: The Final Chapter** (1984), and two hard man Chuck Norris vehicles, **Missing In Action** (1984) and **Invasion U.S.A.** (1985), one time distributor-turned-director Joseph Zito made his feature debut with this definitive grindhouse edition of the headline-grabbing Patty Hearst kidnapping. Despite the filmmakers' disclaimer in the titles, and the fact it was based on Harrison James's semi-porno novel 'Black Abductors', written before socialite Hearst's abduction by a revolutionary cell, it is obviously based completely on the tabloid frenzy event. The facts: newspaper heiress Hearst joined the Symbionese Liberation Army after they kidnapped

her and, in the classic case of Stockholm Syndrome, identified with her captors so much she helped them rob a bank. Imprisoned for two years, she was eventually pardoned and began to make guest appearances in John Waters movies from **Cry-Baby** (1990) onwards. The film sticks close to the facts but warps them slightly in order not to incur libel lawsuits. So Patricia here comes from moneyed landlord stock, and her father likes nothing more than to rewind footage of his daughter being raped. Strong stuff for the time, yet completely inept and determinedly squalid.

ILSA, SHE-WOLF OF THE SS

Canada, © 1974, first public screening 1975
Director: Don Edmonds. Producer: Herman Traeger [David F. Friedman].
Screenplay: Jonah Royston [John Saxton]. Cinematography: Glen Rowland [Glenn Roland].
Cast: Dyanne Thorne, Sandy Richman, Jo Jo Deville, Gregory Knoph, Wolfgang Roehm [Richard Kennedy].

"Who's that woman with Hitler?" screamed one of the best teaser campaigns for the most notorious Nazisploitation classic of all time, directed by one of the most extraordinary showbiz legends ever. Don Edmonds began his Hollywood career acting in TV sit-com fluff like 'Green Acres' (1965) and 'Gidget' (1965) before directing the softcore features **Wild Honey** (1972) and **Tender Loving Care** (1973). As vice president of the Producers Sales Organization, alongside Roger Corman's Poe series actor Mark Damon, Edmonds was responsible for getting movies like **Short Circuit** (1986) and **The Clan of the Cave Bear** (1986) produced and helped give Quentin Tarantino's career a leg up. But he is most revered by exploitation fans for this hilariously offensive slab of concentrated camp starring statuesque Dyanne Thorne, who turned her S&M loving anti-heroine into an autograph-signing convention career. As warden of a Nazi medical camp, Ilsa prepares prisoners for Gestapo brothels and experiments on her female inmates to see if they can withstand more pain than men. At night she forces the male prisoners to satisfy her kinky lust and then kills them when they can't fulfil her needs. Her downfall comes when she falls for a studly US POW.

THE MOST DREADED NAZI OF THEM ALL!

She committed crimes so terrible ... even the SS feared her!

ILSA

She wolf of the SS

starring
DYANNE THORNE as ILSA
with SANDI RICHMAN · JO JO DEVILLE · USCHI DIGARD
Directed by DON EDMONDS   Produced by HERMAN TRAEGER
An AETAS FILM PRODUCTION · Color

KISS OF THE TARANTULA

USA, 1975
Director: Chris Munger. Producer: Daniel Cady. Screenplay: Warren Hamilton Jr.,
Daniel Cady. Music: Phillan Bishop. Cinematography: Henning Schellerup.
Cast: Eric Mason, Suzanne Ling, Herman Wallner, Patricia Landon, Beverly Eddins,
Jay Scott Neal.

Very much in the **Willard** (1971) tradition – tormented teen unleashes deadly
pets onto her enemies – director Chris Munger's cheap chiller sported two poster
designs. One had bigger spiders depicted for the hardcore horror crowd, the
other smaller ones so as not to turn off those suffering arachnophobia altogether. Those in the latter
category will still wince and cover their eyes at the creatures creeping through the mortuary owned by
Susan's (Suzanne Ling) parents. Killing her mean mother after learning she's having an affair with her
Uncle Walter by placing a tarantula by her bed
to cause a heart attack, Walter's turn comes
when he falls down a flight of stairs and
is buried alive under a classmate's
corpse. Always great fun in these
kinds of movies is seeing how none
of the spiders get squashed for
real despite being put in cars and
heating ducts with actors carefully
flailing around because they are
expensive hires from the animal
wrangler! Producer Daniel Cady,
who also co-wrote the project,
was the partner of John Hayes,
director of the emblematic
Grave of the Vampire
(1972) and **Garden of the
Dead** (1972). **Shudder** was
the title when released
outside of America.

She had POWER with her
LIPS and her pet SPIDERS!

RACE WITH THE DEVIL

USA, 1975
Director: Jack Starrett. Producer: Wes Bishop. Screenplay: Lee Frost,
Wes Bishop. Music: Leonard Rosenman. Cinematography: Robert C. Jessup.
Cast: Peter Fonda, Warren Oates, Loretta Swit, Lara Parker, R.G. Armstrong,
Clay Tanner.

Exploitation veteran Lee Frost's loss was Jack Starrett's gain
when the actor seen in lots of Hells Angels movies took over the
directing reins from the **Love Camp 7** (1969) helmer. 20th Century
Fox head Alan Ladd Jr. hated the dailies Frost was delivering so
moved Starrett into pole position based on the decent reviews
he received for the obscure thriller **The Strange Vengeance of
Rosalie** (1972). It was the best shift Ladd could have possibly
made because Starrett's gift for low-budget magic shone through
this terrific merging of the chase and chiller genres, turning it into
quite a sizeable hit. Peter Fonda, Warren Oates, Loretta Swit and
Lara Parker (Starrett's ex) are the married friends on a road trip
vacation to Aspen, Colorado, when they witness a ritual killing by
a devil-worshipping cult. The police aren't interested and after a
couple of nasty incidents – their dog is butchered, a rattlesnake
is put in their RV – they are forced to take on the Satanists or die.
Although he later admitted he only starred in the movie because
he was guaranteed a percentage of the profits, counterculture
favourite Fonda is super in this horror hybrid that used real
Satanists as extras.

From The Director of "Coffy" and "Foxy Brown"

SO EASY TO KILL.
SO HARD TO LOVE.

JACK HILL'S

SWITCHBLADE SISTERS

ROLLING THUNDER PICTURES and JOHNNY LEGEND present
Robbie Lee   Joanne Nail   "SWITCHBLADE SISTERS"
Asher Brauner   Kitty Bruce   Janice Karman   Marlene Clark   and Monica Gayle as "Patch"
music by Medusa   costume design by Jodie Tillen
production design by Robinson Royce and B.B. Neel   edited by Mort Tubor
director of photography Stephen Katz   executive producers Frank Moreno and Jeff Begun
screenplay by F.X. Maier   produced by John Prizer   directed by Jack Hill

MIRAMAX
FILMS

RESTRICTED
UNDER 17 REQUIRES ACCOMPANYING
PARENT OR ADULT GUARDIAN

Visit THE MIRAMAX CAFE on the web at: http//www.miramax.com

ROLLING THUNDER
PICTURES

THE SWITCHBLADE SISTERS

USA, 1975
Director: Jack Hill. Producer: John Prizer. Screenplay: F.X. Maier.
Music: Les Baxter. Cinematography: Stephen M. Katz.
Cast: Robbie Lee, Joanne Nail, Monica Gayle, Asher Brauner,
Kitty Bruce, Marlene Clark.

Jack (**Spider Baby**, 1967) Hill's girl gang cartoon is a high-
energy exercise in self-aware trash. Something chic cinephile
supremo Quentin Tarantino recognised when he championed
its comeback as part of his Rolling Thunder distribution deal
with Miramax. Emblematic of Hill's erratic kitsch aesthetic,
it begins with a shot of two back alley trash cans – it's later
learned via tabloid headlines the entire flick takes place
during a "12 week garbage strike" – the formula story
involves gang wars and in-fighting between the Dagger Debs
(renamed The Jezebels mid-way through the action, Hill's
original title). A rival gang leader wants them dead, there's
a traitor in their midst and a couple of pigs are desperate
to bust them as Lace (Robbie Lee) and Maggie (Joanne
Nail) fight over head Silver Dagger (Asher Brauner), who has made one pregnant and raped the other.
Leaders of the Pack, kinky boots, roller derby, bell-bottoms, groovy slang, Afros, cat-fights, Maoist
slogans, shoot-outs and a 'Right On' feminist message. It's all present and correct in this kinetic and
colourful turf war combo of **All About Eve** (1950) and Shakespeare's 'Othello'. Co-starring Kitty Bruce
(daughter of icon comedian Lenny), who pig squeals in fine **Deliverance** (1972) fashion.

TEENAGE SEX KITTEN

USA, 1975
Director: S.B. [Ann Perry]. Producer: S.B. [Ann Perry].
Cast: Lilly Lovetree [Rene Bond], Threda Bara [Eve Orlon], Doug
Fartbank [Gary Schneider], Max Init, Long Hangey [Walt Davis],
Robert E. Pearson.

Beginning with an emotive speech on screen censorship,
from porn star Rene Bond no less, and ending with sudden
and violent castration, this hardcore opus hewed close
to what was becoming the contemporary norm for the
burgeoning adult film industry. Sexy women, studly men,
social relevance and shock horror as templated by Gerard
Damiano's game-changer **Memories Within Miss Aggie**
(1974). Directed by Ann Perry who, under a variety of noms-
de-plume (Ann Meyers, Stella Cather), acted in a multitude
of sexploiters from **House on Bare Mountain** (1964) to
Deadly Alliance (1982), this begins as it means to go on
with the first explicit sex act taking place under the opening
credits. Penniless, but not penis-less, Rene and Eve Orlon
(making the star grade from the usual uncredited party guest role under the name Threda Bara) head
to Palm Springs for the weekend with their boyfriends. First Rene seduces The Harlow Haven motel
manager and then blackmails him into giving them free rooms claiming she's under-age. Then they head
to a disco, where the pantie-less Rene gets thrown out for being a hooker, and the nightclub manager is
manoeuvred into position for the bloody and completely left field twist ending.

When he's mad...
he's mean...
he's a
killing machine!

BLACK SHAMPOO

USA, 1976

Director: Greydon Clark. Producer: Alvin L. Fast. Screenplay: Alvin L. Fast, Greydon Clark. Music: Gerald Lee.
Cinematography: Dean Cundey, Michael J. Mileham.
Cast: John Daniels, Tanya Boyd, Joe Ortiz [Joseph Carlo], Skip E. Lowe, Gary Allen, Jack Mehoff [William Bonner].

If Greydon Clark's Blaxploitation sleaze-fest is infamous for anything, it's the moment when camp character Artie (Skip Lowe) is bent over by homophobic thugs and sodomised with a hot curling iron. Even the chainsaw-wielding, hatchet throwing and pool cue-jabbing bloody climax doesn't overshadow that significant genre landmark. Inspired by Warren Beatty's **Shampoo** (1975), afroed superstud hairdresser John Daniels (looking like a black Lou Ferrigno) makes his trendy Mr. Jonathan salon extra popular by blow-drying more than his female customers' hair. But his girlfriend's possessive mobster ex-boyfriend wants her back so he arranges to have Mr. Jonathan's establishment trashed and his gay employees beaten up and tortured. Skilled fighter Daniels moves in for a gangster battle royal in a funky, vulgar, jive-talkin' fan favourite. Clark dabbled in every exploitation genre from horror (**Satan's Cheerleaders**, 1977) and science fiction (**Without Warning**, 1980) to sex comedy (**Joysticks**, 1983) and dance craziness (**Lambada: The Forbidden Dance**, 1990); his previous Blaxploitation foray, **The Bad Bunch/Tom** (1973), was released to drive-ins as **Nigger Lover**, so he was no stranger to adverse critical comment. Future star cinematographer Dean Cundey (**The Thing**, 1982) got his first break here when the original cameraman had an accident a day before shooting.

THE BLACK STREET FIGHTER

USA, 1976
Director: Timothy Galfas, Richard Kaye. Producer: William Larrabure, Richard Kaye. Screenplay: Tim Kelly. Music: Ron Carson. Cinematography: William Larrabure.
Cast: Richard Lawson, Philip Michael Thomas, Annazette Chase, Dabney Coleman, Robert Burr, Nicholas Worth.

Constant fade-ins and outs, and future 'Miami Vice' style icon Philip Michael Thomas playing two roles – a black mob informant and a Puerto Rican hustler – are clues that **The Black Street Fighter/ Black Fist/Homeboy** is actually a combination of two films spliced together. In 1974, Timothy Galfas ('Revenge for a Rape' TV movie, 1976) directed **Bogard**, originally rated X for edgy sexual content. But that wasn't Blaxploitation's mission statement and when it was further revealed the producer had financed it by very dodgy means anyway, another producer, Richard Kaye, exercised damage limitation by incorporating footage shot for **Get Fisk**. So the cobbled together plot has genre regular Richard Lawson (**Scream Blacula Scream**, 1973, **Fox Style**, 1973, **Sugar Hill**, 1974) becoming a bare knuckle fighter for white gangsters to support his pregnant wife. Soon his flashy lifestyle starts attracting attention and crooked cop Dabney Coleman wants a percentage of his earnings or it's jail time. But when a little black book containing all the syndicate's shady dealings comes to light, and his wife gets murdered in a car bomb attack, Lawson goes on a revenge rampage. Lawson's best line: "I'm going to rearrange your plumbing so you piss out your mouth!"

BROTHERHOOD OF DEATH

USA, 1976
Director: Bill Berry. Producer: Richard Barker, Bill Berry. Music: John Lewis. Cinematography: Fritz Roland.
Cast: Roy Jefferson, Le Tari, Haskell Anderson, Mike Thomas, Michael Hodge, Ron David.

Way down the list of must-see Blaxploitation comes this drossy Black Man vs. While Klan amateur affair that poorly hangs together. Brothers Junior and Raymond and their best friend Ned (Le Tari, Haskell Anderson and real life Washington Redskins American Football player Roy Jefferson) join the army after living in a broken down bus in Hicksville and being bad-mouthed by the racist white trash locals. A grainy spool of scene-setting Vietnam War stock footage later, the three bros in badly-fitting soldier gear are doing their tour of duty in obvious Maryland scrublands, smoking some spliff, dodging some guerrilla bullets and saving each other's asses. Back in the good ole USA, the Ku Klux Klan have taken over

their hometown, and after the rape of a young black girl goes unpunished, their only white friend gets murdered and their efforts to register to vote are thwarted by white supremacists (a very drawn out sequence indeed), they hit the streets to take long-festering revenge. How they do that does show some creative initiative on the part of director Bill Berry. They dress in stolen KKK robes to sneak up on their enemy and then make them wear blackface masks to confuse their opponents.

FEMALE CHAUVINISTS

USA, 1976
Director: Jay Jackson [Jourdan Alexander]. Producer: Jay Jackson [Jourdan Alexander]. Screenplay: Jack Holtzman. Cinematography: Fred Goodich.
Cast: Roxanne Brewer, Rick Dillon, Uschi Digard, Nora Field [Nora Holliday], Deborah McGuire, Sue Kaftal, Candy Samples.

After appearing in **Dr. Dildo's Secret** (1970), **Sexual Kung Fu in Hong Kong** (1974) and **Deep Jaws** (1976), buxom Roxanne Brewer finally made the grade to headline star in this erratic satire on the women's liberation movement. She plays Boopsie, sent undercover by her photographer boyfriend to infiltrate an education boot camp run by militant lesbian feminists. When Boopsie reports back how the Sapphic sect break down new recruits using sex toys and anti-male scare tactics, he decides to pose as a mute gardener to see for himself. Obviously, one gaze of his stud-muffin self will turn even the most hardened diesel dyke straight. And indeed he ends up being gang-raped by the busty mob, which includes such top heavyweights as Russ Meyer stars Uschi Digard (**Beneath the Valley of the Ultra-Vixens**, 1979), Deborah McGuire (**Supervixens**, 1975), an ex-wife of comedian Richard Pryor, and porn queen Candy Samples (**Up!**, 1976). With plenty of topless action – Brewer rides a horse chasing her lover for maximum jiggle value – and a few laughs between the bad acting and poverty row direction by sexploitation veteran Jourdan Alexander/Jaacov Jaacovi/Jay Jackson, the 'script' came courtesy of Jack Holtzman, writer of **A Fistful of 44s** (1971).

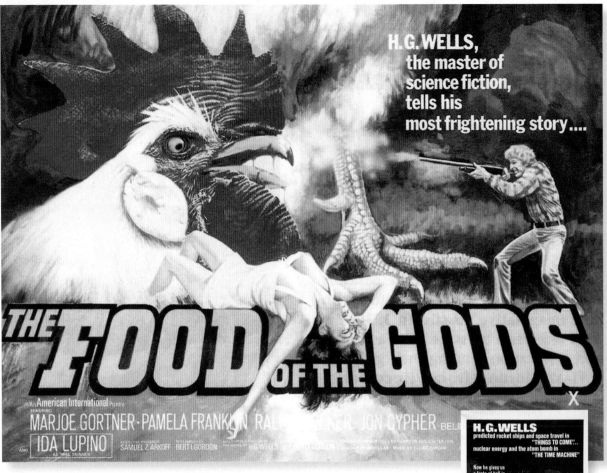

H.G. WELLS, the master of science fiction, tells his most frightening story....

THE FOOD OF THE GODS

H.G. WELLS predicted rocket ships and space travel in "THINGS TO COME".. nuclear energy and the atom bomb in "THE TIME MACHINE"

Now he gives us a taste of hell in the terrifying prediction of an ecology gone berserk!

THE FOOD OF THE GODS

USA, 1976
Director: Bert I. Gordon. Producer: Bert I. Gordon. Screenplay: Bert I. Gordon. Music: Elliot Kaplan. Cinematography: Reginald H. Morris.
Cast: Marjoe Gortner, Pamela Franklin, Ralph Meeker, Ida Lupino, Jon Cypher, Belinda Balaski.

The highest-grossing movie of the year for the American International Pictures B movie powerhouse saw the return of the infamous Bert I. Gordon (affectionately called Mr BIG) to the exploitation table. Up to his old crappy enlargement special effects tricks that saw him stagger through such variable items as **The Amazing Colossal Man** (1957), **Attack of the Puppet People** (1958), **The Spider** (1958) and **Village of the Giants** (1965), here those dodgy techniques liven up a madly hilarious adaptation of a portion of the 1904 H.G. Wells novel 'The Food of the Gods and How It Came to Earth'. The 'Ecology Strikes Back' genre was very much in vogue when Gordon put his competent cast, led by football player Marjoe Gortner and old-timers Ida Lupino and Ralph Meeker, in harm's way hunting enormous wasps, extra-large chickens, huge worms and overgrown rats. Bad superimposition, obvious matte lines, transparent cinematography and clumsy split screen only add to the fun as Gordon's 'trendy' script shows his age. Seventies Scream Queen Pamela Franklin (**And Soon the Darkness,** 1970, **Necromancy**, 1972, **The Legend of Hell House**, 1973), to Gortner: "I shouldn't talk to you when you're doing your thing", "What's my thing?", "Facing danger!"

THE RAPE KILLER

Greece, 1976
Director: Dacosta Carayan [Kostas Karagiannis]. Screenplay: Thanos Leivaditis. Music: Yannis Spanos. Cinematography: Vasilis Vasileiadis.
Cast: Larry Daniels [Lakis Komninos], Dorothy Moore, Vagelis Seilinos, Dimitris Bislanis, Fragoulis Fragoulis, Jane Paterson.

In the same year prolific Greek director Kostas Karagiannis helmed the Satanic cult horror **The Devil's Men**/**Land of the Minotaur** under the alias Costa Carayiannis, he also made this tawdry psycho thriller as Dacosta Carayan. Originally titled **He Murdered His Wife**, then **Death Kiss** before Euro-sleaze exporters Joseph Brenner Associates (**Virgin Witch**, 1972, **Torso**, 1973, **Eyeball**, 1975) settled on this ultra-provocative label, it's a standard 'Where there's a will, there's a kill!' drama given a splashy twist with enough sex and violence to keep it interesting. Handsome oilrig worker Dimitris/Jim Preston (Greek actor Lakis Komninos as Larry Daniels) marries the rich, older Eleni/Helen (Dorothy Moore) and strikes up a deal with sadistic psycho Mike (Angelo Cilento/Vagelis Seilinos giving a truly slimy performance) to murder her so he can inherit and divvy up her fortune between them. To make sure this rape murder goes to plan, the drug-addicted sex maniac carries out a rehearsal kill with a lookalike victim (also played by Moore). But then Mike decides he likes torturing Helen too much and substitutes the lookalike's corpse for her body in order to keep her prisoner as an insurance policy Jim will pay up. All this and Zorba dancing too!

YOU WILL NEVER SEE THIS ON TV

He forced his victims to submit to abnormal sexual behavior!

TRAUMA

UK, © 1975, first public screening 1976
Director: James Kenelm Clarke. Producer: Brian Smedley-Aston. Screenplay: James Kenelm Clarke. Music: Steve Gray. Cinematography: Denis C. Lewiston, Phil Meheux [uncredited].
Cast: Udo Kier, Linda Hayden, Fiona Richmond, Patsy Smart, Karl Howman, Vic Armstrong.

A grief-crazed widow seeks revenge on the best-selling novelist who plagiarised her husband's work and drove him to commit suicide in this re-titling of the controversial British shocker **Exposé**. The problem with this James Kenelm Clarke directed opus, produced by Brian Smedley-Aston of **Vampyres** (1974) renown, was it never gelled into a consistent whole. On one hand you had a gory psycho thriller complete with shootings, mutilation and shower stabbings, on the other a softcore sex melodrama highlighting rape, masturbation and lipstick lesbianism. No one could ever work out the right audience for it as the original title **The House on Straw Hill** proved. The casting was equally off-centre; sex-kitten Linda Hayden had hit the headlines in the nymphet saga **Baby Love** (1968) but was a popular horror regular in such fear fare as **Taste the Blood of Dracula** (1970). Eurotrash favourite Udo Kier bounced between the **Andy Warhol's Dracula** (1973) and **The Story of O** (1975) extremes too. Only glamour model Fiona Richmond commandeered the sex niche – **Not Tonight Darling** (1971). But even her gratuitous nude slashing failed to pull in the punters, yet it was the still photo that was used in most of the PR material.

ANOTHER SON OF SAM

USA, 1977
Director: Dave Adams. Producer: Dave Adams. Screenplay: Dave Adams. Cinematography: Harry M. Joyner.
Cast: Bonnie Schrier, Bob McCourt, Russ Dubuc, Cynthia Stewart, Garland Atkins, Larry Sprinkle.

With the 'Son of Sam' hogging all the headlines in August 1977, when David Berkowitz was arrested for a series of summer 1976 shooting attacks, it's hardly surprising stunt-man Dave Adams decided to retitle his bland solo directing effort **Hostages** to cash in. One of the best examples of no-budget regional cinema (it was lensed in Charlotte and Belmont, North Carolina) and showing clear signs of hurriedly being adapted to piggy-back on a media sensation, this starts with a roll call crawl of real serial killers and mass murderers from East End butcher Jack the Ripper to nurse-slayer Richard Speck. Then the snail-paced police procedural story begins with Lieutenant Setzner (Russ Dubuc, a local TV weatherman) and his psychiatrist girlfriend Dr. Daisy Ellis (Cynthia Stewart) endlessly waterskiing. Returning to work after their mini-break, Setzner goes back to cop desk-jockeying while Daisy gives shock treatment to mental patient Harvey, who breaks free of his restraints and goes on the psycho rampage. A SWAT team is called in as we learn Harvey was sexually abused by his mother and has no intention of being taken alive. Further torture is provided by the on screen Johnny Charro musical number 'I Never Said Goodbye'.

GESTAPO'S LAST ORGY

Italy, 1977
Director: Cesare Canevari. Producer: Cesare Canevari.
Screenplay: Antonio Lucarella, Cesare Canevari. Music:
Alberto Baldan Bembo. Cinematography: Claudio Catozzo.
Cast: Marc Loud [Adriano Micantoni], Daniela Levy
[Daniella Poggi], Maristella Greco, Fulvio Ricciardi,
Antineska Nemour, Caterina Barbero.

Did Liliana Cavani ever expect her nihilistic art-house
hit **The Night Porter** (1974) to spawn a new Italian
exploitation genre? Doubtful, but Cesare Canevari's
L'ultima orgia del III Reich is one of the better
examples, mainly because it copies its basic framing
device – a concentration camp commandant and his
Jewish lover meeting five years after the war has ended
– before developing it into the more reprehensible end
of the gory torture and S&M erotica market. Sadistic
Conrad von Starker (Spaghetti Western mainstay Adriano Micantoni) is
cleared of war crimes thanks to a very sympathetic testimony by one of his
love slaves, Lise Cohen (Daniela Poggi in her first starring role). But it's all
a ruse on her part to invite him back to the scene of his bloody misdeeds
to apparently "refuel old passions" and exact a nasty revenge on her hated
Gestapo master. Flashbacks to skull-crushing, gourmet flesh-eating and acid
baths are the crux of the narrative, with the promised title orgy more a **Salon
Kitty** (1976) clone. Shot under the working title **Caligula Reincarnated
As Hitler**, Canevari helmed
the very first Emmanuelle
film, **Io, Emmanuelle**
(1969) starring Erika
Blanc, glimpsed in **The
Bird with the Crystal
Plumage** (1970).

MIRACLE FILMS present

CANNIBAL x

THE LAST SURVIVOR

Italy, 1977
Director: Ruggero Deodato.
Producer: Giorgio Carlo Rossi.
Screenplay: Tito Carpi, Gianfranco Clerici,
Renzo Genta. Music: Ubaldo Continiello.
Cinematography: Marcello Masciocchi.
Cast: Massimo Foschi, Me Me Lai, Ivan Rassimov, Sheik
Razak Shikur, Judy Rosly, Suleiman, Shamsi.

The dress rehearsal for his gut-wrenching **Cannibal Holocaust**
(1980), Ruggero Deodato got this directing gig after Umberto Lenzi,
the man who started the whole Italian cannibal cycle with **Deep River
Savages** (1972), passed on the similar project. Noted stage actor Massimo
Foschi gives a raw and startling full-frontal performance as an oil prospector
caged by a primitive tribe. Native woman Me Me Lai (wearing way too much eyeliner) takes pity and joins him when he escapes his captors' cave dwellings. But he soon
learns he must resort to the savage laws of the jungle himself if he is to survive. Released
in Italy as **Ultimo mondo cannibale**, in the UK as just **Cannibal**, former Roberto Rossellini
assistant Deodato piles on the violent sex, gruesome gore and animal cruelty. Two stand-out scenes:
Foschi stripped, humiliated, strung up in a harness and repeatedly dropped to see if he can fly like the
plane he arrived in, and Lai beheaded, sliced open, gutted, hot coals put inside her chest cavity and
her cooked flesh eaten. Sold in surprisingly muted fashion considering how Lenzi's eventual riposte
Cannibal Ferox (1981) was advertised with huge hoardings on 42nd Street as **Make Them Die Slowly**.

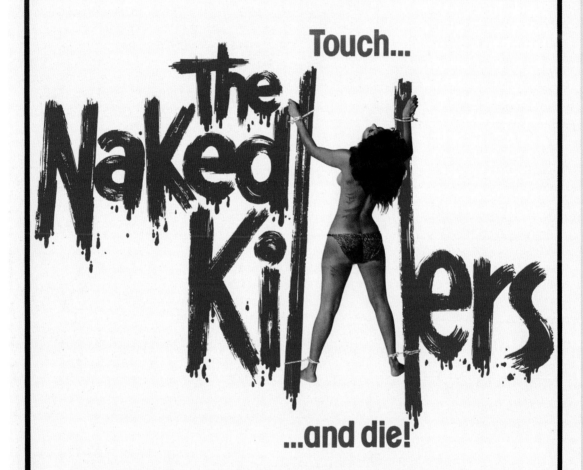

EVERY MAN WHO TOUCHED THEM DIED IN AN ORGY OF BLOOD!

Touch...

The Naked Killers

...and die!

Starring Sita Sadafi · Roxana Dipre · Inca Maria as 'THE NAKED KILLERS'
Directed by M.I. Bonns   ·   Filmed in Widescreen & NakedColor
Released by AMS Films, A DIVISION OF A MAJOR STUDIO, INC.

R	RESTRICTED
	UNDER 17 REQUIRES ACCOMPANYING PARENT OR ADULT GUARDIAN

Copyright © MCMLXXIX · A Major Studio Inc.

THE NAKED KILLERS

Spain, 1977
Director: M.I. Bonns [Miguel Iglesias]. Screenplay: Miguel Cussó, M.I. Bonns [Miguel Iglesias].
Cinematography: Julio Pérez de Rozas.
Cast: Sita Sadafi, Roxana Dipre, Inka María, Alejandro de Enciso, Luis Induni, Antonio Molino Rojo.

Two years after directing Spanish horror icon Paul Naschy in the Werewolf vs. Yeti potboiler **Night of the Howling Beast** (1975) and the erotic adventure **Kilma, Queen of the Amazons** (1975), Miguel Iglesias put his M.I. Bonns insignia on this curio, originally titled **Island of the Wild Virgins**. Sita Sadafi, Roxana Dipre and Inka/Inca María are castaways from a cruise ship disaster stranded on a tropical Pacific desert island for 20 years. The only other inhabitant is an elderly Japanese fighter pilot shot down during World War II who still thinks the battle is raging. So he's been training the scantily clad shipwrecked lovelies for imminent invasion. But the only intruders to come their way turn out to be two bumbling treasure hunters searching for a Japanese freighter that sank during the conflict, supposedly containing a fortune in gold and silver. Let the muted mutiny, bondage, bloodshed and torture begin! Filmed in the technological marvel of NakedColor (did anyone ever think that was anything other than normal colour?), this was released by AMS Films, 'a division of A Major Studio, Inc.', a bit like when 20th Century Fox released Dario Argento's **Suspiria** (1977) under the International Classics banner in embarrassment.

PELVIS

USA, 1977
Director: Robert T. Megginson. Producer: Lew Mishkin, Robert T. Megginson. Screenplay: Straw Weisman.
Cinematography: Lloyd Freidus.
Cast: Luther 'Bud' Whaney, Mary Mitchell, Cindy Tree, Billy Padgett, Chris Thomas, Carol Baxter.

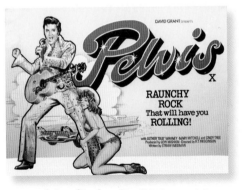

Before he wrote the nifty special effects thriller **FX** (1985), writer Robert T. Megginson directed this squalid rags-to-bitches comedy about a Southern hick musician (Luther 'Bud' Whaney) leaving home to make it big in New York. The news spreads he has a massive penis so he's soon attracted the attentions of agent Cindy Tree, who changes his name to Pelvis to accent his 'talent'. With his repertoire consisting of such bad taste ditties as 'Nazi Lady' (with the chorus line "love, so Aryan") he battles pimps, ageing groupies and crooked promoters before having an obvious epiphany. With gags about sleeping with 14-year-old girls and burning down the World Trade Center (both more toe-curling in hindsight retrospect), this crude showbiz parody is poorly made and shoddy. One of many movies of the day that would pass through the hands of myriad exhibitors, in some places it was re-titled **Toga Party** with a framing device added featuring students getting stoned and laid watching the main footage unfold. Whaney proved a pretty gormless lead but he did look good in Vegas-style costumes and silver face, so much so that for a while he did become quite famous as an Elvis Presley impersonator.

PUNK ROCK

USA, 1977
Director: Malcolm S. Worob [Carter Stevens]. Producer: Carter Stevens. Screenplay: Al Hazrad [Carter Stevens, Rich Jaccoma]. Cinematography: Bruce G. Sparks. Cast: Wade Nichols, Richard Bolla [Robert Kerman], Susaye London, Bobby Astyr, Crystal Sync, Don Peterson.

It began life as X-rated Mickey Spillane-style porn before becoming the first R-rated movie to exploit the punk phenomenon once it had made money on the hardcore circuit. Carter Stevens (aka Malcolm Stephen Worob, aka adult movie actor Steven Mitchell) used the burgeoning New York City punk rock scene, and its Warholian Mecca Max's Kansas City, as the backdrop for this seedy kidnap/homicide/frame-up melodrama starring Wade Nichols (**My Sex-Rated Wife**, 1977) as hopeless detective Jimmy Dillinger. But stripped of its graphic erotica (including turns by **Cannibal Holocaust**, 1980, star Robert Bolla/Kerman and Susaye London, **Teenage Pajama Party**, 1977), extra footage of such local bands as Spicy Bits and The Fast joined featured headliners Edna and the Stilettos, whose bondage gear cabaret points the way to solving the crime mystery. According to Stevens, Edna took over as lead singer from a certain Debbie Harry just before filming took place. Written by Stevens and 'Screw' magazine editor Rich Jaccoma under their Al Hazrad alias, gumshoe Nichols would change his name to Dennis Parker and have a sizeable disco hit with 'Like an Eagle' in 1979 on the banner Casablanca Records label, produced by the Village People creator and mastermind Jacques Morali.

I SPIT ON YOUR GRAVE

USA, 1978
Director: Meir Zarchi. Producer: Joseph Zbeda, Meir Zarchi. Screenplay: Meir Zarchi.
Cinematography: Nouri Haviv.
Cast: Camille Keaton, Eron Tabor, Richard Pace, Anthony Nichols, Gunter Kleemann, Alexis Magnotti.

One of the most infamous flagship exploitation movies ever, with a poster campaign to match, this notorious rape revenge shocker was originally titled **Day of the Woman**. Until multi-tasking Meir Zarchi (writer, producer, director, editor) had the brilliant brainwave of dusting off the title of Michel Gast's 1959 race potboiler so a new audience could appreciate its grungy impact. Camille Keaton, a distant relative of silent comedian Buster, already had a B movie career going in Italy (**Tragic Ceremony**, 1972, **Sex of the Witch**, 1973) when she played writer Jennifer Hills on a backwoods vacation. Raped twice by four

local thugs, she's left for dead but recovers to wreak brutal revenge on her attackers via castration in a bath, axe chopping, hanging, and slicing with outboard motor. Although the direction is nondescript, the look grainy and rough, and the editing done with a trowel, it's often a powerful piece of accidental art, the lack of background music giving it an added pseudo documentary layer. Supposedly based on a true story, Zarchi hit the residual motherlode with this grisly opus, remade in 2010, followed by **I Spit on Your Grave 2** (2013) and **I Spit on Your Grave: Vengeance Is Mine** (2015).

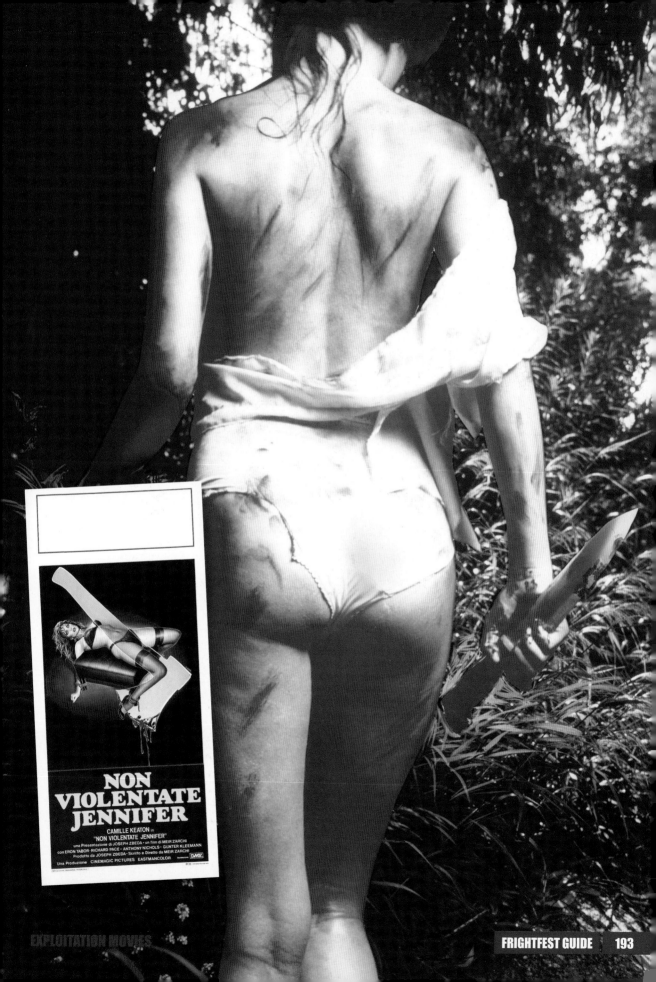

NON
VIOLENTATE
JENNIFER

CAMILLE KEATON in
"NON VIOLENTATE JENNIFER"
una Presentazione di JOSEPH ZBEDA • un film di MEIR ZARCHI
con ERON TABOR · RICHARD PACE · ANTHONY NICHOLS · GUNTER KLEEMANN
Prodotto da JOSEPH ZBEDA · Scritto e Diretto da MEIR ZARCHI
Una Produzione CINEMAGIC PICTURES EASTMANCOLOR

THE MANITOU

USA, © 1977, first public screening 1978
Director: William Girdler. Producer: William
Girdler. Screenplay: William Girdler, Jon
Cedar, Thomas Pope. Music: Lalo Schifrin.
Cinematography: Michel Hugo.
Cast: Tony Curtis, Michael Ansara, Susan
Strasberg, Stella Stevens, Jon Cedar, Ann
Sothern.

Based on the bestselling novel by Scottish
horror author Graham Masterton, this
was to be one-man-exploitation industry
William Girdler's last movie. Shortly before
its release, the **Three on a Meathook**
(1973), **Abby** (1974), **Grizzly** (1976)
director was killed in a helicopter crash in
the Philippines while scouting locations for
his next project, 'The Overlords'. Although
it was put into production within three
months of Girdler stumping up the $50,000
film rights, and allegedly written in three
days by himself, Jon Cedar (tumour
specialist Dr. Jack Hughes in the movie)
and Tom Pope (**Hammett**, 1982), it had
the benefit of time, money ($3 million) and
the semi-major AVCO Embassy (cash rich
from such blockbusters as **The Cassandra
Crossing** and **Voyage of the Damned**,
both 1976) backing him. The goofy plot
has Susan Strasberg (**Psych-Out**, 1968)
finding out the large lump on her back is
the continually growing reincarnation of a
400-year-old Piscatawayan spirit known
as Misquamacus. It ends with modern
medicine man Michael Ansara (**It's Alive**,
1974) and fortune-teller Tony Curtis (**The
Boston Strangler**, 1968) calling down the
Manitou of Love from heaven for a cosmic
battle royal. AVCO cut a bloody scalpel
sequence to make it more teen marketable.

SEX & VIOLENCE

Spain, 1978
Director: Leopoldo Pomés. Screenplay: Leopoldo Pomés, Román Gubern, Oscar Tusquets.
Music: Ricard Miralles. Cinematography: Juan Suriñach.
Cast: Marina Langner, Xabier Elorriaga, Llorenç Santamaria, Ricardo Masip, Jordi Vilajoana.

Before Neil Jordan's **The Crying Game** (1992), came the Spanish import **Ensalada Baudelaire**, the first movie to pull down a girl's bikini bottom to reveal a cock and the hard fact that 'she' was really a he. Directed by Leopoldo Pomés, who would later work with Bigas Luna on the horror-film-within-a-horror-film **Anguish** (1987), this Radley Metzger-esque art-sex imitation tells the shaggy dog tale of a wealthy man taking his dominating wife on a luxury Mediterranean cruise to indulge their S&M leanings a bit more. Inviting another couple on board, things get out of hand in the role-playing department until it's revealed the guests are really a drag queen and his hustler boyfriend employed by the husband to spice up their static B&D relationship. The verbal humiliation includes some bitchy one-liners about transvestites being better than real women, with mild torture, fetish sex and golden showers on the erotic menu. Weirdest scene of all finds the wife forced to grovel in a pincer-tastic congregation of crayfish. Originally called **Andrea** for the US market, until the title change clearly sold it better to the right demographic, completely random glowing reviews by nobodies were used on every poster for additional hype.

In the glitter and glamour world of the very rich, there's a new kind of terror

SEX & VIOLENCE

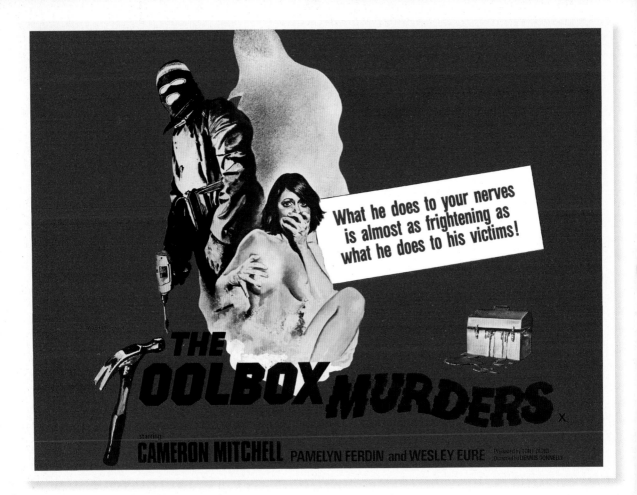

THE TOOLBOX MURDERS

USA, © 1977, first public screening 1978
Director: Dennis Donnelly. Producer: Tony DiDio. Screenplay: Neva Friedenn, Robert Easter, Ann Kindberg.
Music: George Deaton. Cinematography: Gary Graver.
Cast: Cameron Mitchell, Pamelyn Ferdin, Wesley Eure, Nicolas Beauvy, Marianne Walter [Kelly Nichols].

A complete abberration in the career of series TV director Dennis Donnelly ('Charlie's Angels', 'Hart to Hart'), who made this controversial exploitation horror moonlighting from shooting episodes of 'Man from Atlantis' and 'The Amazing Spider-Man'. Cameron Mitchell, entering the super-crazed lunatic phase of his profession, plays the deranged superintendent of a Californian apartment block killing off his tenants with an array of trusty tools – power drill, nail gun, hammer and screwdriver – while constantly singing 'Sometimes I Feel Like a Motherless Child' wearing a ski-mask. In his warped mind he blames the death of his 15-year-old daughter on the evil, exhibitionism and corruption of his victims, hence the reason for his gruesome revenge. A butcher's knife, scissors, carcrash and fire also augment the toolbox killing range supposedly based on a true story. Penthouse Pet of the Month and future hardcore porn star Kelly Nichols is the casualty viciously nail-gunned in the nude. Playing Joanne Ballard is Aneta Corseaut, star of **The Blob** (1958), who met Donnelly when he was directing her in the medical TV series 'Emergency!' For all its edgy gore, this trashy opus is remarkably suspenseless and dull, something Tobe Hooper's remake would fix in 2004.

VAMPIRE HOOKERS

USA/Philippines, 1978
Director: Cirio H. Santiago. Producer: Robert E. Waters.
Screenplay: Howard R. Cohen. Music: Jaime Mendoza-Nava.
Cinematography: Carding Remias [Ricardo Remias], John Araojo [Johnny Araojo].
Cast: John Carradine, Bruce Fairbairn, Trey Wilson, Vic Diaz, Leo Martinez, Karen Stride.

If at first you don't succeed, try and try again. In 1978, ultra-prolific Filipino hack producer/director Cirio H. Santiago (**Ebony Ivory & Jade**, 1976, **Up from the Depths**, 1979) helmed this tame sex horror about vampires disguising themselves as prostitutes to get a willing supply of victims. As he had done so many times in the past, B movie horror icon John Carradine played another Count Dracula clone (Richmond Reed, Carradine's actual first two Christian names) sending out his bevy of bloodsuckers to lure the unsuspecting to his crypt. Carradine steals the show in this sleaze fiasco reciting Shakespeare, positing the notion the Bard was also undead and delivering the poorly scripted punch lines with weary largesse. But the movie was a commercial disaster, so three posters were designed to try and sell it. First it was tagged "Warm blood isn't all they suck", then in the wake of a certain Steven Spielberg blockbuster it was hyped with "They're a close encounter of a different kind!" It still didn't connect with the grindhouse audience, so an old Paul Naschy starring Spanish shocker from 1973 had its US title purloined and **Vampire Hookers** became **Cemetery Girls**. Busted again.

BOG

USA, 1979
Director: Don Keeslar. Producer: Michelle Marshall. Screenplay: Carl N. Kitt.
Music: Bill Walker. Cinematography: Wings.
Cast: Gloria De Haven, Aldo Ray, Marshall Thompson, Leo Gordon, Glenn Voros, Jeff Schwaab.

Old-timers Gloria DeHaven (**Thousands Cheer**, 1943), Aldo Ray (**The Centrefold Girls**, 1974), Leo Gordon (**The Haunted Palace**, 1963) and Marshall Thompson (**It! The Terror from Beyond Space**, 1958) got corralled in 1978 to make a cheapo monster movie similar to the sort made popular by Thompson and director Roger Corman with **Attack of the Crab Monsters**

(1957). The fact there was still a contemporary market for such nostalgia-based nonsense was proven when this quaint Don Keeslar directed zip-up-suit creature feature became a popular attraction for years on the drive-in circuit. Shot in Harshaw, Wisconsin, Carl Kitt's moribund screenplay, containing such dialogue gems as, "We'll get the fire department. They've got hoses. They'll spray anything", and pronunciation mistakes – "hypodeemic (sic) needle" – was bog-standard stuff about a green, bug-eyed mutant awakened by locals fishing in a lake with dynamite. While a biologist desperately wants to learn all about its evolutionary nature as it goes on a killing spree searching for human females so it can breed, the sheriff wants it tracked down and killed. The silly-looking Bog monster was played by 30-year-old Radisson native Thomas 'Jeff' Schwaab, who was 6' 7" tall, weighed 247 pounds and wore size 16 shoes.

DISCO GODFATHER

USA, 1979
Director: J. Robert Wagoner. Producer: Rudy Ray Moore, Theodore Toney. Screenplay: J. Robert Wagoner, Cliff Roquemore. Music: Ernie Fields Jr. Cinematography: Arledge Armenaki.
Cast: Rudy Ray Moore, Carol Speed, Lady Reed, Jimmy Lynch, James H. Hawthorne [Hawthorne James], Julius J. Carry III.

Spurred by the success of **Saturday Night Fever** (1977), one-man Blaxploitation factory Rudy Ray Moore set his sights on mirrorballs after producing and starring in the low-brow classics **Dolemite** (1975) and **The Human Tornado** (1976), based on the kung-fu fighting pimp character from his stand-up comedy routines. The result is a demented cross between **Gordon's War** (1973) and **Can't Stop the Music** (1980), with Moore playing ex-cop Tucker Williams, the rapping owner and main attraction of the Blueberry Hill disco. Called back into police action when his nephew Bucky (Julius J. Carry III) gets hooked on Angel Dust, Williams and Girl Friday Noel (Carol Speed, star of **Abby**, 1974, the Blaxploitation rip-off of **The Exorcist,** 1973) declare war on super-pusher Stinger (James H. Hawthorne) and his cronies using his nightclub to peddle the drug. Skid-row production values meet hefty Moore's skin-tight studded disco ensembles to create a funky fiasco packed with roller disco sequences, cheap psychedelic freak-outs (with zombies and skeletons), hilarious exorcisms to rid addicts of their evil spirits and jaw-droppingly awful kung-fu choreography by martial arts champion Howard Jackson. With no recognisable disco hits even the soundtrack was third-rate wallpaper in this solo J. Robert Wagoner directed effort.

EXPLOITATION MOVIES

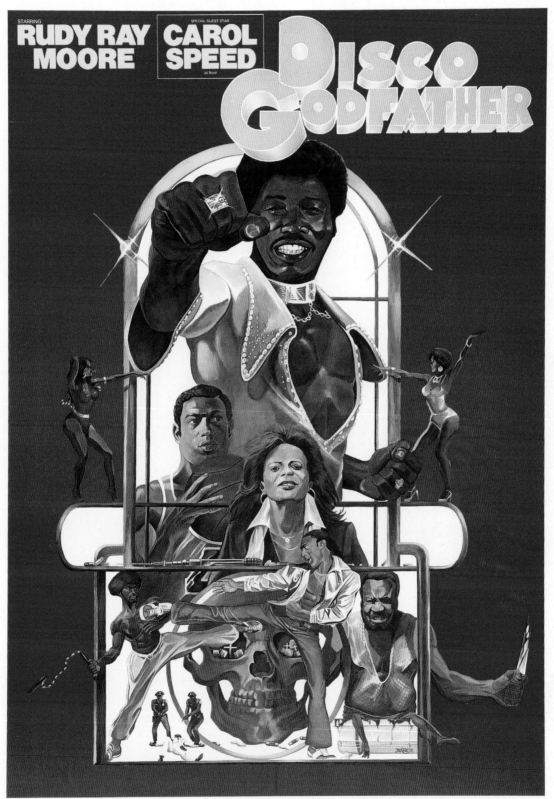

GUYANA, CULT OF THE DAMNED

Mexico/Spain/Panama, 1979
Director: René Cardona Jr. Producer: René Cardona Jr. Screenplay: Carlos Valdemar, René Cardona Jr.
Music: Alfredo Diaz Ordaz, Jimmie Haskell. Cinematography: Leopoldo Villaseñor.
Cast: Stuart Whitman, Gene Barry, John Ireland, Joseph Cotten, Jennifer Ashley, Yvonne De Carlo.

Like father, like son. In 1976, Mexican horror wrestling movie genius Rene Cardona gave the world **Survive!**, his version of the 1972 Andes plane crash tragedy where survivors ate the dead passengers. Three years later his son Rene Cardona Jr. was at the true-life horror game with this seedy version of the 1978 mass suicide of People's Temple members engineered by cult leader Jim Jones. The names might have been changed – bible-thumping Jones became Jim Johnson – but the story was accurate to every lurid detail, showing the public humiliation, the electric shock genital torture and the deadly Kool-Aid climax. Incredibly Cardona Jr. managed to enlist an impressive array of ageing Hollywood stars for his penny-dreadful sleaze. Stuart Whitman, Bradford Dillman, Joseph Cotten, John Ireland, Yvonne De Carlo, Jennifer Ashley and Gene Barry were rounded up to play congressmen, mistresses and lawyers, and all looked embarrassed. Ending with actual photographs of the real victims was the final straw for many who were incredulous that Universal Pictures had the temerity to release it. But this was at the time Paramount was making a fortune from **Friday the 13th** (1980) and every major distributor was looking to exploitation for easy money.

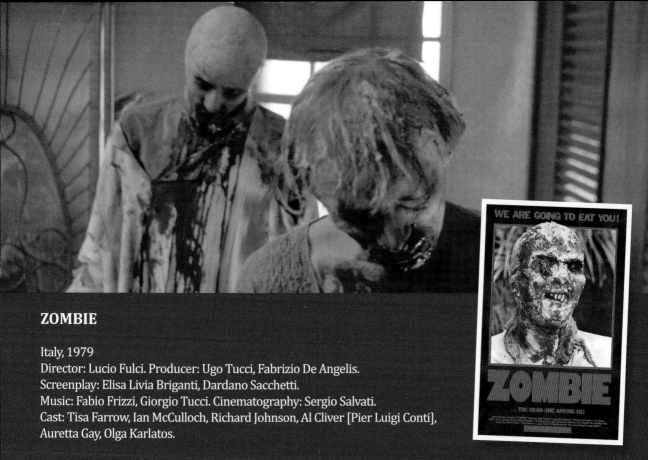

ZOMBIE

Italy, 1979
Director: Lucio Fulci. Producer: Ugo Tucci, Fabrizio De Angelis.
Screenplay: Elisa Livia Briganti, Dardano Sacchetti.
Music: Fabio Frizzi, Giorgio Tucci. Cinematography: Sergio Salvati.
Cast: Tisa Farrow, Ian McCulloch, Richard Johnson, Al Cliver [Pier Luigi Conti],
Auretta Gay, Olga Karlatos.

One of the immortal posters of all time, the George Romero-influenced knock-off American title for **Zombi 2/Zombie Flesh-Eaters** kicked off director Lucio Fulci's second wave of genre popularity after a notable early Giallo career with **Perversion Story** (1969), **A Lizard in a Woman's Skin** (1971) and **Don't Torture a Duckling** (1972), all 42nd Street favourites. Supposedly inspired by a fumetti/comic strip where cowboy hero Tex Willer remote-controls corpses, this throwback to the walking dead's voodoo roots featured exemplary no-budget work by make-up maven Gianetto De Rossi, who smeared actors in red clay and stuck live maggots in their eye-sockets. As a result, Fulci referred to these 'dead' extras as "walking flowerpots". Infamous for two iconic moments of horror cinema legend: the masterpiece of madness where an underwater zombie attacks a shark, and the excruciating gore sequence where actress Olga Karlatos has her eye slowly skewered by a wooden splinter. US distributor Jerry Gross made sure his target audience got the message with the barefaced "We Are Going to Eat You" tag-line, something he was a past master at since combining **I Drink Your Blood** (1970) and **I Eat Your Skin** (1964) for one of the greatest ever double-bill attractions.

BARE BEHIND BARS

Brazil, 1980
Director: Oswaldo de Oliveira.
Producer: A.P. Galante, Alexandre Adamiu.
Screenplay: Oswaldo de Oliveira.
Music: Estudios Galante.
Cinematography: Oswaldo de Oliveira.
Cast: Maria Stella Splendore, Neide Ribeiro, Marcia Fraga, Danielle Ferrite, Martha Anderson, Serafilm Gonzalez.

Four years after John Waters' muse Divine starred in an Off-Broadway spoof of trashy Women In Prison movies entitled 'Women Behind Bars', the Brazilians caught up with the Z-movie zeitgeist. The controversial result was **A Prisão,** directed and written by Oswaldo de Oliveira the same year he helmed **A Filha de Emmanuelle**. Sick of being mistreated, molested and pimped out to wealthy lesbians by warden Sylvia (Maria Stella Splendore, **Brisas do Amor**, 1982), three inmates in a rat-infested women's prison escape incarceration under Carnival cover. But once on the outside they soon resort back to criminal form, becoming prostitutes and penis-razoring crazies as the authorities close in. Badly dubbed, but with copious nudity and offensive titillation, this is a prime example of the Pornochanchada, popular during the 1970s and early 1980s. Its name derived from porno and chanchada, translated

as light comedy, most were produced in the downtown quarter of São Paulo nicknamed Boca do Lixo or Garbage Mouth. But if made in Rio de Janeiro the genre was called Pornochanchada Carioca. Sônia Braga was one of the few actresses on show here who crossed over to the big time in more mainstream fare such as **Kiss of the Spider Woman** (1985) and **The Rookie** (1990).

CANNIBAL HOLOCAUST

Italy, 1980
Director: Ruggero Deodato. Producer: Franco Palaggi, Franco Di Nunzio. Screenplay: Gianfranco Clerici. Music: Riz Ortolani. Cinematography: Sergio D'Offizi.
Cast: Robert Kerman, Francesca Ciardi, Perry Pirkanen, Luca Giorgio Barbareschi, Salvatore Basile, Gabriel Yorke.

If you thought the 'found footage' craze began with **The Blair Witch Project** (1999), Ruggero Deodato's infamous shocker irrefutably proves otherwise. Banned in 33 countries and the cause of protests

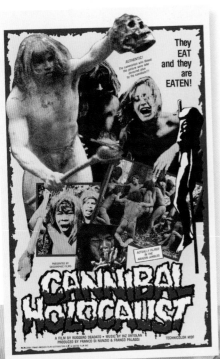

forcing the **Concorde Affair '79** (1979) director to defend his filmmaking methods in Italian law courts, Deodato's visceral epic is the apotheosis of the mutilation extravaganza begun by Umberto Lenzi's **Il paese del sesso selvaggio/Deep River Savages** (1972) combining fake human torture with real animal killing. A film crew led by Gabriel Yorke goes missing in South America while shooting a documentary on tribal cannibalism. Anthropologist Robert Kerman (aka porn star Robert Bolla) is assigned to lead another expedition back into the 'Green Inferno' to establish their fate and finds sealed film cans being kept by the feared Tree People. On the reels are details of the crew being hunted down, maimed and eaten, complete with amateurish zooms, scratches and graininess. Animal butchery includes a live turtle being cut into pieces while prosthetics convey castration, hand forced abortion and vaginal impaling. It's because Deodato imitates the cynical art form he seeks to condemn that his barrage of barbaric set pieces is so challenging and repugnant to watch.

A fast drive to Paradise turns into a nuclear nightmare

THE CHAIN REACTION

THE CHAIN REACTION

Australia, 1980
Director: Ian Barry. Producer: David Elfick. Screenplay: Ian Barry.
Music: Andrew Thomas Wilson. Cinematography: Russell Boyd.
Cast: Steve Bisley, Arna-Maria Winchester, Ross Thompson, Ralph Cotterill,
Patrick Ward, Mel Gibson.

A suspensefully taut slice of Ozploitation that took four years to get to the screen thanks to first-time writer/director Ian Barry's resilience and the fact **The China Syndrome** (1979) became a hit in the interim. Originally titled **The Man at the Edge of the Freeway**, Barry's tense plot has German engineer Ross Thompson, working for the unscrupulous multinational company WALDO (Western Atomic Long-term Dumping Organisation) being exposed to a fatal dose of radiation after an earthquake causes a disastrous nuclear waste spill. Suffering from

THE CHAIN REACTION

memory loss, he goes on the run and encounters vacationing racing car driver Steve Bisley (Goose in **Mad Max**, 1979) and his nurse wife Arna-Maria Winchester. As they both try and keep the fugitive from dying before he can whistle-blow on WALDO, shadowy operatives follow in hot pursuit desperate to keep the leak a secret. On location in Glen Davis, New South Wales, the inexperienced Barry fell way behind in the shooting schedule. So executive producer George Miller stepped in to direct the second unit, lending his fast and furious **Mad Max** know-how to the car chases, which every reviewer pointed out, plus talking Mel Gibson into a cameo role as a garage mechanic.

DOCTOR BUTCHER M.D.

Italy, 1980
Director: Frank Martin [Marino Girolami]. Producer: Gianfranco Couyoumdjian, Fabrizio De Angelis. Screenplay: Romano Scandariato. Music: Nino Fidenco. Cinematography: Fausto Zuccoli.
Cast: Ian McCulloch, Alexandra Delli Colli, Sherry Buchanan, Peter O'Neal, Donald O'Brien, Dakar.

A legendary patchwork job, a totally gory mess, but a staple 42nd Street attraction that began life as an Italian island-set bloodbath entitled **Queen of the Cannibals**, shot by veteran director Marino Girolami/Frank Martin (**My Friend, Dr. Jekyll**, 1960, **2 RRRingos no Texas**, 1967) on the same sets Lucio Fulci used in **Zombie Flesh-Eaters**. With a title change to **Zombi Holocaust**, and the addition of purloined cues from Nico Fidenco's score for **Emanuelle and the Last Cannibals** (1977), this Living Dead/gut-muncher combo opened in Italy and flopped badly. It was second to last in the 1980 box-office charts with only 29,909 spectators. So when American distributor

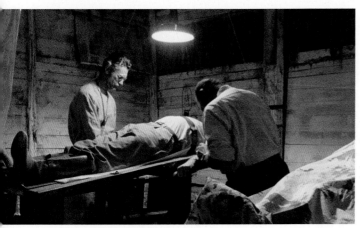

Aquarius picked it up they added unrelated opening footage by director Roy Frumkes from an unfinished anthology, **Tales That Will Tear Your Heart Out**, trimmed all the talk, dropped the stolen soundtrack, replacing it with a catchy synthesizer score, and changed the title to one of the all-time exploitation greatest, the 'Medical Deviate' appendage the icing on the cake. That story is far better than the one on screen of course, something to do with a madman stealing body parts from a Manhattan hospital traced back via tattoos to a tribe of Indonesian pygmies.

THE EXTERMINATOR

USA, 1980
Director: James Glickenhaus. Producer: Mark Buntzman.
Screenplay: James Glickenhaus. Music: Joe Renzetti.
Cinematography: Robert M. Baldwin.
Cast: Christopher George, Samantha Eggar, Robert Ginty,
Steve James, Toni di Benedetto, Dick Boccelli.

It was the talk of the Cannes Film Festival that year.
Everyone who had seen director James Glickenhaus's urban
vigilante melodrama couldn't stop
discussing how the opening
flashback to a Vietcong prison featured the most incredibly realistic
decapitation shock on film – and in slow motion. Naturally all that
buzz, whether impressed or outraged, translated into massive success
when the **Death Wish** (1974) variation opened commercially. Fresh
off that eye-opening traumatic experience, veteran Robert Ginty
returns to Manhattan to lead a normal life working in a meat packing
plant. But when his best friend Steve James is assaulted and murdered
by the most sadistic gang of criminals imaginable, Ginty moves into
flame-throwing, meat-grinding, shotgun blasting and scrotum shooting
action. While the general public applauds his crime-busting techniques
the police, led by city cop Christopher George (**Pieces**, 1982), and vicious
government agents are on his trail. **The Exterminator** put Ginty on a virile
action hero roll and he formed his own production company that distributed
his vehicles worldwide. After directing further action adventures – **The Soldier**
(1982), **The Protector** (1985) – and executive producing **Maniac Cop** (1988)
and **Frankenhooker** (1990), Glickenhaus quit the film business to
become a Wall Street fund manager.

MACABRE

Italy, 1980
Director: Lamberto Bava. Producer: Gianni Minervini, Antonio Avati. Screenplay: Pupi Avati, Roberto Gandus, Lamberto Bava, Antonio Avati. Music: Ubaldo Continiello. Cinematography: Franco Delli Colli.
Cast: Bernice Stegers, Stanko Molnar, Veronica Zinny, Roberto Posse, Ferdinando Orlandi, Fernando Pannullo.

Just like his father, maestro Mario Bava, was rewarded for saving **I vampiri/The Devil's Commandment** (1957) when director Riccardo Freda walked out, his son Lamberto attracted financing for his feature debut when he helped ailing Mario complete his last movie **Shock/Beyond the Door II** (1977). From the Avati brothers, Pupi and Antonio (of **La casa dalle finestre che ridono/The House with the Laughing Windows**, 1976, fame), to be precise who also felt his assistant direction on their production of Mario Lanfranchi's **Il bacio/The Kiss** (1974) saved it from being a complete write-off. Bernice Stegers, wife of **Harry Potter and the Goblet of Fire** (2005) director Mike Newell, stars as deranged Jane Baker, estranged from her husband Fernando Pannullo, who develops a bizarre sexual obsession with the severed head of the lover she murdered and keeps in the refrigerator. Stanko Molnar is her increasingly suspicious blind landlord, while Veronica Zinny plays her malicious daughter who puts a rotting earlobe in her soup to drive her mother completely over the edge. Complete with **Carrie** (1976) inspired twist ending and shot on the same Italian locations as Pasolini's **Salò** (1975) masquerading as New Orleans, it's a grisly guilty pleasure.

MANIAC

USA, 1980
Director: William Lustig. Producer: Andrew W. Garroni, William Lustig. Screenplay: C.A. Rosenberg, Joe Spinell. Music: Jay Chattaway. Cinematography: Robert Lindsay. Cast: Joe Spinell, Caroline Munro, Gail Lawrence [Abigail Clayton], Tom Savini, Kelly Piper, Hyla Marrow.

The last great horror exploitation poster is this one for the landmark psycho sicko by one-time grindhouse movie theatre usher William Lustig, director of **The Violation of Claudia** (1977). So iconic would the poster prove to be – many commented on its shock impact at the time of release – director Franck Khalfoun paid homage to it in his 2012 remake as star Elijah Wood's reflection in a car door distorts into an approximation of the same image. Shot in Manhattan and featuring state-of-the-art gore by then rising special effects make-up star Tom Savini, this package of sleaze, sexism and slashing managed to offend everybody. Brilliantly cast character actor Joe Spinell (**The Godfather**, 1972, **Taxi Driver**, 1976, **Cruising**, 1980) plays Frank Zito, a middle-aged, overweight, Italian-American loner. Landlord of a small apartment complex, his tenants don't realise Frank is a schizophrenic serial killer who spends his nights stalking, killing and scalping women to decorate his steadily growing supply of mannequins, used to carry on one-sided conversations with his deceased mother, an abusive prostitute who constantly physically abused him before dying in a car accident leaving him orphaned. British Scream Queen Caroline Munro is the photographer Frank tries to romance rather than slaughter.

MOTHER'S DAY

USA, 1980
Director: Charles Kaufman. Producer: Michael Kravitz, Charles Kaufman. Screenplay: Charles Kaufman, Warren Leight. Music: Phil Gallo, Clem Vicaro Jr. Cinematography: Joe Mangine.
Cast: Nancy Hendrickson [Nancy Lowenthal], Deborah Luce, Tiana Pierce, Holden McGuire [Frederick Coffin], Billy Ray McQuade [Michael McClerie], Rose Ross [Beatrice Pons].

Few splatter movies can honestly say they were based on truth. And while Charles Kaufman's Troma movie had a trendy calendar date for the times, it was actually taken from events that happened to the director himself. In college Kaufman (**The Secret Dreams of Mona Q**, 1977) and his closest classmates vowed that once through graduation they would spend all their vacations together every year afterwards. One summer they went on a camping holiday, pitched their tents in a remote country spot and spent the entire sleepless night scared to death convinced

they were being watched by lurking undesirables. This occurrence, gender-swapped, with the unknown threat sublimated as two sub-normal psychos ruled by the iron hand of their mother ('Car 54, Where Are You?', 1961, star Rose Ross) and taken to its horrific conclusion, forms the central theme of this gleefully gory Stalk and Slasher. With its EC comic-style humour, **Deliverance** (1972) in-jokes, great performances all-round and cheeky satirical messages, this deranged delight features rape 'charades', **Texas Chain Saw Massacre** (1974) décor and an array of inventive weaponry including radio aerials, electric meat carvers, cans of sink cleaner and a TV set. The 2010 remake was pretty good too!

I WARNED YOU NOT TO GO OUT TONIGHT MANIAC

"Maniac" Starring Joe Spinell · Caroline Munro

Associate Producer John Packard · Special Make-Up Effects by Tom Savini · Music by Jay Chattaway · Screenplay by C.A. Rosenberg and Joe Spinell · Executive Producers Joe Spinell and Judd Hamilton

Produced by Andrew Garroni and William Lustig · Directed by William Lustig

A Magnum Motion Picture · Copyright © 1980 Maniac Productions
Color by TVC
RECORDED IN DOLBY STEREO
Distributed by ANALYSIS FILM CORPORATION
A NEW FILM DISTRIBUTION COMPANY

There is no explicit sex in this picture.
However, there are scenes of violence which may be considered horrifying.
No one under 17 will be admitted.

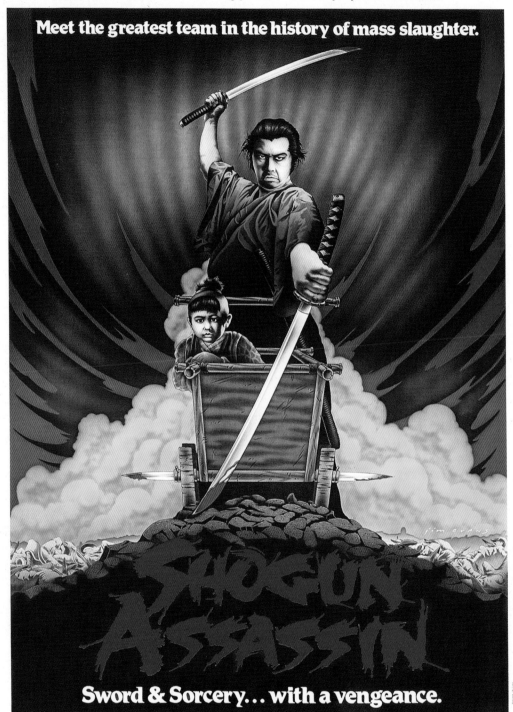

David Weisman & Peter Shanaberg present a Toho Company-Katsu Production

Meet the greatest team in the history of mass slaughter.

SHOGUN ASSASSIN

Sword & Sorcery... with a vengeance.

Starring Tomisaburo Wakayama as Lone Wolf · Music by Mark Lindsay & W. Michael Lewis
Screenplay by Robert Houston · David Weisman · Kazuo Koike · Exec. Producer: Peter Shanaberg
Original Version Produced by Shintaro Katsu & Hisaharu Matsubara · Directed by Kenji Misumi
American Version Produced by David Weisman · Edited by Lee Percy · Directed by Robert Houston
Also Starring Kayo Matsuo as The Supreme Ninja & Masahiro Tomikawa as Daigoro · Photographed by Chishi Makura
Associate Producers: Larry Franciose, Michael Maiello, Albert Ellis Jr., Joseph Ellis · Creative Consultants: Igor Dimont & Nelson Lyon

WARNING: This film contains scenes depicting
graphic violence which may be considered shocking.

A New World Pictures Release

RESTRICTED
UNDER 17 REQUIRES ACCOMPANYING
PARENT OR ADULT GUARDIAN

DOLBY STEREO

ONE SHEET

SCHIZOID

USA, 1980
Director: David Paulsen. Producer: Menahem Golan, Yoram Globus.
Screenplay: David Paulsen. Music: Craig Hundley [Craig Huxley].
Cinematography: Norman Leigh.
Cast: Klaus Kinski, Marianna Hill, Craig Wasson, Donna Wilkes,
Richard Herd, Christopher Lloyd.

Once they had bought the Cannon Films company name (from 1967 founders Dennis Friedland and Chris Dewey), Israeli producers Menahem Golan and Yoram Globus set about establishing their credentials as leaders in exploitation fare. **Schizoid** was one of the first to hit the market place. It was also one of the first films Klaus Kinski made in America after a hugely successful European sleaze/art-house career, ranging from the German Edgar Wallace-based Krimis (**The Secret of the Red Orchid**, 1962) and Spaghetti Westerns (**For a Few Dollars More**, 1965) to Giallo (**Death Smiles on a Murderer**, 1973) and Werner Herzog (**Nosferatu, the Vampyre**, 1979). The Polish-born curmudgeonly superstar plays psychiatrist Dr. Pieter Fales, whose female therapy group is being stalked by a scissors-wielding maniac. Could the killings be related to a series of threatening letters, completely randomly using cut-up and pasted words from newspaper adverts for director David Paulsen's previous movie **Savage Weekend** (1979), distributed by Cannon!? That's really the only point of interest in this slow-paced, bloodless affair featuring Marianna Hill (**Messiah of Evil**, 1973, **Blood Beach**, 1980), Richard Herd (**Trancers**, 1984), Craig Wasson (**Ghost Story**, 1981), Donna Wilkes (**Angel**, 1984) and Christopher Lloyd (the **Back to the Future** trilogy, 1985-90).

SHOGUN ASSASSIN

Japan/USA, 1980
Director: Robert Houston, Kenji Misumi [uncredited].
Producer: Shintarô Katsu, Hisaharu Matsubara.
Screenplay: Kazuo Koike, Robert Houston, David Weisman. Music: Michael W. Lewis, Mark Lindsay.
Cinematography: Chikashi Makiura.
Cast: Tomisaburô Wakayama, Akihiro Tomikawa, Kayo Matsuo, Minoru Ôki, Shôgen Nitta, Shin Kishida.

One of 42nd Street's most popular attractions was this cut-and-paste job edited together by Robert Houston (Bobby in **The Hills Have Eyes**, 1977) and David Weisman (director of **Ciao Manhattan**, 1972). In the early 1970s six films were made in Japan from the popular Samurai manga 'Lone Wolf and Cub'. The first two were **Sword of Vengeance** and **Baby Cart at the River Styx**, both 1972 and both directed by Kenji Misumi. Eleven minutes of footage from the first were intercut into the second, redubbed (one voice belongs to comedian Sandra Bernhard), rescored by Mark Lindsay, singer with Paul Revere and the Raiders, and famed disco producer W. Michael Lewis, and retitled to become this grindhouse favourite. Once a famous court executioner, Lone Wolf (Tomisaburô Wakayama) is framed for his wife's murder by the Yagyu Clan and hits the road with his young son, Daigoro (Akihiro Tomikawa), in a wooden pram rigged with blades and other weapons. Earning his living as a mercenary for hire, the end game is to make the Clan pay for their crime. Fast-paced, bloody and incredibly violent, it's the movie the Bride and her daughter watch at the end of **Kill Bill: Vol. 2** (2004).

BUTTERFLY

USA, 1981
Director: Matt Cimber. Producer: Matt Cimber. Screenplay: John Goff, Matt Cimber. Music: Ennio Morricone. Cinematography: Eduard van der Enden.
Cast: Stacy Keach, Pia Zadora, Orson Welles, Edward Albert, Stuart Whitman, June Lockhart.

The same year Faye Dunaway chewed the scenery in **Mommie Dearest**, but a full 14 years before **Showgirls** launched a thousand quips, the camp classic came of age with this astonishingly awful adaptation of James M. Cain's 1947 noir dwelling on incest. Adapted for the screen by Matt Cimber/ Matteo Ottaviano (doomed sexpot Jayne Mansfield's husband, responsible for her swansong **Single Room Furnished**, 1966), starring Orson Welles and a host of lesser has-beens, the story has Lolita-like Kady tracking down her distant white trash father who gets accused of sexual interest in his new-found kin. But the big story here was all about headlining Pia Zadora, the Kim Kardashian of her day, who appeared in **Santa Claus Conquers the Martians** (1964), had a short-lived disco career, married billionaire Meshulam Riklis and became a pop culture punchline. It was Riklis who flew the foreign press to Las Vegas for a lavish junket to endorse his wife for a 'New Star of the Year' Golden Globe. And she won, beating out Kathleen Turner in **Body Heat** (1981), but also winning the Worst Actress Razzie too. Zadora would endure rape by garden hose in **The Lonely Lady** (1983) before claiming cult fame in **Hairspray** (1988).

FIRECRACKER

USA/Philippines, 1981
Director: Cirio H. Santiago. Producer: Syed Kechik. Screenplay: Ken Metcalfe, Cirio H. Santiago. Music: Nonong Buencamino. Cinematography: Ricardo Remias, Ben Lobo [uncredited].
Cast: Jillian Kesner, Darby Hinton, Reymond King [Rey Malonzo], Ken Metcalfe, Peter Cooper, Don Gordon Bell.

Prolific – and Poe-lific – exploitation legend Roger Corman never missed a trick either as director, producer or company CEO for both New World Pictures and New Horizons/Concorde. Apart from getting future luminaries like Francis Ford Coppola, Martin Scorsese, Jack Nicholson and Robert De Niro to work for peanuts and inventing Teensploitation that didn't exist until he came along, he was also fond of cheaply remaking tried-and-tested hits. As far back as **A Bucket of Blood** (1959) to **Dance of the Damned** (1989), if the concept wasn't broke and had earned enough box office cash, it was remodelled and refashioned into a brand spanking, sparkling All-New entertainment. **TNT Jackson** (1974) was ubiquitous Filipino producer/ director Cirio H. Santiago's second collaboration with Corman following the stewardesses vs. kung-fu fighters **Fly Me** (1973) and concerned a black karate expert going to Hong Kong to take revenge on her brother's killers. Also released as **Naked Fist**, this virtual remake removed the outmoded Blaxploitation element and upped the T&A and topless fighting as karate champion Jillian Kesner (**Starhops**, 1978) arrives in the Philippines searching for her missing reporter sister doing a story on a seedy martial arts club owned by returning star Ken Metcalfe that's a front for a heroin smuggling cartel.

CLASS OF 1984

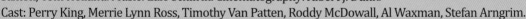

Canada, © 1981, first public screening 1982
Director: Mark L. Lester. Producer: Arthur Kent. Screenplay: Mark Lester, John Saxton, Tom Holland. Music: Lalo Schifrin. Cinematography: Albert J. Dunk.
Cast: Perry King, Merrie Lynn Ross, Timothy Van Patten, Roddy McDowall, Al Waxman, Stefan Arngrim.

For a while it looked like director Mark Lester would amount to an exploitation master of iconic note. With the glorious **Truck Stop Women** (1974), **Bobbie Jo and the Outlaw** (1976) and **Roller Boogie** (1979) behind him and the higher grade efforts **Firestarter** (1984), **Commando** (1985) and **Armed and Dangerous** (1986) ahead, he moved into the development, directing and distribution of such genre filler as **Pterodactyl** (2005) and **Sinbad and the Minotaur** (2011) for American World Pictures and Titan Global Entertainment. This violent update of **Blackboard Jungle** (1955) for the punk generation layers on the dated Sex Pistols aesthetic as student Timothy Van Patten (future director of the TV series 'The Sopranos', 1999, and 'Boardwalk Empire', 2010) terrorizes Abraham Lincoln High School. Especially long-suffering music teacher Perry King (**Mandingo**, 1975), who takes on the cocaine-dealing punk gang without any support from the faculty and retaliates in the most brutal way possible. Both chilling – Roddy McDowall teaching his class at gunpoint – and crass – a flagpole drug death with the tripping victim wrapped in the Stars and Stripes – this **A Clockwork Orange** (1971), **To Sir with Love** (1967) and **The Wanderers** (1979) combo spawned the sci-fi sequel **Class of 1999** (1989).

"WE ARE THE FUTURE! ... AND NOTHING CAN STOP US."

EATING RAOUL

USA, 1982
Director: Paul Bartel. Producer: Anne Kimmel.
Screenplay: Richard Blackburn, Paul Bartel.
Music: Arlon Ober. Cinematography: Gary Thieltges.
Cast: Mary Woronov, Paul Bartel, Robert Beltran, Susan Saiger,
Lynn Hobart, Richard Paul.

EATING RAOUL

One of the exploitation genre's underrated heroes, gay icon Paul Bartel did it all. From directing such superior fare as **Private Parts** (1972), **Death Race 2000** (1975) and **Lust in the Dust** (1985) to appearing in memorable outings like **Hollywood Boulevard** (1976), **Rock 'n' Roll High School** (1979) and **The Usual Suspects** (1995), Bartel had taste, class and nerve, all put to brilliant use in this wonderful cult black comedy. Tired of having every project rejected by mainstream Hollywood, Bartel borrowed from friends and family to finance this remarkable fable about strait-laced Paul and Mary Bland's (Bartel and Warhol cult actress Mary Woronov) desire to open a gourmet restaurant. After the bank refuses funds – one of the funniest gags in the movie has the manager saying "No" in front of a sign saying "We Never Say No" – to raise money they advertise Mary as a dominatrix in newspaper sex adverts. But when one of the kinky sessions ends in accidental death, and the corpse is loaded, robbery kills seem the easiest fund-raising option. Then street hustler Raoul (Robert Beltran) muscles in on the business leading to myriad erotic and murderous complications. The Off-Broadway musical adaptation was equally splendid.

YOU'VE READ THE COMIC BOOK, NOW SEE THE MOVIE!

Bon Appetit!

RAW FORCE

It's nourishment~human flesh
It's guardian~the undead
It's sanctuary~the island

RAW FORCE

USA, © 1981, first public screening 1982
Director: Edward D. Murphy. Producer: Frank E. Johnson. Screenplay: Edward D. Murphy. Music: Walter Murphy.
Cinematography: Frank E. Johnson.
Cast: Cameron Mitchell, Geoffrey Binney, Hope Holiday, Jillian Kessner, Carla Reynolds, Rey King [Rey Malonzo].

Kung fu fighting, warrior zombies, cannibal monks, strippers, women in cages, prostitutes, rape, torture, Hitler lookalikes, piranhas, 'Any C Movie will do' veteran Cameron Mitchell and a soundtrack composed by disco legend Walter Murphy of 'A Fifth of Beethoven' **Saturday Night Fever** (1977) fame. Yes, it's all here in this weird flesh-and-fantasy extravaganza of sex, violence and silliness ticking every exploitation box and so much more. When the Burbank Karate Club and a group of mismatched stock characters – including LAPD cop Jillian Kessner (**Firecracker**, 1981), her cousin Carla Reynolds (**Maniac Cop**, 1988) and chef Rey Malonzo (**They Call Him Bruce Lee**, 1979) – take a cruise to Warriors Island, where legend has it

disgraced fighters go to commit suicide but are resurrected as the living dead to redeem themselves, they fall foul of jade smugglers who provide kidnapped girls to the local monks for their flesh-eating rituals. Directed by ex-military boxer Edward D. Murphy, who also helmed **Heated Vengeance** (1985) before reverting to his acting career (**Goodfellas**, 1990, 'Law and Order', 1991-2000), it's a showcase for frenzied martial arts, softcore erotica and slow-motion shambling zombies. The piranha footage was actually a steal from Joe Dante's **Piranha** (1978).

SATAN'S MISTRESS

USA, © 1980, first public screening 1982
Director: James Polakof. Producer: James Polakof.
Screenplay: James Polakof, Beverly Johnson.
Music: Roger Kellaway. Cinematography: James L. Carter.
Cast: Britt Ekland, Lana Wood, Kabir Bedi, Don Galloway, John Carradine, Sherry Scott.

Frustrated housewife Lana Wood (Natalie's younger sister) can't understand why her husband is more interested in swimming at their fabulous beachfront house than making love to her. But help is soon at hand in the guise of an invisible ghost who continually beds her before transforming into Bollywood superstar Kabir Bedi (**Octopussy**, 1983). Soon her family sport glowing eyes, bleed a lot, experience weird visions and meet alleged Devil's advocates. Trying to make spiritual sense of it all is Lana's psychic friend Britt Ekland (**The Wicker Man**, 1973) who despite being top-billed appears in four scenes only; one has her nearly hot-tubbed to death, another sees her drunken husband decapitated and then she asks the advice of priest John Carradine in his only scene. It turns out Bedi is caught in a netherworld between Heaven and Hell and Satan is using Lana to tempt him to Hades. And that's indeed where he chooses, so great is Lana's turbo nymphomania. Does this mean the forces of evil are defeated? Who knows in this demonic farrago, aka **Demon Rage**, **Fury of the Succubus** and **Dark Eyes**. James Polakof also directed the rapist melodrama **Sunburst** (1975) and the Valley Girl comedy **The Vals** (1983).

One by one he killed them until
he was trapped in his own game.

THE SCAREMAKER

USA, 1982
Director: Robert Deubel. Producer: Anthony N. Gurvis.
Screenplay: Gil Spencer Jr., Kevin Kurgis, Joe Bolster,
Anthony N. Gurvis. Cinematography: Joe Rivers.
Cast: Hal Holbrook, Julia Montgomery, James Carroll,
Suzanne Barnes, Rutanya Alda, Al McGuire.

After **Halloween** (1978) gained critical plaudits
plus a place in the highest-grossing independent
movie history books, and **Friday the 13th**
(1980) cashed in big-time with more gore and
future franchise glory, everyone jumped on the
slasher bandwagon. But most couldn't muster
John Carpenter's artistry or Sean Cunningham's
chutzpah and here's a good example of the sorry
flotsam in the oceans of splatter clichés, aka
Girls Nite Out. Robert Deubel wasn't someone
you'd associate with the genre anyway, having
directed documentaries on Norman Rockwell,
and historic women of courage. But here he
was trying to put an original spin on the old
chestnut of a university basketball win leading
to costume party celebrations. A killer dresses up in a goofy cartoon bear suit and starts slaughtering
all the co-eds indulging in campus slut behaviour. Who's the bruin out to ruin? Well, you should have
paid closer attention to the Weston Hill
Sanatorium prologue for the clue
to the onesied maniac. Featuring
veteran actor Hal Holbrook
as a security guard trying to
solve the murders and his
son David Holbrook as a
suspect, the neatest aspect of
the entire misbegotten affair
is the bubblegum soundtrack
featuring Ohio Express and
The Lovin' Spoonful.

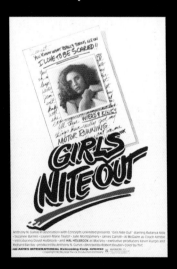

What these women did to get into this prison is nothing compared to what they'll do to get out.

2000 chained women stripped of everything they had... except the courage to survive.

CHAINED HEAT

USA/West Germany, 1983
Director: Paul Nicolas. Producer: Billy Fine, Monica Teuber. Screenplay: Vincent Mongol, Paul Nicolas.
Music: Joseph Conlan. Cinematography: Mac Ahlberg.
Cast: Linda Blair, John Vernon, Sybil Danning, Tamara Dobson, Stella Stevens, Henry Silva.

A dream team exploitation cast – count 'em – Linda Blair (**The Exorcist**, 1973), Stella Stevens (**The Manitou**, 1978), Sybil Danning (**Battle Beyond the Stars**, 1980), John Vernon (**Animal House**, 1978), Edy Williams (**Beyond the Valley of the Dolls**, 1970), Henry Silva (**The Italian Connection**, 1972), Tamara Dobson (**Cleopatra Jones and the Casino of Gold**, 1975), plus tongue-in-cheek direction by Paul Nicolas, a terrific ear for hardboiled dialogue and loads of campy violence. Yes, let's hear it for one of the best, if not the sleaziest, of the chicks-in-chains repertoire. Women In Prison flicks rarely get as good as this, with born innocent Blair sentenced for 18 months after a hit-and-run accident learning all about penitentiary life the hard way. If it's not razor attacks in the nude showers and lesbian rough-and-tumble, it's cocaine dealing by the prison doctor and violent death to those who snitch on any of the corrupt practices going on behind these bars. Vicious Vernon is a hoot as the venal warden who videotapes inmates in his office Jacuzzi while forcing them to snort coke. It might not be the movie Blair signed up to make – she blames constant rewriting on set – but it's one of her top-tier greatest.

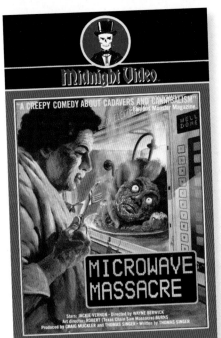

MICROWAVE MASSACRE

USA, 1983
Director: Wayne Berwick. Producer: Thomas Singer, Craig Muckler.
Screenplay: Thomas Singer. Music: Leif Horvath. Cinematography:
Karen Grossman.
Cast: Jackie Vernon, Loren Schein, Al Troupe, Claire Ginsberg, Marla
Simon, Lou Ann Webber.

Stand-up comedian Jackie Vernon was discovered when he appeared on Steve Allen's hit television show 'Celebrity Talent Scouts' in 1963 and became a regular on the likes of 'The Ed Sullivan Show', 'The Dean Martin Show' and 'The Tonight Show with Johnny Carson'. Although he played assorted parts in various TV series and forgettable movies, his lone starring role was as the hen-pecked husband driven to desperate cannibal measures in this grotesquely good-natured horror comedy shot in 1978 and taken off the shelf for grindhouse playoff five years later. Very much tapping into Vernon's Las Vegas lounge persona of the self-deprecating hapless loser, Donald is a construction worker sick of his routine and boring life. His bartender dumps on him and his nymphomaniac neighbours only highlight the fact he hasn't had sex with his nagging wife May since 1962. Eventually snapping, he murders May, cuts her up and stores the body parts in the freezer. After inadvertently cooking a piece of her in the microwave, he develops a taste for female flesh that begins a sex, murder and meal spree. Wayne Berwick, an actor in **The Monster of Piedras Blancas** (1959) only directed one other movie, **The Naked Monster** (2005).

STREET LOVE

USA, 1983
Director: Rosemarie Turko. Producer: Rosemarie Turko, Mark Borde.
Screenplay: Rosemarie Turko. Cinematography: Michael Miner.
Cast: Jennifer Mayo, Jackie Berryman, David Dean, L. Rico Richardson,
Debra Dion, Lili.

Originally a UCLA film course project completed with American Film Industry and National Endowment for the Arts grants, student Rosemarie Turko must have been gutted when her realistic look at the relationships between prostitutes, pimps and their punters ended up with a title change from **Scarred** on the grindhouse circuit after the hooker fantasy **Angel** (1984) became a hit. For hers was a gritty chronicle of the daily degradations suffered by 16-year-old runaway Ruby Starr (Jennifer Mayo) in the effort to support her 2-year-old son and pay the rent. Befriended by seemingly decent pimp Easy (David Dean), she's soon on the treadmill of turning $20 tricks, dodging cop busts and considering starring in the porno 'Sex Wars'. Shot cine-vérité style on 16mm using available light, Turko incisively balances the sidewalk solidarity of her street sisters (note the background graffiti declaring "Women Rule Now" and "Castration Squad") with their cynical male counterparts, the latter hilariously depicted as preening gossipers at a hairdressing salon. Enlightening and depressing, this potent snapshot of Hollywood Boulevard flotsam and jetsam was Turko's one missed shot. After directing the 'Ice Gallery' segment of **The Dungeonmaster** (1984) for trash tycoon Charles Band she completely disappeared.

THE MICROWAVE MASSACRE

FOR HUMAN CONSUMPTION

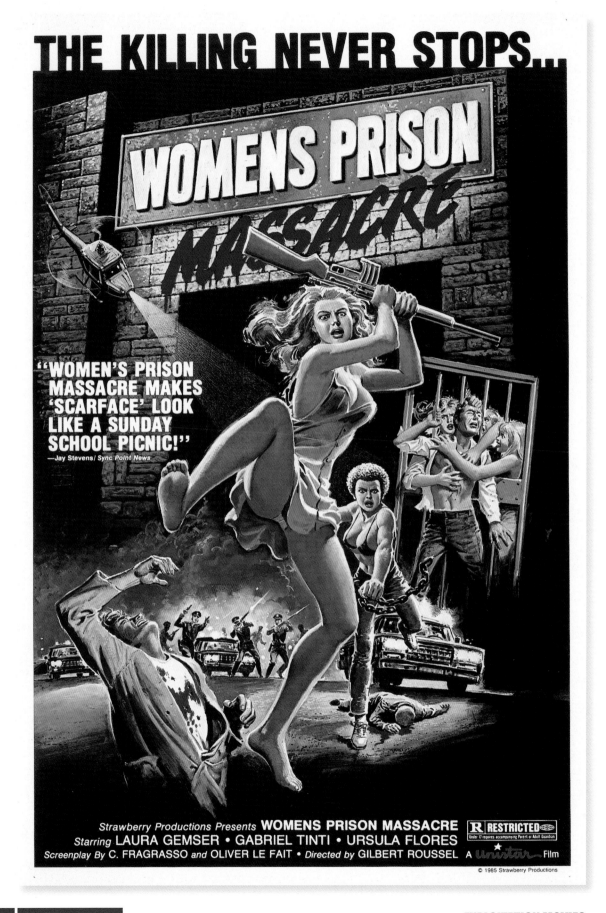

WOMEN'S PRISON MASSACRE

Italy/France, 1983
Director: Gilbert Roussel [Bruno Mattei]. Producer: Jean Lefait.
Screenplay: Claudio Fragasso, Olivier Lefait. Music: Luigi
Ceccarelli. Cinematography: Henry Frogers.
Cast: Laura Gemser, Gabriele Tinti, Ursula Flores, Maria Romano, Antonella Giacomini, Raul Cabrera.

The Italian Ed Wood, Bruno Mattei (**Casa privata per le SS/Private House of the SS**, 1977, **Virus/Zombie Creeping Flesh**, 1980, **Caligula and Messalina**, 1981, **Shocking Dark**, 1989, and a raft of gutter extremes) strikes again with **Blade Violent – i violenti**, shot back-to-back with **Violenza in un carcere femminile/Violence in a Women's Prison** (1982), hence the almost identical cast. Here **Black Emanuelle** (1975) career star Laura Gemser plays, yes, you guessed it Emanuelle, a reporter investigating a corrupt politician, who has drugs planted on her by said sinister official and gets sent to prison to rot away. There she falls foul of the both the sadistic warden who happily tortures her scantily clad charges and hardened jailbird Ursula Flores in endless lesbian power struggles. Life gets even worse when four convicts heading to Death Row, led by 'Crazy Boy' Henderson (Gabriele Tinti, Gemser's husband and regular **Emanuelle Nera** co-star), hijack their police escort and take the entire female penitentiary hostage. It's up to Emanuelle to galvanize the caged harlots and fight back. While lurid and slapdash Eurotrash, it's so good to see the razor-blade-in-vagina revenge from **Deported Women of the SS Special Section** (1976) getting another welcome outing.

COMBAT SHOCK

USA, 1984
Director: Buddy Giovinazzo. Producer: Buddy Giovinazzo.
Screenplay: Buddy Giovinazzo. Music: Ricky Giovinazzo.
Cinematography: Stella Varveris.
Cast: Ricky Giovinazzo, Nick Nasta, Veronica Stork, Mitch Maglio, Asaph Livni, Michael Tierno.

The best movie Troma ever released was this indie pick-up retitled from **American Nightmares**. It introduced 42nd Streeters to a world right on their doorstep and the world to the inestimable talents of director Carmine 'Buddy' Giovinazzo, who has alternated German TV cop series with **No Way Home** (1996), **The Unscarred** (2000), **Life Is Hot in Cracktown** (2009), **The Theatre Bizarre** (2011) and **A Night of Nightmares** (2012). Best described as **The Deer Hunter** (1978) meets **Eraserhead** (1977), it's a moody, shocking and defiantly downbeat look at what's now diagnosed as Combat Stress Reaction. Directed in gritty vérité style, the appalling existence of Vietnam veteran Frankie (Ricky Giovinazzo, Buddy's brother) snaps into focus as he relives the horror of his Saigon tour of duty. Living in a seedy New York apartment with his nagging wife and deformed baby son, Frankie can't get a job and won't call his father for money, who presumed he died in action anyway. Hustling in the street, standing in unemployment lines and coping with his junkie friend (the coat-hanger heroin fixing scene is a gut-wrencher), Frankie's life eventually implodes. There's only one escape route open to him, but will the baby fit in the oven?

DON'T OPEN TILL CHRISTMAS

UK, 1984
Director: Edmund Purdom, Alan Birkinshaw [uncredited].
Producer: Dick Randall, Steve Minasian. Screenplay: Derek Ford.
Music: Des Dolan. Cinematography: Alan Pudney.
Cast: Edmund Purdom, Alan Lake, Belinda Mayne, Mark Jones,
Gerry Sundquist, Caroline Munro.

The link between Christmas and horror goes back to King Herod but it was Charles Dickens's 'A Christmas Carol' that created the popular image of the holiday season as one populated by ghostly terror. Aside from numerous film adaptations of that Dickens classic other shockers include **Christmas**

Holiday (1944), **Santa Claus** (1959), **Santa Claus Conquers the Martians** (1964), **Silent Night, Bloody Night** (1972), **To All a Goodnight** (1980) and the controversial **Silent Night, Deadly Night** (1984) franchise. Among the best in the 'Stalking in a Winter Wonderland' genre are **Black Christmas** (1974, not the 2006 remake), **You Better Watch Out** (1980), **36-15 Code Père Noël** (1989), **Saint** (2010) and **Rare Exports** (2010). Amongst the worst this cheapjack chiller, British matinee idol-turned Euro-horror (**Pieces**, 1982) mainstay Edmund Purdom's one and only movie as director. A madman is murdering all the deadbeats, drunks and tramps dressed as Santa Claus during the holiday season. Purdom is the Scotland Yard detective assigned to track down the psycho before he can castrate another Saint Nick in a public restroom. Caroline Munro, the grande dame of Hammer femmes fatales, pops in briefly to sing a disco tune wearing a skintight pink dress and a glitter-dusted hair-do.

FRANKENSTEIN'S GREAT AUNT TILLIE

Mexico/USA, © 1983, first public screening 1984
Director: Myron J. Gold. Producer: Myron J. Gold. Screenplay: Myron J. Gold.
Music: Ronald Stein. Cinematography: Miguel Garzón.
Cast: Donald Pleasence, Yvonne Furneaux, June Wilkinson, Miguel Ángel
Fuentes, Aldo Ray, Zsa Zsa Gabor.

Director Myron J. Gold – **Temporada salvaje/The Wild Season** (1971) – tempted a fabulous has-been cast down to Mexico City to appear in this fright farce considered one of the worst ever. Baron Victor Frankenstein (Donald Pleasence, **Halloween**, 1978), his wife Randy (June Wilkinson, **Macumba Love**, 1960) and his 190-year-old Aunt Matilda (Yvonne Furneaux, **Repulsion**, 1965) arrive at their castle in Mucklefugger village in the Transylvanian mountains to find out they owe back taxes. Discovering a possible revenue stream from the Frankenstein Monster they find in the dungeon, they try and halt repossession through tourism, much to the locals' annoyance, sick of Tillie already causing upset with

her orphanage rescue antics and women's rights rallies. Aldo Ray (**Human Experiments**, 1979) plays the Burgermeister, Zsa Zsa Gabor (**Queen of Outer Space**, 1958) is Clara, Victor's first wife, glimpsed only in silent flashback and Miguel Ángel Fuentes is the blue monster. A year later Fuentes would play King Kong in the Mexican comedy **In 'n' Out** (1984). According to Wilkinson, Pleasence hated Gabor, who made off with items of wardrobe once her role had been completed (the reason for her lack of screen time?) and Gold resented Furneaux for not following his directions.

Don't Open Till CHRISTMAS

WARNING
CONTAINS EXPLICIT SCENES OF TERROR
from the makers of Friday the 13th.

R RESTRICTED EXHIBITION
NOT AVAILABLE TO PERSONS
UNDER 18 YEARS

THE MUTILATOR

USA, © 1983, first public screening 1984
Director: Buddy Cooper, John Douglass. Producer: Buddy Cooper.
Screenplay: Buddy Cooper. Music: Michael Minard.
Cinematography: Peter Schnall.
Cast: Matt Mitler, Jack Chatham, Bill Hitchcock, Frances Raines,
Ruth Martinez, Morey Lampley.

Made at the height of the slasher horror craze begun by **Halloween**
(1978), fuelled by **Friday the 13th** (1980) and continued
remorselessly by bastard sons of a million other masked maniacs,
this shocker was filmed as **Fall Break** with a same titled theme
song to match. As a child, Ed Jr. (Matt Mitler) accidentally killed his
mother while cleaning the barrel of his father's rifle. Traumatised
Big Ed returned home to a secluded island and lost his mind. Now
Ed Jr. is taking five college friends to this island for a fall break.
There the 'teenagers' find weird photos of corpses, a huge arsenal
of weapons and Big Ed on a quest to kill his son. In time-honoured
naff slasher tradition they don't leave immediately, but stay to
play Blind Man's Bluff! You literally cannot wait for them all to
be hideously slaughtered and soon unhinged Big Ed shows up with battleaxe, machete and grappling
hook pinning them all to the wall via spikes through their heads. The final title purloined from John 'Bud'
Cardos's original moniker for **The Dark** (1979), the gore effects by Mark Shostrom (**Evil Dead II**, 1987)
and Anthony Showe (**Chopping Mall**, 1986) are a plus.

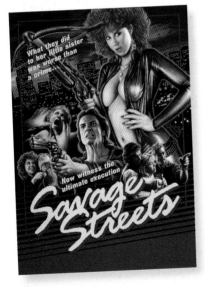

SAVAGE STREETS

USA, 1984
Director: Danny Steinmann. Producer: John Strong. Screenplay: Norman
Yonemoto, Danny Steinmann. Music: Michael Lloyd, John D'Andrea.
Cinematography: Stephen L. Posey.
Cast: Linda Blair, John Vernon, Robert Dryer, Johnny Venocur, Sal Landi,
Scott Mayer.

What's Linda Blair's best performance after her head-turning one in
The Exorcist (1973)? Easy, her role here as Brenda, gang member of
The Satins, whose deaf-mute sister is run over then raped by another
bunch of degenerates, The Scars. Donning commando gear, a crossbow
and bear traps, Brenda moves into vengeance mode and gives The Scars
an overdose of their own venal medicine. Violent 1980s exploitation
doesn't come any more quintessential than this bright and breezy
example but Blair wasn't the first choice for the lead cross between

Mamie Van Doren and Charles Bronson. Cherie Currie of the all-girl
band The Runaways was, and even shot some footage before being
replaced. Blair was brought on by producer Billy Fine, who had cast
her in **Chained Heat** (1983), and helmer Tom DeSimone, who had
directed her in **Hell Night** (1981). Further 'creative differences' caused
those two to depart the production and when it was finally revived
producer John Strong (**The Earthling**, 1980) and director Danny
Steinmann (**High Rise**, 1973, **The Unseen**, 1980) had taken over.
The latter's commendable salvage job secured him the helm of **Friday
the 13th Part V: A New Beginning** (1985), his last credit to date.

THEIR ONLY LAW IS,
"AN EYE FOR AN EYE"

MICHAEL FRANZESE & JOHN L. CHAMBLISS
Present
A JOHN STRONG PRODUCTION
LINDA BLAIR
In
SAVAGE STREETS
ROBERT DRYER • SAL LANDI • JOHNNY VENOCUR • SCOTT MAYER   Special Guest Star JOHN VERNON
Written By NORMAN YONEMOTO & DANNY STEINMANN • Director of Photography STEPHEN L. POSEY
Edited By BRUCE STUBBLEFIELD & JOHN O'CONNOR • Music By MICHAEL LLOYD & JOHN D'ANDREA
Associate Producer CLEVE LANDSBERG • Executive Producers JOHN L. CHAMBLISS & MICHAEL FRANZESE
Produced By JOHN C. STRONG III • Directed By DANNY STEINMANN
R RESTRICTED   Sound Track Album Distributed By MCA RECORDS, INC.
UNDER 17 REQUIRES ACCOMPANYING   Featuring JOHN FARNHAM • REAL LIFE • 3 SPEED • B M W
PARENT OR ADULT GUARDIAN   An MPM Release © 1984

Tonight is what it means to be young.

STREETS OF FIRE

A Rock & Roll Fable.

SILENT MADNESS

USA, 1984
Director: Simon Nuchtern. Producer: Simon Nuchtern, Bill Milling.
Screenplay: Bob Zimmerman, Bill Milling. Music: Barry Salmon.
Cinematography: Gerald Feil.
Cast: Belinda Montgomery, Viveca Lindfors, Sydney Lassick,
David Greenan, Solly Marx, Roderick Cook.

Simon Nuchtern had grindhouse form prior to directing this
stalk-and-slasher devised solely to cash-in on the early 1980s
wave of 3D movies sparked by **Jaws 3-D** (1983). There was
The Girl Grabbers (1968) and **To Hex with Sex** (1969)
before the crowning glory of his entire career – director
of the gore footage added to the finale of the Argentine
produced exploiter **The Slaughter** (1970) turning it into the
grand slam of grift, **Snuff** (1976). At Manhattan's Cresthaven
Mental Hospital the patients seem to come and go as they
please, so hopeless is the disorganized staff. Enter dedicated
psychiatrist Belinda Montgomery (TV series regular and
star of the little seen gem **The Todd Killings**, 1971) who
discovers the bumbling bureaucrats have allowed an insane
maniac to be released due to a false death certificate screw-
up. Too late she learns the co-ed crazy nutjob has gone back to the scene of his crimes, Barrington
College Sorority, and intends to finish what he started. With the deaths shot and edited abruptly with
little blood on show, only the exercise machine demise makes any kind of impact. And there's only one
true 3D angled effect too, a hatchet hurled at the screen.

STREETS OF FIRE

USA, 1984
Director: Walter Hill. Producer: Lawrence Gordon,
Joel Silver. Screenplay: Walter Hill, Larry Gross.
Music: Ry Cooder. Cinematography: Andrew Laszlo.
Cast: Michael Paré, Diane Lane, Rick Moranis, Amy Madigan,
Willem Dafoe, Deborah Van Valkenburgh.

Many contemporary critics noted that it took a
lionised film director to make the best rock-video
inspired movie of all time. On the surface Walter
Hill's innovative groundbreaker would seem to be another of his typical excursions into stylised gang
violence set against a rain-washed, neon-lit landscape. See **The Warriors** (1979). Instead it was much
more an audacious assault on both visual and aural senses that took 1980s cinema
into a whole new exciting future. Hill's urban western uses exaggerated realism
and obvious character ciphers to conjure up a strange 1950s and beyond milieu as
it tells the tale of superstar Diane Lane, kidnapped by one of her psychotic super-
fans, Willem Dafoe. Her manager Rick Moranis must hire ex-boyfriend Michael
Paré (impersonating Gary Cooper to perfection) to rescue her from a downtown
disco hideaway. Hill at the time perfectly summed up his genre-bending Rock 'n'
Roll fable as "The Queen of the Hop captured by the Leader of the Pack and rescued
by Soldier Boy". With its thunderous music score, songs penned by Jim Steinman,
comic book frame recreations and startlingly new stereo frame wipes, Hill set the
seal on future graphic novel adaptations and industry sound design.

YELLOW HAIR AND THE FORTRESS OF GOLD

USA/Spain, 1984
Director: Matt Cimber. Producer: John Ghaffari,
Diego G. Sempre. Screenplay: John Kershaw,
Cimber. Music: Franco Piersanti. Cinematography: John Cabrera.
Cast: Laurene Landon, Ken Roberson, John Ghaffari, Luis
Lorenzo, Claudia Gravi, Aldo Sambrell.

Although pitched in Exploitation Land as a **Raiders of the Lost Ark** (1981) knock-off, this genial variation on the same classic adventures Steven Spielberg pillaged for cliffhangers echoes the lower budgeted end of the sagebrush serial industry as churned out by Republic Pictures. Director Matt Cimber/Matteo Ottaviano clearly wanted to discover another starlet in the mould of his fated wife Jayne Mansfield and statuesque Laurene Landon seemed to fit the bill. ...**All the Marbles** (1981), **I, the Jury** (1982) and **Airplane II: The Sequel** (1982) brought Landon to the public's attention and Cimber hoped his adventure fantasy **Hundra** (1983) would cement her star in Hollywood's firmament. It didn't, so he tried again with this tale of fiery Apache half-breed Yellow Hair (Landon) and her easygoing sidekick the Pecos Kid (Ken Roberson) wanting to get their hands on a fortune in Mayan gold, guarded by the Tulpan tribe who possess the ability to turn into statues. Shot in Spain, camouflaged as Mexico, late, great character actor and Spaghetti Western icon Aldo Sambrell plays mute bandit Flores. Landon endured to feature in many of writer/director Larry Cohen's movies including **The Stuff** (1985), **Maniac Cop** (1988), **Wicked Stepmother** (1989) and **The Ambulance** (1990).

ZOMBIE ISLAND MASSACRE

USA, © 1983, first public screening 1984
Director: John N. Carter. Producer: David Broadnax.
Screenplay: Logan O'Neill, William Stoddard. Music: Harry
Manfredini. Cinematography: Robert M. Baldwin.
Cast: David Broadnax, Rita Jenrette, Tom Cantrell, Diane
Clayre Holub, Ian McMillan, George Peters.

Shot in Jamaica, this non-horror, non-suspenseful, non-anything Troma pick-up is bottom-of-the-barrel fodder hooked on one key element – star Rita Jenrette. The wife of disgraced South Carolina congressman John Jenrette, jailed after being convicted of bribery during an FBI sting operation in 1980, Rita did the talk show rounds, wrote the scandalous bestselling book 'My Capitol Secrets', posed nude for 'Playboy' magazine in their April 1981 issue, headlined the play 'A Philadelphia Story' and attempted a Country and Western music career releasing the single 'It Gives Me the Low Down Blues Ever Since You Found Money Stashed in My Shoe'. There was literally nothing left for her to do but have a go at movies and this was the blinding result. Essentially, after an opening shower scene with Rita languorously soaping her breasts, she joins a Caribbean tour group promised "One of the most exciting and fun-filled evenings of your lives" only to end up watching a local voodoo ritual and getting knocked off one by one. Rita's big emotive moment arrives when she sobs in front of her boyfriend's severed head. She also sings the theme song 'Di Reggae Picnic'.

"... A female
Indiana Jones!"
– The Film Journal

Behind its walls
the treasure of kings.
Getting in is easy.
Getting out ...

IMPOSSIBLE!

YELLOW HAIR

and the

FORTRESS OF GOLD

CineStar Films, Inc. and JOHN GHAFFARI present a Matt Cimber Film
YELLOW HAIR and the FORTRESS OF GOLD

AMERICAN NINJA

USA, 1985
Director: Sam Firstenberg. Producer: Menahem Golan, Yoram Globus. Screenplay: Paul De Mielche.
Music: Michael Linn. Cinematography: Hanania Baer.
Cast: Michael Dudikoff, Steve James, Judie Aronson, Guich Koock, Tadashi Yamashita, Don Stewart.

Fast, dumb formula fun, this martial arts fiesta made a B-movie action star of Michael Dudikoff when he replaced the originally cast Chuck Norris. After a modelling career starring in the Coppertone suntan commercials, Dudikoff rose through the ranks of series television and bit parts in **Bloody Birthday** (1981) and **TRON** (1982) to playing the leading role of GI Joe Armstrong in Polish director Sam Firstenberg's Philippines shot Cannon fodder that began a five part series. Driving through the jungle with an arms convoy, Joe fights off an attack by Black Star Ninja (Tadashi Yamashita, **The Octagon**, 1980) and rescues the base commander's daughter (Judie Aronson, **Friday the 13th: The Final Chapter**, 1984). But Colonel Hickock is furious over the cock-up because he's in cahoots with local gun-smuggling crime czar Victor Ortega (Don Stewart) and makes plans to rid the camp of this upstart jujitsu master. Joe is equally non-plussed because, as he tells Corporal Jackson (action regular Steve James), he has amnesia and can't remember where he acquired his fighting skills. An economy trip to predictable Bruce Lee land, no question, but an engaging one as Joe woos the fair maiden gaining the grudging respect of his muscular platoon.

PSYCHO GIRLS

Canada, 1985
Director: Jerry Ciccoritti.
Producer: Robert Bergman,
Michael Bockner, Jerry Ciccoritti.
Screenplay: Michael Bockner, Jerry Ciccoritti.
Music: Joel Rosenbaum.
Cinematography: Robert Bergman.
Cast: John Haslett Cuff, Darlene Mignacco,
Agi Gallus, Pier Giorgio DiCicco,
Silvio Oliviero [Michael A. Miranda], Rose Graham.

Canadian horror, or Canuxploitation, ranges from the 3D **Eyes of Hell/The Mask** (1961), Ivan (**Ghostbusters**, 1984) Reitman's **Cannibal Girls** (1973) and David Cronenberg's extraordinary body horror works initiated by **Shivers** (1975) to Bob Clark's seminal slasher **Black Christmas** (1974) and its later kin **Prom Night** (1980) and **My Bloody Valentine** (1981). It was during the 1980s that director Jerry Ciccoritti made his mark with indie horrors that established him as a genre cult figure. His first was this makeshift shocker, with a classy poster campaign, made for $15,000 in nine days. In 1966, young Sarah wants to know what God looks like, so poisons her parents hoping they'll come back from heaven to tell her. Twenty years later, after being committed to a mental institution for her crime, she escapes to hunt down her sister and guardian Victoria. Sarah finds her working as a cook for rich and famous pulp fiction writer Richard Foster, who happens to be looking for inspiration for his new novel and is the narrator of this minor gem. Ciccoritti followed this with **Graveyard Shift** (1987), **The Understudy: Graveyard Shift II** (1988) and many episodes of TV series, including 'Deadly Nightmares' before becoming a critically acclaimed mainstream talent.

RE-ANIMATOR

USA, 1985
Director: Stuart Gordon. Producer: Brian Yuzna.
Screenplay: Dennis Paoli, William J. Norris, Stuart
Gordon. Music: Richard Band. Cinematography:
Mac Ahlberg.
Cast: Jeffrey Combs, Bruce Abbott, Barbara
Crampton, David Gale, Robert Sampson, Gerry Black.

Iconic writer H.P. Lovecraft made it very clear
from the start of his legendary status that all the
short stories under the 'Herbert West – The Re-
Animator' banner commissioned for the obscure
publication 'Home Brew' were written solely for the money. How fitting then that Charles Band's cheesy
Empire Pictures outfit (**The Alchemist**, 1983) should help turn them into an all-stops-out exploitation
horror gem that has also stood the test of time. Making a feature debut his career has never really
recovered from, Stuart Gordon's offbeat and perverse masterpiece has West (brilliantly nutzoid Jeffrey
Combs) inventing a luminescent serum that brings the dead back to life. Problem is the revived corpses
only have one thing on their braindead minds – blood lust and gut-ripping slaughter. All this takes place
in Arkham's Miskatonic University where evil Dr. Carl Hill (David Gale) wants to steal the serum, is
decapitated and re-animated as a result, and plots revenge on the Dean of the university, his gorgeous
daughter (the wonderful Barbara Crampton) and her boyfriend (Bruce Abbott). With its basic grimness
offset by a witty script crammed with hilarious one-liners, the most-talked about sequence involves
Hill's severed head getting up to outrageously funny sexual shenanigans.

STORY OF A JUNKIE

USA, 1985
Director: Lech Kowalski. Producer: Lech Kowalski, Ann S. Barish.
Music: Chuck Kentis. Cinematography: Raffi Ferrucci.
Cast: John Spacely, Steven Shingles, Claude du Sorbier,
Osualdo Vasquez, Cliff Weiss, Renee Tenenbaum.

After documenting the rise and fall of the punk movement
with rare interview footage of Sex Pistol Sid Vicious in **D.O.A.**
(1980), filmmaker Lech Kowalski turned his attention to the
heroin addicts infesting Manhattan's seedy underbelly in
this uncompromising look at a junkie's spaced-out lifestyle.
Playing a limited engagement on 42nd Street as **Gringo**
before appearing on the Troma videotape label, it follows
eye-patched smack-addict John Spacely going about his daily
routine on the mean streets of New York, navigating between
Greenwich Village and Alphabet City on his skateboard
scoring bags of his drug of choice. Matter-of-fact and devoid
of any knee-jerk moralizing, Spacely makes for an amiable
guide through the bullet points of addiction – shooting up,
skin-popping, rambling monologues, mellowing out and
interacting with other stoners as tempers flare, cash issues and health problems get raised and early
morning vomiting is the norm. Blaming his girlfriend's miscarriage and death for his addiction, Spacely
did finally kick the habit and moved to Hollywood to pursue an acting career, but only appeared briefly
in **Sid and Nancy** (1986) and other assorted documentaries. Unfortunately, years of sharing needles in
dirty shooting galleries meant he died of AIDS in 1992.

THE STUFF

USA, 1985
Director: Larry Cohen. Producer: Paul Kurta. Screenplay: Larry Cohen. Music: Anthony Guefen. Cinematography: Paul Glickman. Cast: Michael Moriarty, Paul Sorvino, Andrea Marcovicci, Danny Aiello, Patrick O'Neal, Tammy Grimes.

Prolific writer/director Larry Cohen was never off the drive-in circuits during the 1970s. **Black Caesar** (1973), **It's Alive** (1974), **God Told Me To** (1976) and **The Private Files of J. Edgar Hoover** (1977) just the tip of the Cohen iceberg combining provocative concepts, smart execution and unusual shocks in commercial packages. Here Cohen economically sets up the notion of an alien killer dessert being pumped from the centre of the Earth and successfully mass-marketed to a consumer society hungry for the next fast-food experience. The entrepreneurs behind the delicious-tasting sweet don't care that it's addictive and has a habit of taking over the body just as long as those Happy Meals cash registers keep ringing. Cohen stronghold Michael Moriarty stars as the shady ex-FBI agent employed by a panic-stricken ice-cream industry to ensure everyone gets their just desserts. Cleverly updating and inverting the 1950s creature feature as exemplified by Cohen's two main inspirations, **Quatermass II** (1957) and **The Blob** (1958), here the people eat the monster rather than the reverse. Fleshed out with numerous star cameos – Paul Sorvino, Tammy Grimes, Patrick O'Neal, Danny Aiello – many death scenes involving shaving foam were edited in after shooting to up the body count.

TENEMENT

USA, 1985
Director: Roberta Findlay. Producer: Walter E. Sear. Screenplay: Joel Bender, Rick Marx. Music: Walter E. Sear, William Fischer. Cinematography: Roberta Findlay. Cast: Joe Lynn, Mina Bern, Walter Bryant, Corinne Chateau, Angel David, Martha De La Cruz.

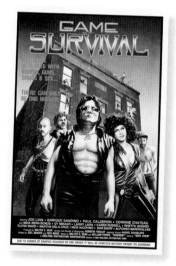

Renamed **Slaughter in the South Bronx** for quick release on that new-fangled platform videotape once it had played 42nd Street, this violent revenge saga – also known as **Game of Survival** – was one of the last movies directed by the true legend of exploitation that was Roberta Findlay. With her husband Michael, she directed, produced, shot, edited, starred in and composed the soundtracks for some of exploitation's most revered releases like **The Touch of Her Flesh** (1967), **The Altar of Lust** (1971), **Invasion of the Blood Farmers** (1972) and **Snuff** (1976). Findlay's first non-pornographic film of the 1980s, branded with an official X-rating in America, sees a multi-ethnic gang of over-age junkies and deadbeat punks kicked out from their rundown tenement apartment when the block superintendent calls the police to evict them. But as **Death Wish** (1974) watchers know only too well, the justice system in Manhattan is pretty slack so the lowlifes are released on a technicality and embark on an orgy of payback with machetes, guns and switchblades. Calling on her **Flesh** trilogy experience for edginess and outrageously inventive deaths, Findlay's vile catalogue of gruesome carnage here includes crotch-stabbing, blood-vomiting, throat-slitting, stair-scalding, TV aerial wounding, sudden lightning strikes and that old favourite, granny raping.

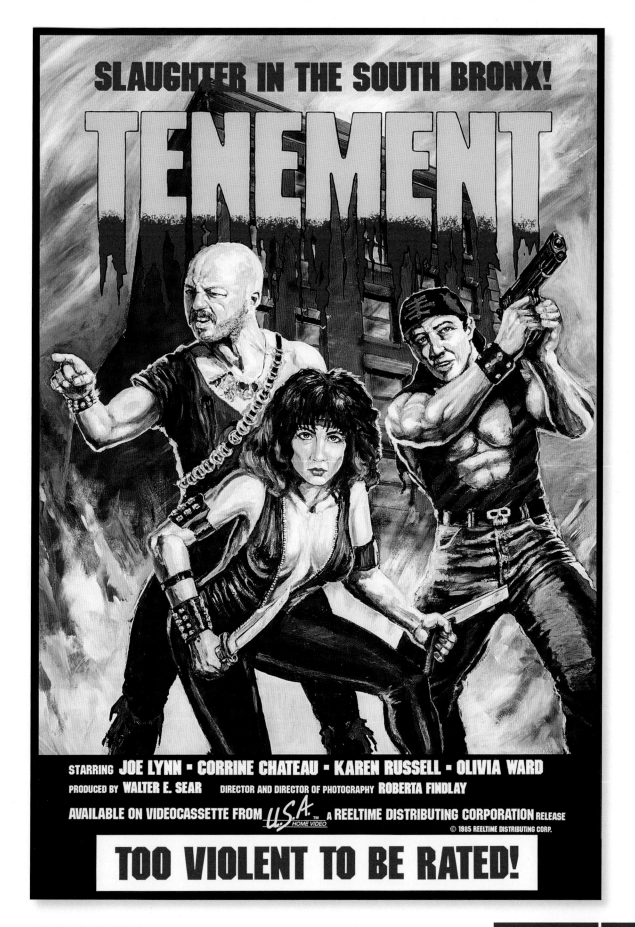

SLAUGHTER IN THE SOUTH BRONX!

TENEMENT

STARRING JOE LYNN · CORRINE CHATEAU · KAREN RUSSELL · OLIVIA WARD
PRODUCED BY WALTER E. SEAR   DIRECTOR AND DIRECTOR OF PHOTOGRAPHY ROBERTA FINDLAY
AVAILABLE ON VIDEOCASSETTE FROM U.S.A. HOME VIDEO ™ A REELTIME DISTRIBUTING CORPORATION RELEASE
© 1985 REELTIME DISTRIBUTING CORP.

TOO VIOLENT TO BE RATED!

INDEX OF FILM TITLES

Page references in **bold** refer exclusively to illustrations.